Opened Time Capsules

My Vintage Conversations with Show Business Personalities

by David Rothel

BearManor Media
2010

Opened Time Capsules: My Vintage Conversations
With Show Business Personalities
© 2010 David Rothel

For information, address:

BearManor Media
P. O. Box 71426
Albany, GA 31708

bearmanormedia.com

Cover design by John Teehan

Typesetting and layout by John Teehan

Published in the USA by BearManor Media

ISBN—1-59393-530-7

Table of Contents

Preface i

Milton Berle 1
  "I've got the first penny thrown at me."

Lloyd Bridges 19
  *"When I went to New York, they weren't hiring any classical actors at
  that time, so I had to brush up on my dees, does, and dems."*

Hans Conried 39
  "I remember I played eighteen parts in thirty minutes on one occasion."

Dennis Day 55
  "Sing, Dennis." – Jack Benny

Henry Denker 77
  *"If you wait for inspiration to hit you, you will die very old and
  very unhappy."*

Phyllis Diller 97
  "A lot of people think that I'm truly the harridan they see on stage."

Tony Dow & Jerry Mathers 113
  *"There haven't been any shows on TV that depicted what the adult
  world is like viewed from a child's eyes, and that's what* Leave It To
  Beaver *was."*

Tom Ewell 131
  "I had twenty-seven failures before I had a success."

Walter Gibson 149
  "Who knows what evil lurks in the hearts of men?"

Myrna Loy 171
"I was pretty much just playing myself in The Thin Man *series."*

Jock Mahoney 187
"Every boy, no matter how old you get, wants to play Tarzan."

Virginia Mayo 217
"Let me be candid, if I may."

Roddy McDowall 257
*"Plays happen to have the chance of disappearing sooner than
movies because the emulsion stays around."*

Spanky McFarland 275
"I am Spanky. That's the only role I ever played."

Molly Picon 287
"Wherever I can make people laugh, that's the job I want to do."

Vincent Price 309
"A man who limits his interests limits his life."

Gordon Scott 323
"I like sex, although it's very difficult on a vine."

George Takei 341
*"Takei means 'warriors well,' so I suspect my ancestors ran the
local pub for the Samurai way back when."*

Victor Sen Yung 359
*"He who takes whatever Gods send with smile has learned life's
hardest lesson." –Charlie Chan*

About the Author 375

Notes 377

Preface
How It All Came About

Back in the late 1970s I had a radio program on WQSA in Sarasota, Florida, entitled *Nostalgia Newsbreak*. It was a five minute pre-news-on-the-hour feature not unlike Garrison Keillor's current *Writers' Almanac* on NPR radio, the difference being that I visited with show business celebrities regarding their careers. The conversations were edited to run for a week or more with each person.

Most of the conversations with the famous actors, singers, writers, or whomever were career-type interviews which endeavored to hit the main career points which I thought would be of interest to my audience. Occasionally, I would talk with them about some aspect of their life or career that an audience would probably not be aware of, such as Vincent Price's love of radio drama, *Suspense* and *Escape* for example, and his own radio series as *The Saint*.

The tapes that accumulated while doing the program were stored away after the series concluded many years ago. In early 2008 I decided to transfer the audio cassettes to CD so that they would be better preserved. In the process I was reminded of what a treasure trove of show business history resided in those tapes—now CDs.

They were very much like show business time capsules of a bygone era. I also began to realize that most of the conversations were unlike any that the personalities gave at other times, since they were one-on-one and intimate, usually done in a backstage theater or nightclub setting, and the subject was rarely promoting a current project that he/she needed to tout.

It was at that time I thought of *Opened Time Capsules: My Vintage Conversations with Show Business Personalities* as a book, a sort of oral history of a cross section of American popular culture that would cover much of the Twentieth Century. I transcribed the conversations and wrote

i

a "wrap-around" for each conversation—pre and post segments that briefly detailed what led up to the meeting and conversation and what happened to the personality during the many years following our conversation. It seemed quite evident that for anyone who has an avid interest in the show business history of the Twentieth Century, the book should be of considerable interest.

– David Rothel
March 2010

Milton Berle

May 23, 1978

"I've got the first penny thrown at me!"

This composite of Milton Berle shows him at the time of our conversation in 1978.

One of my first remembrances of television was in the winter of 1948 when my folks and I (not yet in my teens) visited friends in the nearby country community of Belden, Ohio. It was a Tuesday evening and shortly after we arrived, our friends interrupted the conversation to mention that it was just about eight o'clock and that we should go into the living room to watch the *Texaco Star Theater* with Milton Berle on their new TV. I had heard about the show, but since we did not have a television, I had never seen it.

We adjourned to the living room where a ten-inch television set was sitting atop an upright piano. I remember the living room lights were turned off as the show was beginning, and I sat enraptured by the magic which I beheld on that tiny television screen.

The show began with four gentlemen dressed as service station attendants singing a song about Texaco gasoline and the show:

"Oh, we're the men of Texaco
We work from Maine to Mexico
There's nothing like this Texaco of ours!
Our show is very powerful
We'll wow you with an hour full
Of howls from a shower full of stars

[And so forth, finally ending with]

And now, ladies and gentlemen,
America's number one television star, Milton Berle!

Out popped Milton from behind the curtain, dressed bizarrely as Brazilian samba singer Carmen Miranda with a two-foot chapeau of tropical fruit perched atop his head as he gushed out half-a-dozen comedy zingers about Carmen, fruit, and maneuvering in high heels. As Milton wiggled off the stage to the music of the Brazilian bombshell, pitchman Sid Stone rushed out with his derby hat on, rolled up sleeves, and small, collapsible stand to pitch some Texaco to us.

What followed the commercial, as I remember it, was a raucous, razzmatazz of zany, slapstick sketches; a couple of songs by a current popular singer; and a wacky, windup sketch which featured Milton as Cleopatra—

Milton is pictured here as a Super-duper Man and engaged in a typical slapstick TV sketch with one of his favorite funny men, Henny Youngman.

again in full drag—chugging down the Nile as the curtain closed. Following another break with Sid Stone, Milton was back, still in Cleo garb, to sing a sentimental closing, "There's just one place for me, near you," as he waved goodbye to the studio audience and me. Wow, what an hour, and I was missing it every Tuesday because we didn't have a television set. It was that night I started my campaign to get my parents to buy a television, and a few months later they gave in.

Jump ahead almost forty years to 1978 and a phone call informing me that Milton Berle would be performing the next week at *Les Club*, a fancy new nightspot in St. Petersburg, Florida. "Would you like to see the show and talk with Milton after?" "You bet I would," I told their press rep as I made a mental note to review Milton's autobiography[1] that I had read a few years back and had on my library shelf. One always needs to do his homework before talking with a big star.

The intervening forty years from 1948 had not always been kind to Milton Berle's stardom—even with the commonly accepted appellation of "Mr. Television" and a 1951 thirty-year, one hundred thousand dollars a year, television contract from a grateful NBC[2] for being TV's first star and for selling so many TV sets during his pioneering years. Milton's reign on television only lasted for eight years—not bad, but there was a steep "over-exposure" decline after that until by 1960 he was reduced to hosting a game show called *Jackpot Bowling* and throwing in an occasional quip to keep things moving.

Milton had never really been a major movie star although in the 1940s he was a supporting comic in *Sun Valley Serenade*[3] and starred in several "B" comedy movies such as *Whispering Ghosts*[4] and *Over My Dead Body*.[5] In the late forties he starred with Virginia Mayo in *Always Leave Them Laughing* [see the Virginia Mayo conversation] just before the *Texaco Star Theater* arrived to brighten his career. Following his TV years, Milton was featured in several films, the most outstanding being *It's a Mad, Mad, Mad, Mad World*.[6]

Milton's popularity in nightclubs and in Las Vegas remained strong after his halcyon television years. He appeared all over the country in clubs and starred at the Sands, Caesar's Palace, the Desert Inn, and other casino hotels in Nevada. By the late 1970s his career had wound down some, but now he was a senior-citizen "legend" in show business and had nothing to prove to anyone, least of all to me because I was a believer and had followed his career throughout those years and read his autobiography.

I could see that it was a packed house as I arrived at Les Club and met with my PR contact before dinner and Milton's show. She handed me a press release and promised that it would be "helpful" in tracing Milton's career. I folded the "cheat sheet" and put it in my pocket as I was taken to my table. To paraphrase Gold Hat's comment to Bogart in *The Treasure of the Sierra Madre*, "I don't need to study no stinking press release."

Dinner was great and so was Milton's show. He knew how to play with the audience, build the laughs, and go off to a standing-ovation climax. He certainly hadn't lost his touch with a live audience. The word-of-mouth comments I overheard as I was ushered to the lobby and then to Milton's dressing room were the kind that performers live for—and certainly this performer's ego thrived on it. How else could you explain his presence at age sixty-nine in a small nightclub in St. Petersburg, Florida. He certainly shouldn't need the money.

Anyway, there he was in his dressing room, stripped of his tuxedo and still perspiring from his performance, encased in a huge, multi-colored-but-mostly-green paisley robe, chomping on an unlit huge cigar, and looking ready to wind down with a good smoke and a little talk.

David: Is it really true that you first appeared in the silent film serial *The Perils of Pauline*?[7]

Milton: That's right, with Pearl White.

David: And they were going to throw you off a train.

Milton: Some comics had something to do with it! *[Laugh]* The Pearl White thing was done over at Fort Lee in New Jersey.

David: And the situation was that they had a little kid on a train and they were going to throw him off and you. . .

Milton: I was the child they were going to throw off.[8]

David: *[Laugh]* You also did Buster Brown about that time.

Milton: Well, I was also a Buster Brown model, but there were a lot of them. I had the Buster Brown hair, and I had the Buster Brown collar, and dog. I was a Buster Brown boy, a boy model, and my mother schlepped me and dragged me around [to auditions]. I want to tell you something. I just did a show about three days ago that's called *Hey, Abbott*,[9] which was [a documentary about] Abbott and Costello's black and white film and television clips. They tied them all together for ninety minutes, and I was the narrator and host of it.

David: It sounds like an enjoyable ninety minutes!

Milton: It was kind of done on a good basis with me walking around doing narration, talking to the camera. They did all the famous Abbott and Costello bits—Who's *on First*, and *The Cheating Dice Game*; it was hilarious, and they are going to tie it all together. I walked into this studio where they shot my part, a place called Gotham Studio. I thought I was doing *Batman* again![10] *[Laugh]*

It was located at Santa Monica and Van Ness in Hollywood. I walked into this dingy-looking place where they had the sound stage; then, as I walked into the dressing room to put on my tuxedo, I thought, "This seems very, very familiar. It wasn't smelly, but it was like a flee bag. So I said to a grip, a stage hand, what studio was this? Then I said, "Hold it! I think I know. I worked there in 1915, the same studio, with Mary Pickford in *Rebecca of Sunnybrook Farm*."[11] He said, "This was originally the Mary Pickford studio before it became United Artists with Fairbanks and Chaplin."[12] Is that strange?

David: My goodness!

Milton: The last time I was in there I was with my mother in 1915, and I was seven years old.

David: Well, jumping ahead for what must seem about a hundred years for you, you ushered in television in the late 1940s. I think it is safe to say that you wrote the book on TV variety shows starting in 1948 with the *Texaco Star Theater*,[13] and that went on for a good many years.

Milton: Yeah, eight years.

David: What did it cost to produce the *Texaco Star Theater* then?

Milton: I'm glad you asked that. That show—which I discussed in my book that you read—for the first year only cost fifteen thousand dollars for the whole hour including the actors, the scenery, the costumes, the time, everything. You couldn't get Vicki Carr to sing four bars today for fifteen thousand. *[Laugh]*

I met Jack Dempsey about four weeks ago, okay, who is eighty-five years old and not feeling too well. I said, "How you feeling, Jack?" He said, "Not so hot." I said, "Is anything bugging you?" He said, "Yep, I was born sixty years too early." Now what does he mean by that? A Muhammad Ali can get twenty million and fifteen million [for boxing matches] and Jack Dempsey got a hundred and fifty thousand for maybe the first million dollar gate against [Gene] Tunney. The inflation, the salaries, the moneys have gone up.

So I would say if I was thinking only of money, which I'm not: I started in television thirty years too early, okay! *[Laugh]* Even though I get paid for the rest of my life by NBC—which is a pittance compared to what Red Foxx got when he moved over to NBC from ABC, six million dollars just to get him to go over there—I was thirty years too early! But I don't care because I got mine from vaudeville! *[Laugh]* And I've got the first penny thrown at me! *[Laugh]* I got the big dollar bills!

David: In your book you comment on television being a devil for standup comedians because of over exposure.

Milton: Well, all I can say is this: I think it's easier today for a comic to get a shot than it was when I was around as a young comic, because we have the exposure of television. They can work at a place like The Comedy Club or Improve and somebody can catch them on the *Tonight Show* or any of the other late night or talk shows on the air. They hear them do a routine. Now they have, let's say, four good, solid blocks of routines. They need exposure, but it's very dangerous for them. They better be *very* good the first time now [on television].

They didn't have a shot like I did playing vaudeville in St Petersburg and Tampa in 1920 and dying. Then changing my act and doing the same act for eight years; it took me maybe four years to get three or four good minutes by weeding out the junk. So they better be ready!

Milton's NBC series had sold a lot of black and white TV sets in the late 1940s and early fifties. By the mid 1950s he was telecasting in color and helping to push color TV sets.

But, in answer to your question, the exposure of doing the material on one show being watched by millions, then doing it on another talk show, you can be eaten up in three appearances. That's the dangers. They have four, good, solid routines and people say, "Oh, I heard that one!"

David: Do you really steal jokes?

Milton: No, I just find them before they're lost. No, we started that notion years ago, Richie Craig and myself. He was a standup comedian back in the thirties, and at that time Jack Benny had a setup feud with Fred Allen, and they got a lot of publicity on it. Ben Bernie[14] had a setup feud with Walter Winchell. We figured that we'd try to cash in on that kind of publicity, so we set it up ourselves—Richie and myself—you know, saying we were stealing jokes from each other.

David: Do you know who first called you "The Thief of Bad Gags"?

Milton: Sure, it was Winchell, Walter Winchell was the one. And they called me "Milton Burglar." It didn't stunt my career in any way. All the notoriety and the image made for jokes and everything and still does. And when you get branded with some kind of a label which you're known for, even if it's a put on, it's a fake, it can develop into something that you can build laughs on and be identifiable with.

The name of this game, I think, is style and identity. "Who am I, and what am I doing here, and why?" These are the three questions we always ask ourselves when it comes to style and identification that actors are known for. That is the difference between being a comic and a comedian. I think it was Ed Wynn who responded when asked the difference between a comic and a comedian said, "A comic is a guy who says funny things and a comedian is a guy who says things funny."

So, actually, you've got to have a character going for you. I think if you ever read a Jack Benny script, radio or television script, and it said Benny, colon [:] "Well." I don't think that looks very funny on paper, and I don't think it's funny unless Jack Benny was saying it. Meaning that it depends solely on characterization and "Who am I, what am I doing here, and why?"

The strongest vote for that today, I think, is the success of one of the geniuses, and that's Woody Allen, who makes his whole move towards success built on one word and that's "incongruity." When you see a guy with glasses wearing dungarees, sneakers, a sweatshirt, and ruffled hair walk out on the stage or even his characters in his pictures, he's always the "patsy." He's always the hero a la Harold Lloyd or Buster Keaton where there is something lurking over him, either danger or putting him in a spot.

But his success is one word and that's "incongruity," because if you see this type of a guy dressed the way Woody Allen dresses, and you hear him speak in an incongruous way, you've got to laugh at him even if it isn't a joke—it can be a straight line. When he dreams of sleeping with Sophia Loren, talking about having a date with her, it's incongruous. That's what makes the juxtaposition work. So he doesn't need "joke" jokes. What I mean by "joke" jokes, for example: "I'm so unlucky; if they sawed a woman in half, I'd get the part that eats." There's the joke; it's a joke that can be said by anybody.

Now let's talk about me, which is what we're [supposed to be] talking about—getting down to the fine form of it. This character that I do is not the character that's talking to you now. The flippancy, the brashness, the wise guy, the smart ass, the aggressor, the put-downer, the insulter—that is a character that I made up myself on myself. The offspring is [Don] Rickles now, who is my protégé. *[Laugh]*

Like I said to Rodney Dangerfield—you've seen him—he does lines like, "I get no respect." I told him once, "Rodney, if you ever get off that path of deviating away from 'I get no respect' and being the butt of your own jokes, you're really going to be in trouble. Then you'll be like any standup comic. So that's the way we separate the men from the boys, the comics from the comedians—the indelibility, the identifiable tag which goes with their personality—what are they representing and who are they?

We have a lot of young—you didn't ask me these questions, but I figure you may. Can I have a match, please? I want to burn this dressing room [Lighting his cigar]—we have a lot of young new comedians around, a young, new breed—from David Brenner to Chevy Chase to Steve Martin to George Carlin. Some of them are very, very good, and some of them are not very good—and some of them should be in the furniture business.

I don't say that bitterly; I say that advisedly because I get a lot of young guys coming over to me—and young girls too—saying that they want to be a comedian or a comic. The first thing I say to them is, "Do you have a funny bone?" You know, you just can't manufacture a comic attitude; it just can't be made. Like when they were kids in school, did people say, "Oh Charlie, he's the clown of the school; he's always clowning and kidding"? Well, I wouldn't put a stop to that; I'd encourage that because he's got a funny bone at least. So if these young would-be comics haven't got a funny bone to start with, I don't think they should be in the business.

Now, where are they to start? Catch a Rising Star, The Comedy Store, improve places. They do get shots. Some of them that come out of those places are very good. I think the ones that get the big breaks are the ones who maybe get a part in a sitcom. And that part that they get makes them that "character." They didn't have it before they created that character. That goes for the "Fonz," Henry Winkler. He's a straight actor, but he played the Fonz and it became comedic. Now that is identifiable.

Of course, television and movie actors always say, "I don't want to be typed." After he played the Fonz, Winkler went on to play Hamlet." All right, that's fine, but if Winkler is a big success as the Fonz, I don't see anything wrong with cashing in on that success. I don't think Mr. Bogart or Edward G. Robinson or Errol Flynn or Sidney Greenstreet or Cary Grant or Gary Cooper were hurt by type casting. It only made them individual.

And there are a lot of guys around today that have comedic ability, but they won't let themselves be a comedian. Let me explain that: I usually say that a comedian is a guy who isn't afraid of silence, meaning he can take the beats. The funniest line that was ever done was written by Milt Josefsberg[15] for a radio show for Jack Benny. It wasn't a joke; it was a situation: a heavy comes out of the shadows and says to Jack Benny, "Your money or your life!" After several long beats Benny says, "I'm thinking about it." *[Laugh]*

But it took forty-five years for Jack to set up that character so the joke would work. So jokes should come out of character. If I'm flippant and aggressive and brash with a putdown, the audience knows my character, that I'm kidding. I think they know that it is not my real character, but for that time they're seeing it, it's funny because that is the character I'm playing: the wise guy.

Now, Don Rickles is a pussy cat; he's personally very different when he's not "on." And I must, without being hammy or hamm*ier,* say that I'm not "on" until the spotlight hits me. I think it's imperative for the young boys [comics] today to get themselves a character. Look in the mirror and ask, "Does this joke fit me?"

Take Alan King, for instance, who I started. Some twenty, twenty-two years ago—no, it's more than that; it must be twenty-five years ago—my mother was the president of The Troupers, a female Friars

Club. We gave her a dinner at the Latin Quarter in New York, and I was master of ceremonies and every comedian was on. Alan King was just starting, and Alan King at that time was doing the me that I did years ago: Ted Healy.[16] Everybody has to have someone they look up to, to be *like* someone before they have their own style.

So Alan King got there very late at this benefit, and I took him on the side, being a friend of mine, "Alan, this was said, that was said, this joke was told, that joke was told." He said, "Oh, my gosh, what am I going to do?" I said, "Just go out there and thank them, tell them that you're glad to be here for Saundra, my mother."

So I introduced him, and he went out there and he said, "Sorry I'm late, but I just played a club date and a benefit at the Biltmore Hotel, and do you know how long it took me to come from the Biltmore Hotel to the Latin Quarter? Fifty-five minutes! It's only five blocks away!" Now he starts to get mad. He says, "This damned taxi driver; he wanted to go where he wanted to go. So I asked him, 'Where do you want to go? Do you want to go to Newark?'"

So as Alan gets madder and madder, and by getting mad and putting down the problem that he had, the audience started to laugh. He did about four or five minutes, and they were laughing at him because he had gotten mad and was saying some funny things.

As he came off, I took him aside and said, "Alan, throw out all the junk and get somebody to write in that style for you. I want you to be mad at the world, at the insurance companies, and airplanes. That's what I think you should do." And that's how he got his style. Now that's identification, strictly identification. Right now I'm doing a symposium on comedy for you.

David: Please continue!

Milton: I'll tell you who didn't get enough credit and that's Desi Arnaz—for the success of *I Love Lucy*. It was Desi Arnaz who was the editor at that time for *I Love Lucy* and said to the writers what Lucy *couldn't* say [in the scripts] even though the line might have been a big laugh, because it wasn't [appropriate] for the character that Lucy was playing. George Burns was the same way with Gracie, and Jack Benny was the greatest editor for *himself* than anyone. He'd say [to the writers], "That's a funny line, but I wouldn't do it in my character."

Then there's the old formula that was true—and I think it was Buster Keaton or Chaplin who said it—regarding how to make the hero of the piece funny. He said there're three stages of making your hero funny—if it was Harold Lloyd in *Safety Last* or Keaton in *The General* or Chaplin in *City Lights*—it is to get the hero [or comic] up a tree, throw rocks at him, and try to get him out. That's opening, middle, and end. If you're writing a column, you've got to have an opening, a middle, and a finish; if you're doing a motion picture, you've got to have an opening, a middle, and an end—right?

And that's the same with the one-liner. Even if it's one line—a remark like I said [on stage tonight], "I need this like Jimmy Carter needs another brother."[17] That was the opening. Little laugh, but it was the setup—exposition-wise. Then I said, "I don't know why everybody's picking on Jimmy Carter; he hasn't done anything." That's the second part of the joke. The third part of the joke was, "Yes, he has. He's done the work of two men: Laurel and Hardy." *[Laugh]*

Now that's the three parts of that one joke, and they are all one-liners, all on the same subject matter. So a one-liner has to have three parts. If Neal Simon has a Broadway play, it has got to have an opening, a middle, and an end. That's my symposium for today. *[Laugh]*

No, but I do symposiums in colleges, and I hope I can get down here to a Florida college and do a symposium and seminar—it's a two-hour thing I do by myself with Q and A's and open forums. It's kind of interesting [the symposiums] because they ask questions like "Why is this or that funny? What makes it funny?" You didn't ask me these questions, but I think this is more important than "Where were you born and how long have you been on the stage?" *I* think so, anyway.

I'm in the middle of a book now—I've been on the book a year and a half. It's going to be the largest comedy text book written, I think. It's called *The Comedy Bible*.[18] It'll have about two thousand pages, and it will be for perpetuity or infinity, we hope. And it will go into libraries and colleges and high schools for art classes and drama classes. It's comedic—whys and don'ts and why nots. These are my points of view, what has happened to me in my [show] business, and what I learned. Next question: I don't think there are any more.

David: Oh, I've got a couple if you've got the time.

Milton: Yeah, but they better be strong—I mean following that symposium on comedy.

David: I'll try. I wanted to ask you . . .

Milton: How old am I?

David: No. *[Laugh]* I know how old you are; I read your book. By the way I recognized the lines you quoted earlier—as a matter of fact I have them written down here—about "flippant, aggressive, a wise guy, and the real me" because I read it in your book, and I found it fascinating.

Milton: Well, you see, in the book there are no holds barred. In the book I said, "Gee, they say that I am flippant, aggressive, a wise guy." Well, I say, "I made it up [my comedy character]! I know this, because I created it myself." That's the passage you're talking about.

David: Yes. In your book you also say, "Retire? To what?"

Milton: Right! "Retire to what?" What would I do, open a Lum's or McDonald's? I don't know anything but makeup and show business. As I said out there sitting on the stool [during the show on stage], I said, "This is my sixty-fifth year in show business. You know, I started when I was five years old and I'm going to be seventy July 12th. I know politics somewhat. I know what's going on, but I don't know any other business. I think that's enough. *[Laugh]*

David: Thank you very much, Milton Berle.

I didn't ask Milton anything about his personal life in our conversation; it just seemed out of place to get into that area of his life as he was winding down after a nightclub performance. And, anyway, most of it was pretty much common knowledge. He'd been married twice to a Broadway showgirl named Joyce Mathews, and they had adopted a daughter named

Milton Berle was seldom seen on or off stage without his trademark cigar.

Victoria. After his second divorce from Mathews, he married publicist Ruth Cosgrove, adopted a son named Bill, and was happily married for more than thirty-five years until her death in 1989 of cancer—more than ten years after he and I had talked in his dressing room.

Milton was to marry once again. In 1991 at the age of eighty-three, he married a much younger woman, a fashion designer named Lorna Adams. By all accounts the marriage was a success; family and friends credited this late marriage to keeping Milton "young and vital" for the last decade of his life. The marriage with Lorna included two stepdaughters: Leslie and Susan Brown.

Milton continued playing Vegas and nightclubs and made frequent guest appearances on television shows. In 1979 he was guest-host of *Saturday Night Live* in an apparent ill-fated attempt to recreate his old *Texaco Star Theater* antics and mugging which did not sit well with the regular cast members. In addition, his take-charge ways also alienated the show's producer Lorne Michaels.

But that situation was just a bump in the road and did not mitigate against his appearances on other shows of the eighties and nineties such as *Fantasy Island, Diff'rent Strokes, Murder She Wrote, The Love Boat, Matlock,* and *Roseanne,* just to name a few.

Milton had been one of the first to receive the television Emmy award back in 1949. As he entered his late "golden years," the accolades commenced at a faster pace. He was given another Emmy in 1979 for Lifetime Achievement. In 1984 he was inducted into the Television Hall of Fame. In 1991 he became the first entertainer inducted into the International Comedy Hall of Fame.

In 1996, five years into his fourth marriage and at eighty-eight years of age, Milton proclaimed that he never felt better. But that was not to last, of course. Two years later in December of 1998 it was reported that he suffered a mild stroke. He recovered enough to perform twice more: In 1999 he participated in a filmed tribute to his beloved Friar's Club which he had helped found in 1947, and in 2000 he made his last television appearance in a TV movie entitled *Two Heads Are Better than None.*[19]

In April of 2001 it was announced that Milton had been diagnosed with a cancerous tumor in his colon but that no surgery was planned because it was growing at such a slow rate that it would not affect his overall health for ten to twelve years. But the doctors were wrong. Milton Berle died while taking a nap less than a year later of colon cancer on March 27, 2002, at age ninety-three. His wife Lorna was at their Beverly Hills home with him when he died.

Milton's contemporary, comedian Sid Caesar, said, "When television was a new medium and the networks were skeptical, Milton Berle proved that one man could do a new show every week for thirty-nine weeks a year. He is going to be sorely missed." Bob Hope (then ninety-eight) and his wife Dolores (then ninety-three) said of Milton's passing,

"Eighty-eight years in show business, a brilliant comedian, an accomplished actor, a lifelong friend. We are among the select few who could call him 'kid.'" Actor/comedian Tony Randall, noting that director Billy Wilder and actor/comedian Dudley Moore died on the same day as Milton Berle, called it "the day comedy died."

Lloyd Bridges

October 25, 1977

"When I went to New York, they weren't hiring any classical actors at that time, so I had to brush up on my dees, does, and dems."

Lloyd Bridges posed outside his trailer on the set for *The Great Wallendas* just after our conversation back in 1977.

Sarasota, Florida, has been a circus town since 1927 when the Ringling Bros. Barnum & Bailey Circus made the city its winter headquarters for "The Greatest Show on Earth." The circus influence became so prolific in the area that Sarasota High School in 1949 created its own Sailor Circus [the sailor is their mascot] as part of the athletic program, and over the years the Sailor Circus became world famous and is officially known as "The Greatest Little Show On Earth." In 1951 director Cecil B. DeMille came to Sarasota to film *The Greatest Show on Earth*, which went on to win the Academy Award for Best Movie the next year. Because of its circus aura and history, the area also became a mecca for circus people who made it their home during the off season and then later retired there.

Thus it was not a surprise when NBC announced in the fall of 1977 that a production company was coming to Sarasota to make a television film about one of the greatest high-wire circus acts of all time, The Flying Wallendas—only the film would be called *The Great Wallendas*.[20] Lloyd Bridges, Britt Ekland, and Cathy Rigby were named as the stars of the two-hour movie.

The film was to be shot at the Karl Wallenda home where there was high-wire rigging they rehearsed on for their shows, and Lloyd Bridges was set to play Karl Wallenda in the film. In addition, they would film staged shows at Sarasota's Robard's Arena where they would recreate the Wallendas' tragic accident from 1962 and their comeback with the seven-person high-wire pyramid in 1963.

I had admired the film work of Lloyd Bridges for many years, having first noticed him in bit parts in Columbia pictures during the forties, and his later leading man roles in mostly low-budget Westerns and adventure pictures. In the fifties he began to appear in some excellent A pictures alongside some of our stellar actors, such as Gary Cooper, Burt Lancaster, Katherine Hepburn, and Kim Stanley. Later, of course, there were his television series.

With Lloyd Bridges practically in my backyard for the next couple of weeks, I, naturally, decided he should be my next radio guest. I contacted the public relations person for *The Great Wallendas* and was told that she would check with Mr. Bridges and get right back to me—and she did. Our meeting was set for three o'clock the next afternoon in his trailer on the Wallenda property where they were filming.

Lloyd was on a break from filming when I arrived, and I was told he was in his trailer waiting for me. Lloyd's trailer was just off the side street where the Wallendas lived. It was parked in an area adjacent to the large backyard area where the high-wire rigging was set up. I could see several people working on the wire as the assistant director and I walked to the trailer. As he held the door open for me, he quietly cautioned me that we might have to stop our conversation if Lloyd got called back to the set.

Lloyd greeted me warmly, assuming, I'm sure, that we would talk mostly about the present film he was shooting, not his long history in show business. He thus seemed a bit taken aback and a touch bemused that I obviously knew a lot more about his career than he expected. We sat side by side on the sofa-like seat in the back of the modest [to say the least] trailer with the recorder and mike between us.

David: Are you one of those actors who knew from an early age that acting was the only field of endeavor for you?

Lloyd: Yes. That was what I was mainly interested when I was at UCLA. I graduated from UCLA, and I took part in all of the Greek drama, played Oedipus there, and Hamlet and other Shakespearian plays. I had a kind of a classical background. When I went to New York, they weren't hiring any classical actors at that time, so I had to brush up on my "dees, does, and dems." [Laugh]

When I went to New York, there weren't that many parts, and so I had a rough time. I worked for United Parcel Service and any odd job I could get. My wife Dorothy also went to UCLA, and we would play leads opposite each other. I liked the way she kissed in the plays, so we decided that we were meant for each other and we got married in The Little Church around the Corner in New York. .

We stuck around New York for a couple of years. There was not much work there. A bunch of us actors who weren't working said let's get our own theater. So we got an iron foundry and made it into a theater—it was off Broadway quite a ways. We redecorated this foundry, moved everything around, and got some chairs. I think it was the beginning of the Off Broadway theaters. We put on a couple of seasons of plays there. We had the critics down to review us, and we did very well with that. But things were rough there.

David: If I'm not mistaken, your first film was *The Lone Wolf Takes a Chance*[21] for Columbia Pictures in 1941.

Lloyd: Oh, my gosh. That goes way back.

David: You were under contract with Columbia for a few years. How did you get that Columbia contract?

Lloyd: Well, I was doing summer theater at Green Mansions,[22] and Sidney Buckman, who was then the right-hand man to [Harry] Cohn,[23] saw me in a show and he wanted to know if I would be interested in a test. We put on quite a few plays at the time; we put on *Liliom*, *Green Grow the Lilacs*—oh, and I did an adaptation of *Othello* at that time. I played Iago and directed. He was impressed and said, "If you are interested in doing anything in pictures, I'll make a test of you." So I did make a test and, as a result, was put under contract to Columbia Pictures.

David: And *The Lone Wolf Takes a Chance* was your first picture.

Lloyd: Yes. It seems a long time ago. It *was* a long time ago.

David: You appeared in most of the Columbia B series pictures during the early forties. I know you were in Boston Blackie pictures, Blondie pictures, and some of the westerns. I was checking the other day and discovered that you were in an old Tex Ritter and Wild Bill Elliott picture.

Lloyd: And a Charlie Starrett picture. You've done a lot of research. *[Laugh]* That's fantastic!

David: Harry Cohn, the notorious head of the studio, has been described as autocratic, intimidating, and something of a tyrant by many who worked at the studio. What was it like for you to be a contract player on Cohn's lot, Columbia Pictures?

Lloyd: It was rough! He tried to get his money's worth out of me as he did all of the contract players. I think we only got about $72.50 a week or something like that. I was sometimes in three or four pictures at the same time doing small parts. Maybe in one day I'd be in two different pictures.

The only thing that saved me as a sort of an artist, you might say, was that I was a part of a thing called The Actors Lab, which was an offshoot of the Group Theatre.[24] I worked at my craft there and studied and learned a lot. I was in plays there at The Actors Lab; we put on some very good productions: *Volpone* and *All My Sons*, for example.

That was the only thing that kept me alive artistically. It was just rough doing that type of work [in the Columbia Bs]. But I did observe, and I worked with people like Ronald Coleman and Spencer Tracy, Loretta Young, Paul Muni, some of the greats. So it was great in that respect. It was a good experience.

David: I don't know how much radio you did. I have a *Suspense* radio program with you starring entitled "Deep, Deep Is My Love." Does that maybe ring a bell?

Lloyd: Yeah, sure!

David: That's a great *Suspense* program.

Lloyd: Yes, yes it was. When I was going to UCLA, I used to make some money doing those shows on the side. That's another era, that whole radio thing, and it really kept the actors in pin money because the [stage] plays were few and far between, but if you got into radio, you could do a lot of that radio work. That helped!

David: I wrote a book on one old-time radio program, *The Lone Ranger*.

Lloyd: Oh, my gosh! Well, I played a lot of heavies on *Red Ryder*. Tommy Cook[25] was Little Beaver.

David: Reed Hadley[26] played Red Ryder for a while; I don't know whether that was when you were on it.

It looks as if Gary Cooper and Lloyd Bridges are about to mix it up in this staged scene from the classic western *High Noon*.

Lloyd: Yes, he did. But I used to talk in a [providing an example] mean, kind of lowdown voice, like that. *[Big laugh]* God! Tommy Cook, now I see him all the time. He's quite a tennis player, and I'm into the whole tennis thing, the pro-celebrity tennis circuit. There's a certain group of actors who love to play tennis, and we go all over playing for worthy causes. Last year we made over $400,000 for Muscular Dystrophy.

David: Getting back to your film career, you worked your way up the ladder in films with major supporting roles in such films as *A Walk in the Sun,*[27] *Canyon Passage,*[28] *Home of the Brave*[29] until you received starring roles in films like *Rocket Ship X-M*[30] and *Little Big Horn.*[31] Your role as the deputy in *High Noon*[32] with Gary Cooper and Grace Kelly seemed to mark a turn in your acting career to more dramatic roles in major productions.

Lloyd: Well, I'd done heavies and interesting characters before. I think it was because Gary Cooper was in it and because *High Noon* was a first for a very special type of western and it was a big success. I think that was the main reason that I was recognized a little.

David: I've got to ask this question; it's a pretty stock question: what was it like to work with Gary Cooper in a western?

Lloyd: It was fabulous. He was a beautiful, beautiful person and he was so nice to me. It's one of the very special memories that I have of having worked with some of the great actors of the past, great personalities. It was a strange experience working with Coop. Sometimes I felt that scenes with him just weren't working; he doesn't seem to be doing anything more than talking—it's all so simple. It [Cooper's acting] comes across like gangbusters, of course, as we all know, because that was kind of Cooper's personality; it was all sort of off-the-cuff.

David: He won an Academy Award for that role, of course, and it has been said that Cooper was suffering from an ulcer when *High Noon* was made and that the pained expressions and looks of anguish he so eloquently expressed were really only the pain of the ulcer. What do you know about this?

Lloyd: [Laugh] Well, I think the one who wrote that wanted to call attention to himself, probably, instead of Cooper. Writers have said that the closest I ever got to water was a dry Martini [referring to *Sea Hunt*]. It makes a good sort of line, good story. I do know that Coop had a bad back at the time. It took a lot of courage to do that fight [with me] under the horse. He said, "Oh, gosh, let's do it; it'll be something kind of special." But I don't remember any ulcers.

David: It seemed for a few years that you were forever to be typed as the cowardly or jealous or cruel or animal-like second lead in a lot of movies. I'm thinking of your roles in *High Noon, The Rainmaker,*[33] *The Goddess,*[34] for example. Were you ever concerned that you were getting typed in these unsympathetic roles?

Lloyd: Oh, no. And I did a lot of baddies in westerns too, B westerns that most of us have never seen. You've probably checked on those too; you probably know some of the baddies I played.

But, you know, it's all in an actor's handbag; I didn't have any choice in those days too much, and sometimes those characters can be just as interesting as the leads. It was a nice experience, for example, working in *The Rainmaker* with the stars of that picture.

David: Burt Lancaster, Katharine Hepburn. Yeah, those are pretty good people to be working with. The TV series *Sea Hunt* certainly turned your screen image around and made you a hero in the eyes of the public. How did you happen to get into *Sea Hunt?*[35]

Lloyd: Well, there again it was a job. It seemed like it would be a very interesting series, going into the water. That had never been done before. The thing that I was fearful of, as most of the actors were at that time, was if you got into a successful series that you'd be typed. I guess the money and the unusual kind of quality of the series attracted me, and I wasn't working that much either at the time,[36] so I took a plunge, so to speak. *[Laugh]*

I hadn't dived or done that sort of thing before; in fact, Ivan Tors, the producer, didn't even ask me if I knew how to swim. I had done a lot of swimming, but I had never dived before, but I learned about that. It's like a lot of other things an actor does; I never rode a horse either until I got into westerns.

Lloyd played the role of Mike Nelson in the *Sea Hunt* TV series.

David: Luke Halpin, the actor who played the older boy on the *Flipper* series, told me a while back that you were his biggest hero when he was a little kid and that your character, Mike Nelson, inspired him as he worked in the *Flipper* series. Did you realize the impact the *Sea Hunt* series was having on a generation of youngsters back there in the late 1950s and early sixties?

Lloyd: Yes, I am acquainted with that. The fringe benefits of having done *Sea Hunt* are tremendous. Wherever I go anyone who is involved with underwater work naturally knew about *Sea Hunt* and Mike Nelson, and I do get to talk with a lot of people who are involved with underwater work: oceanographers and people who have been turned on to oceanography and all kinds of things that are happening under water today that are very exciting.

David: I have a person in my office, as a matter of fact, who has gotten into scuba diving, and he was quite interested in the fact that I was going to talk to you because you spurred his interest in it back in the early 1960s.

Lloyd: I'm really delighted, of course, because there is so much to be learned and so much for the world to gain by what we have to offer under water if we don't pollute it before it's being used for what we need. I'd like to make a plea for people to do something about the pollution that's going on under water.

Lloyd and Ivan Tors, the producer of *Sea Hunt*, received Certificates of Appreciation from the Greater Miami Fiesta Committee, Inc. for their work on *Sea Hunt*.

I know it's bad above, too, especially in a place like Los Angeles and a lot of the big cities. You haven't got it here in Sarasota, but it's miserable in Los Angeles; it used to be a beautiful place to live, and they're ruining it now with all the pollution, and the same thing is happening in the water.

We have a place in Malibu and I go swimming and diving out there a lot, and it's nothing like it was ten years ago. I used to have fifteen, twenty feet of visibility, and now I'm lucky if I can see my fingernails.

David: Well, *Sea Hunt* certainly provided you a platform for your environmental concerns, and it's great that you've taken advantage of that opportunity. Mike Nelson was an interesting character for you to play. What do you look for in a role when you're deciding on a project?

Lloyd: I like to play characters that have a lot of dimension to them, that aren't cardboard characters, that are a little unusual. I like to play comedy; I like to play drama just so that I keep working, doing all different kinds of characters.

That's the only problem with doing a series; you have to do the same character all the time. I did play in a series that Aaron Spelling produced that was called *The Lloyd Bridges Show*.[37] It was about a writer who would see somebody, and it would trigger his imagination and, all of a sudden, he'd be a butcher, a banker, a wirewalker, something, you see. So I played a different character every time. It was more difficult but more interesting than playing the same character all the time.

David: And then you did a series called *The Loner*,[38] I believe, right after that.

Lloyd: Yeah. Rod Serling was responsible for that. You're really up on all my credits. It's fantastic!

David: Of the different television series that you've starred in, which is your favorite?

Lloyd: I guess the most interesting was the one I did for Spelling where I did play different characters. It was very interesting.

David: With your busy schedule of film and TV work, have you had time to do much stage work in recent years?

Lloyd: That was one of the things that *Sea Hunt* did for me—made me a kind of known personality, a star, so to speak. I was then offered parts on Broadway that I'd never had an opportunity to do before. I did *Oh, Men, Oh, Women,* and then *Man of La Mancha.*

David: Did you do that; I didn't know that!

Lloyd: I took over for Dick Kiley.[39] He was leaving for his vacation, and I was about to go into a picture. They said it was a good time to get my feet wet; no pun intended there. So I did it for two weeks, got up on the part. I'm not that much of a singer, but, you know, you've got a character to hide behind, a very interesting, great character [Don Quixote]. So I did it for two weeks and then I was prepared to go on again as soon as I finished my picture and Kiley finished his run, but at that time my girl [daughter Cindy] had a very serious operation and I had to be with her, so I couldn't do the run.

Jose Ferrer[40] tells me that's the greatest thing I ever did for him, not to do the show, because he got to do it and said he had a wonderful time doing it. I saw Jo in it; he was great. I also did *Cactus Flower* for nine months on Broadway in New York.

David: I directed that show a few years ago here in Sarasota.

Lloyd: Did you? That's a good comedy, full of laughs.

David: It seems that show business parents are sometimes hesitant about their kids going into show business. Were you pleased when your sons Jeff and Beau indicated they wanted to follow in your footsteps as actors?

Lloyd: Well, my wife and I always like to spend a lot of time with our kids. When an actor works, he has pretty long hours, but there's a lot of time off, so we spend a lot of time with our kids, my wife and I. This was a chance to be with the kids even at work, and they were fascinated because kids at that age are always interested in what their daddy's doing—and my work was kind of special.

Every once in a while I'd be coming home in cowboy clothes, and they'd want to try on the guns and the belt and the hat and the boots, and everything. They got interested in an insidious way like that, and then, of course, when *Sea Hunt* came, they were always interested in the swimming and the ocean. They wanted to know about the use of the mask and the fins and snorkel and all that. They kind of got into it in an easy, gentle way. Whenever there was a part for a kid in anything I was involved in, I'd always say, "My kid can do it." We always checked on them first to see if they could cut the mustard, and they usually did. They always enjoyed it.

Neither Beau nor Jeff was that crazy about acting. Beau wanted to be a baseball coach; he was always into coaching and baseball. The Dodgers had touted him, as a matter of fact. Jeff has written about sixty songs, lyrics and the music. They're both very talented as far as music is concerned. Their interest wasn't really that much into acting until fairly recent.

My daughter, as a matter of fact, Lucinda—Cindy, we call her— she was more into painting and writing; she went to the University of California at Santa Barbara, and it's only recently that she decided she's going to get into acting too. She did a couple of guest star roles in my series, and we also did a play together, *Anniversary Waltz.* And now this, she's going to be in *The Great Wallendas* with me. She's going to be playing the nurse. She's a good little actress. The boys think that she is better than they are. *[Laugh]*

David: You're on location here in Sarasota filming *The Great Wallendas.* Tell me a little bit about the film.

Lloyd: Well, it's a very unusual film; it's not every day that you see a picture about wirewalkers. The people who work in this world are unusual people. I feel so close to the Wallendas now, Karl and Helen, his wife and all the kids, Edith and Herman and Jennie and Karla and Gunther. They're all here.

I saw a documentary film about them a long time ago and to see them here and their ups and downs is tremendous. They're way high and then they're way low, some tragedy happens. The other day it happened to Karl . . .

[At this point there was a knock on the door of Lloyd's trailer, and we paused in our conversation as the assistant director of *The Great*

Wallendas spoke to Lloyd.]

The assistant director said I'm through for the day, so we can relax and take our time.

We're shooting here right in Karl Wallenda's back yard. They've got all the wire apparatus up here. It was back here that Karl fell off

Four of the Flying Wallendas are seen here rehearsing at their home in Sarasota. Second from the left is Karl Wallenda, the patriarch of the family.

the wire the other day, and he was up twenty feet high. There were two men underneath him on bicycles and they had a bar on him and he was on top of this bar, balancing the bar with his pole and a chair. He rested the pole on his knee and then put the chair in the back and as he was sitting down, the pole started to roll off and he grabbed for the pole and went down.

It was the worst moment that I've ever gone through. I've learned to love the guy and to see him fall and on the back of his head. I thought that's it, that's the end of him. He was unconscious for just a beat, I think. But when he came to, immediately he wanted to go back up on the wire. It took about three of us to say, "No, you can't do that." There were no bones broken from this miracle that happened. He does have pain now; he's *got* to have a little pain. He's got a brace on his neck now.

It was just a miracle [he didn't get hurt seriously]; they are very religious people. I think there *was* a miracle there; he had a lot of outside help. They're tremendous people and it's an exciting kind of life, and I have a feeling we've captured it.

We've got a very good director, Larry Elikann, and producer Danny Wilson has done a lot of very good shows out of New York, and the cast, I think, is just fine. With a little help from God we should really do a great job on this, and he seems to be around. He had to be there when poor Karl Wallenda hit that ground. Karl is such a wonderful guy, and I feel so honored to be playing Karl Wallenda in this script. He's very helpful; and he's very eager too to see that we do the right kind of job and authentic kind of a job.

David: Are you going to try some of those tricks yourself on the high wire?

Lloyd: I don't know that I'm going to get *that* high up. These wirewalkers got there after years of training. All of them started when they were three or four years old, I guess. The Wallendas started their grandchildren when they were three or four, and they are just beautiful up there on the wire. You know, when he fell, before the ambulance had left the grounds, they were back up on that wire again, working. This is the way they've been trained, and this is what he would want them to do. Fabulous people!

David: After such a full show business career, do you still have worlds you want to conquer? Is there something that you haven't done yet that you still strive to do?

Lloyd: Well, I did something a few days ago; I got on this wire here, walking on the wire. *[Laugh]* But I think that's part of living an exciting life; leaving that door open and trying something new all the time. It doesn't have to be anything that you risk your life for, but keeping your eyes and ears and all your senses open and enjoying everything in life. There're a lot of wonderful, exciting things to see and to do.

David: Have you ever thought of retiring; do actors retire?

Lloyd: I don't know. I feel just like Karl Wallenda does about that. He said, "I'll die on the wire." And I'll die on the boards, I guess, or in front of the camera. I think a person should always keep active; I think retiring is for the birds unless you're doing the kind of work you don't want to do and you're miserable. I think the mistake that's made sometimes is people work so hard and slave away to get the money to someday take it easy and knock off. Well, today, now, is very important, and I think sometimes a person may look too far ahead. You've got to live now, today.

David: Thank you, Lloyd Brides, very much.

Lloyd: Nice being with you.

Lloyd's closing comments regarding retirement and Karl Wallenda turned out to be very prophetic. Five months after our conversation Karl Wallenda *did* die on the wire. On March 22, 1978, the seventy-three year old Wallenda attempted to walk between the two towers of the ten-story Condado Plaza Hotel in San Juan, Puerto Rico, on a wire stretched one hundred and twenty-one feet above the pavement. In winds that exceeded thirty miles per hour during his attempted wire walk, he fell to his death. The Wallenda family did not attribute his fall to the winds but to "several misconnected guy ropes along the wire."

Lloyd Bridges is Admiral "Tug" Benson in *Hot Shots!*, an outrageous send-up of flyboy films directed by Jim Abrahams, who directed Lloyd in several such film spoofs.

The Great Wallendas was telecast on NBC February 12, 1978, just a little over a month before Karl's death. The film got respectable ratings for the network and was years later released on videotape. As of this writing there is still no DVD of the film.

Lloyd remained busy in films and television work throughout the next two and a half decades, doing some of his finest work, and delighting in the fact that his two sons also became famous and respected actors in films and television. Lloyd got to work with his sons several times over the years. Most notably he worked with Jeff in *Tucker: The Man and His Dream*[41] in 1988. Older son Beau had a short-lived [fifteen episodes], delightfully offbeat, dramedy TV series in 1993 entitled *Harts of the West*[42] in which a bearded Lloyd had a recurring comedy role as a ranch hand. Beau's mother Dorothy even made an appearance in the pilot episode in a dream sequence. Lloyd also got to work with ten-year-old grandson Dylan Bridges [Beau's boy] in a 1995 episode of *The Outer Limits* TV series.

In the 1980s Lloyd Bridges began to display a late-in-career knack for wacky, off-the-wall comedy, especially for director Jim Abrahams. It first manifested itself when he played a drug-addled air traffic controller in Abrahams' *Airplane*[43] and its follow-up *Airplane II: The Sequel*.[44] Later examples include *Hot Shots*[45] (1991), a *Top Gun/Rambo* parody in which he plays hard-as-nails Admiral Thomas "Tug" Benson, and its sequel *Hot Shots! Part Deux*,[46] both directed by Abrahams, in which his "Tug" character has now been promoted to President. Lloyd also made his comedy mark on the *Seinfeld* TV series as the zany "Izzy Mandelbaum."

Lloyd continued working right up to the end. He told the *Los Angeles Times* in 1994, "I really exist when I'm working as an actor, and next to my family, that's my greatest joy in life." His last film was another comedy send-up, *Jane Austin's Mafia*,[47] which took the *Godfather* trilogy of films to task.

Lloyd Bridges was known to have a heart condition and there were rumors of possible prostate cancer, but when he died on March 10, 1998, his death was listed as "natural causes." He was eighty-five years old. Lloyd's wife Dorothy, son Beau, and daughter Cindy were at his side. It was later reported that he was cremated and his ashes were given to the family. Beau Bridges said to the press that day, "We all feel really blessed to have been with my dad for these eighty-five years. If dad could speak to those people who are thinking about him right now, he would want you to all think about family."

Hans Conried

September 27, 1977

"I remember I played eighteen parts in
thirty minutes on one occasion."

— on radio acting

This is the portrait shot that Hans Conried was using for personal appearances at the time of our conversation in 1977.

As a radio kid growing up in the forties and fifties, I gradually became accustomed to hearing a voice that seemed to be everywhere on my radio dial. If the character I was listening to was pompous, blustery, a stuffed shirt, or hammy Shakespearean actor in style, it would usually belong to that one voice. If the character were Russian, French, German, Polish, Jewish—whatever the accent—I recognized the hidden voice behind the accent as *that voice*. Finally, as I visited my local movie theater, I began to notice a tall, skeleton-thin young actor who could spruce up an otherwise run-of-the-mill "B" and sometimes "A" picture with delightful, frequently eccentric, characterizations. I was then able to put a face and body to the voice—and a name: Hans Conried.

I don't remember exactly why Hans Conried happened to be in Sarasota on September 27th of 1977, but I do know that I got a call early that morning informing me that he was in town and might be available to talk with me if I could get to the Boys' Club by eleven o'clock. It seemed a strange place to rendezvous with one of the great character actors and dialecticians of radio, motion pictures, television, and the stage, but, as Hans would later say, "Be that as it may."

Anyway, as near as I can recall, there were mostly adults at the club and Hans, I seem to remember, was to present an award to someone. That's the best I can do on the remembrance front. But the point at this late date is that Hans Conried *was* there and, yes, he was amenable to talking with a radio journalist, as we were sometimes called back in the day.

Tape recorder in hand I promptly arrived a few minutes before eleven and sought out the contact person who had promised to put me in the presence of the actor I had long admired and was eager to talk with. I was told that Mr. Conried was waiting in a side office until the time of his award presentation (or whatever) and that I should go right in.

I found him seated behind the desk in the small but serviceable side office that had been designated, probably the daily abode of a conscientious secretary who was now engaged with the crowd that was gathering in the main hall of the club. Hans was dressed conservatively in a dark gray suit, white shirt, and subdued bowtie, and looked, for all the world, like a stern, bean-counting executive from some high-level financial institution.

He gave me an acerbic look as I introduced myself and sat on the opposite side of the desk, suddenly feeling as if I were entering into a job interview for a position for which I was totally unqualified. But then I saw a trace of a smile and felt obliged to get on with my business. As we conversed, I think he was taken aback that I had obviously spent a fair amount of time researching his career or perhaps that I was a biographical stalker. Either way, we got on well.

David: You were one of the top character actors on big time, old time radio, performing on many of the most popular programs. What's the first network radio program you can remember performing on?

Hans: The first network radio program I performed on was a show called *First Nighter*[48] with Barbara Luddy. I performed with a young man who was brought out from Chicago to be a movie star in the season of 1936, Don Ameche, who was appearing in Atlanta last week and we renewed our acquaintance between acts where he was performing. He came to see me the night he had off, and I went to see him the night I had off. I remarked [to Ameche] on the elegance—I did that for the benefit of my daughter who was sitting in the room—of early radio; that we were obliged, with an audience, to wear dinner jackets, you see.

I was able to win the audition against twenty-four, I think, other actors. The number was significant. They brought the show from Chicago, as I said, and they had their own character man, Cliff Sebea, but they needed a young character actor, and I won the audition. We had two or three day's preparation [for the show].

Now, the salary was magnificent: twenty-five dollars. But I needed a dinner jacket and I had none. I was, I guess, twenty; no, I was nineteen. I bought a dinner jacket for twenty-two fifty—completely outfitted for twenty-two fifty. They realized that investment cost me most of that salary, so they maintained me on the show as second character man for about three years thereafter. But it was a golden, marvelous time with such elegance and propriety, such presentation that a premiere in Hollywood would not presume.

David: My friend Charles Livingstone was a Detroit radio director who years ago directed *The Green Hornet, The Lone Ranger, Sergeant Preston of the Yukon.* . . .[49]

Hans: Those were the only things that came out of Detroit.

David: Right. He said that as stage actors came to town, quite often they'd want to pick up a few bucks working. . . .

Hans: Five or seven-fifty. I doubt more on *The Green Hornet.*

David: That's about right. But he said it wasn't always easy working with stage actors in radio.

Hans: No. It was a different technique. We had a bag of tools, but we applied them quite differently. Most actors begin as stage actors; I had done some stage work, but what can you do when you're seventeen or eighteen? But radio employed me steadily from 1935 on. That was my primary form of self-support other than motion pictures, which was yet another medium.

No, stage actors very often wanted to proclaim, wanted the physical movement, and they were stuck to the microphone. I remember when I supported John Barrymore in the summer of 1937.[50] He was a splendid, a great actor. I did Laertes to his Hamlet [and] Malcolm, which is two lines, in Macbeth. They had to build a little cage around the microphone because in his passion he would take the microphone stand and shake it. Well, that couldn't be permitted!

Radio acting was completely mental. You became accustomed to emphasizing so much vocally, labially, lingually, that you made faces. The problem when you did a motion picture the next week was that you were accustomed to emphasizing so much [on radio] that you made faces for the camera. The camera being so close to you—much closer than a stage audience—you had to be much more subdued on the screen than you were on the stage. Each one has its aspects.

David: Let me say something to you and we'll see if it jogs a memory nerve. Ugga-ugga-boo, ugga-boo-ugga . . . .

Hans: Ugga-ugga-boo, ugga-boo-boo-ugga!

David: I got it wrong! *[Laugh]*

Hans is seen here in a typically grumpy-looking photo from the late 1940s-early fifties.

Hans: You got it wrong! *[Laugh]* "Hello, Mel. Ugga-ugga-boo, ugga-boo-boo-ugga!" That was rather late in life; that was comedy, post-war. We had done nice things, the best literary aspects of radio past with the necessary propaganda in the war. I was gone in the Army myself for almost four years, and when I came back a dear old friend of mine, Mel Blanc[51]—we are still good friends, I'm happy to say—offered me a job as a comedian. It was nothing below my dignity; I had been digging ditches for a while in the Army, but be that as it may, "Ugga-ugga-boo, ugga-boo-boo-ugga" was the entrance of Mr. Cushing, who was the great panjam of some sort of a society. . . .

David: "The Loyal Order of Benevolent Zebras."

Hans: Well, then you know more than my memory permits me to know, and I didn't realize that it had been written down on any Dead-Sea scrolls. But be that as it may, suddenly I hit it hot as a comedian, and whereas I had been a character comedian at worst and a character actor at best, suddenly I began to stooge for everybody in Hollywood. There was a great vogue then for comedy, and I did comedy until the end of radio in 1953.

David: I think probably the two programs that you are most known for are *Life with Luigi*[52] starring J. Carrol Naish and *My Friend Irma*[53] with Marie Wilson. You were "Schultz" on *Luigi* and "Professor Kropotkin" on *Irma*.

Hans: I did one [*Life with Luigi*] for six years and the other for seven years with Marie Wilson.

David: You worked with Alan Reed a lot—the actor who played "Pasquale" on *Luigi* and "Mr. Clyde," Irma's crotchety boss, on *Irma*—and much later, of course, became the voice of Fred Flintsone on television.

Hans: Oh, yes. And Alan just passed this year, you know. And he was a good friend, too.

David: You used to have a stock opening, I believe, on the *My Friend Irma* program. . . .

Hans: Where do you get this, such ridiculous scraps of unimportant miscellanea?

David: People are fascinated by this stuff. You used to come to the door and Mrs. O'Reilly. . . .

Hans: Who [the actress] was the mother in life of Gale Gordon.[54] Gloria Gordon, a lovely lady! [Mrs. O'Reilly came to the door] and I'd say, "It's only me, Professor Kropotkin."

It was so cut and dried. My entrance would always be between page four and six of the first act, and I would come in between twenty-two and twenty-five of the second act. They never varied, you know. People say they liked them [the shows] because they were identical week to week. The situations changed slightly, but the characters had their same appearances and their same function.

David: Say it again, your entrance line the way you did it on the show.

Hans: Well, I can't remember what it was; it's been twenty-five years ago. "It's only me, Professor Kropotkin."

David: *[Laugh]* Beautiful!

Hans: It ran for seven years. The first week of the show Kropotkin was a gypsy violinist who lived in the attic and on whom the landlady, Mrs. O'Reilly, had a crush. That's why he never paid any rent. He answered only with the fiddle; they had the violinist in the orchestra play that part.

Then they said after the first show, "Well, it's a cute idea, but where can we go from there, there's nothing. We've got to get a speaking actor to do that." So they said, "We'll use this guy; he's got dialects." And I got the job. "Kropotkin" is a grand duke name among the Russians, very noble. [With Russian accent] So I played it Russian.

But the political situation was then so unsatisfactory, after the second week they said, "Conried, we think that that's a good character, we think it's funny, we like the way you handle it, but we can't have him Russian." I said, "You're stuck with Kropotkin; what will you do with Kropotkin?" So I then made him what we call a Jew comic, and it became a Jewish dialect thereafter, but maintaining Kropotkin. And it lasted for seven years until the end of radio. The *Life with Luigi* [character that Hans played] was a German, "Schultz."

David: Dialect humor was very popular on radio, and, of course, you were a master at it.

Hans: As a character actor on radio, you see, it was very important to be able to do dialects. In the early days—before we were organized in 1937—you could play any number of roles in a radio show. I remember I played eighteen parts in thirty minutes on one occasion. Anything you could sound you could play. For a character man on radio there is no makeup change, no costume change; you couldn't affect any light differences. You had to change your voice entirely. So it [dialect] was the easiest way to change your voice.

David: If it comes naturally to you.

Hans: If it comes easily. And if they offer to pay you as much as five dollars a performance, why should it not come easily?

David: You performed on *The Jack Paar Show*[55] in 1947, the radio program.

Hans: Yes, when I came home from the war.

David: You played an aging actor on that show, I believe.

Hans: I have no idea. We played different things every week. We'd never met each other—our backgrounds had been similar—we'd heard about each other in the Pacific. I was [affecting a snooty, comic attitude] doing more legitimate work, of course. I was on Armed Forces Radio when they took the shovel out of my hand—after I lost a tank. *[Laugh]*

Be that as it may, he needed people around him, and we had similar backgrounds and were a similar age, and he would utilize me, and we became friends. Jack was always very generous, and whenever he had a show—he was only styled by heaven and nature to be a star; he couldn't support, you understand—he'd have me on it.

One day he called me from New York, saying "Listen, I got a talk show on at night." I said, "What do you mean a talk show? Do you mean like the one that Steve Allen had that flopped?" He said, "Well, a little different and you have a big mouth. Come on out and talk." So I became an irregular regular with Paar on television,[56] and on the strength of that I cannot deny that his patronage afforded me a larger world in which to operate.

David: I have got to ask the greatest cliché question in show business.

Hans: And I will have the greatest cliché answer for you.

David: What is Jack Paar really like?

Hans: Well, he's a really nice fellow. We don't see each other as much as we used to. You know, people grow apart, we're not as active. I bumped into his daughter[57] in Sardi's last year. He's got a charming daughter that's been admitted to the bar. I think she's marrying a young lawyer or has married him by now. We exchange Christmas cards, and when I play Westport, Connecticut, he and Miriam [Paar's wife] will come down and see me. We haven't seen each other since because my family's seldom in the East, and if I'm in the New York area, I'm working.

David: On television, along with the Paar program, undoubtedly people think of you as the stuffed-shirt character "Uncle Tonoose' on the *Make Room for Daddy*[58] show with Danny Thomas.

Hans: Well, if they do, their memory is a long one because I have not done that in some years.

David: Ah, but people remember, and you'd be surprised how often it's seen in reruns—or maybe you wouldn't be surprised.

Hans: Yes, I'm conscious of them. I try to close my eyes since I've long since been paid my last seventh check. You know, we get a progressively smaller check for seven exposures. After that it belongs to the world.

David: You have made quite a career out of playing grouchy stuffed shirts on television situation comedies.

Hans: I don't play them; I *am* a grouchy stuffed shirt.

David: There are people of several generations who have heard you on radio and seen you on television playing these grouchy-stuffed-shirt roles. Are they a little bit afraid of you because of these roles?

Hans: I hope not. I hope they rush to the box office without approaching me personally and buy a ticket. *[Laugh]*

David: I understand that you are going to be playing a similar character on *The Tony Randall Show*[59] this season.

Hans: Yes, yes. I can't tell you much [about it]. I haven't seen it. I may not see any of the ones I do. I'm going to be on the stage now for the next three weeks, and then I'm going to go back to do some more. I've done three shows already—they're being shown on Saturday nights. I must say that we are at a point now of early honeymoon; there's a great deal of mutual love being thrown around.

It's a splendid company of actors and very bright young people writing it. The show has been established a year without my endangering it in any way. It's substantial now and dependent on what its opposition will be on Saturday nights, I would hope it would be a success. It would change my life considerably because I have not worked on television since the Danny Thomas days, and that's seven or eight years ago. It will afford me the opportunity to sleep in my own bed in California for a while.

David: You were in a lot of movies I've enjoyed over the years, usually in a character role: *Summer Stock*[60] with Judy Garland, Disney's *Peter Pan*[61] where you were the voice of "Hook," *Three for Bedroom C*[62] with Gloria Swanson, *The Monster that Challenged the World*[63] with Tim Holt. I've got to ask you about a movie that I've found particularly fascinating in which you played the title character, *The Five Thousand Fingers of Dr. T.*[64]

This press book ad appeared in newspapers at the time of the film's release in 1953. Hans played the title role of Dr. Terwilliker.

Hans: Ah, you have done a lot of [research] work. That was one of the great money losers of all time. It was an opportunity, as we say, a break that didn't pay off. That being a success, my life might have been much changed. It was a great failure. I don't denigrate it in any sense artistically. It was created by Dr. Suess,[65] Ted Geisel, whose latest production, *Halloween is Grinch Night*, will be performed on television with me starring this fall sometime—I guess the end of October when Halloween comes around.

We are still on the warmest basis of friendship, and his efforts [On *Dr. T*] went to naught other than his salary. He designed it and wrote it. I worked on it; Stanley Kramer[66] produced it; and it was a failure.

The Americans were not ready for fantasy.

If you see it in a distressfully cut version on television, you are seeing much less than the original offered. It's been cut with a broken beer bottle. Even so, you will recognize that it had aspects: the dancing, in which I had little part, is still superb. The ballet is still wonderful and the music—much of it is still left—can still be eaten with a spoon, as the entire score could be at that time. It failed.

David: It might have failed, but it's become something of a cult film.

Hans: It's a classic. My children saw it at UCLA and they called it a classic. In its time it never played any theater in the United States more than five days. They stayed away in droves, as we say.

Dr. T (Hans) is instructing young Bart (Tommy Rettig) during his piano lesson in this scene from *The Five Thousand Fingers of Dr. T.*

David: And now it's being shown at film festivals as a classic.

Hans: It's a little late to mend my broken heart, I can tell you.

David: Radio, Television, motion pictures, the stage. Which do you prefer?

Hans: I will give you a professional answer: that which I am doing tonight, which will be next week at the big theater in Miami with Molly Picon in *The Second Time Around*. I'm happy that I've been able to change the blade in whatever tool I utilize in my craft.

David: And you'll be opening in Miami. . . .

Hans: A week from tonight—whether I know the lines or not, whether I should be rehearsing this morning and learning my business or not, we'll open.

David: And where do you go from there?

Hans: Fort Lauderdale for a week. They'll catch on to us in a week, I'm sure, and we'll have to leave town. And then I'll go back to Tony Randall.

David: Thank you very much, Hans Conried.

Hans: Thank you.

Hans was only sixty when we talked in 1977, although he struck me as somewhat older. It was his nature to gently and humorously deprecate his own achievements in the various media in which he worked, but one could not help but sense that Hans felt that his career was somewhat scattershot and that he had not been able to achieve the level of stardom that he hoped for himself in any of the show business areas where he displayed such extraordinary talent.

He was proud of his pre-World War Two radio work where he excelled as a character actor in some of radio's finest drama series and where he was able to perform Shakespeare with Barrymore—high-class stuff for a serious actor—only to follow it after the war in mostly light-weight sitcoms where he was frequently asked to play outrageously over-the-top eccentrics in *My Friend Irma, Life with Luigi* and so many other radio and later television shows—"Suddenly I became a stooge for everyone in Hollywood." If *The Five Thousand Fingers of Dr. T* had been a success "my life might have been much changed," he told me. He was recognized for his extraordinary "voice" work in Disney's *Peter Pan* as "Captain Hook" and the later *Rocky and Bullwinkle Show*[67] on television where he voiced "Snidley Whiplash" to the delight of children (and adults) of several generations. But in that type of work you were just a disembodied voice—it was lucrative but probably didn't do much for self-esteem.

Hans only made a couple of movies after our conversation, Disney's *The Cat from Outer Space*[68] and *Oh, God! Book II*,[69] but did lots of voice work in such animated kids shows as *Drak Pack*[70] where he was the voice of "Dr. Dredd." During the seventies and eighties Hans concentrated more on stage work, appearing, for example, in Neil Simon's *The Odd Couple* in Atlanta for over a year and touring with Molly Picon in *The Second Time Around*,[71] later called *Something Old, Something New* when it opened on Broadway in January of 1977 and flopped. It was nine months later in September of 1977 when we talked, and he was again doing the show, touring with it under its original title and again costarring with Molly Picon.

Hans's last involvement in a network television series was the short-lived and now pretty much forgotten one-hour drama series, *American Dream*, which appeared briefly on ABC in April of 1981 and only ran until June. It was the story of a suburban family that is forced to adjust to inner-city life after they move to Chicago. Hans played "Abe Berlowitz," the old-timer who sold them the house and now was their neighbor.

Hans had married way back in January of 1942, and he and his wife Margaret had four children. By all accounts the marriage had been a successful one despite the fact that his work kept him away from home and family for long periods of time. (His stated hope to me that *The Tony Randall Show* might afford him "the opportunity to sleep in my own bed in California for a while" did not come to be; the show was cancelled in March of 1978.)

Hans Conried died following a heart attack on January 5, 1982, at a hospital in Burbank, California. He was survived by his wife and children. It was reported that his body was donated to medical science. A tireless worker right to the end, he had completed a cable-TV version of Neil Simon's *Barefoot in the Park* only the month before. Hans was only sixty-four when he died.

Fellow radio actor Harry Bartell wrote about his friend: "Hans Conried was born a hundred years too late. He should have been touring the country playing Shakespeare with the likes of Edwin Forrest or Edwin Booth instead of doing most of his work in the confines of a radio studio or TV set. There was an air of sadness that hung around him, but he was one of the warmest, brightest people I ever knew."

Dennis Day

December 8, 1977

"Sing, Dennis."

— Jack Benny

This publicity portrait of Dennis Day was sent to fans who requested a photo of the singing and comedy star when he was on *The Jack Benny Program*.

It was mid-afternoon on Tuesday when I got a call at my office from Bobby Breen[72] of Entertainment Plus, a booking agency that Bobby ran with his wife. "David, Dennis Day is coming to Sarasota on Thursday to start his tour of the Florida West Coast condos and retirement homes and I wanted to let you know. You remember Dennis from *The Jack Benny Program*, don't you?"

I assured Bobby that I remembered Dennis from that show and much more and that I would like to talk with him. "Well, I *thought* you might like to meet with Dennis for your radio show; he's just a great guy and I think you two will get on well. He's staying at the Hyatt House and will be there through Saturday. Can I set it up for you?"

Of course, he could! I wouldn't miss an opportunity to talk with Dennis Day. I had followed his career from the time I was a kid, listening to him on *The Jack Benny Program* but also watching him on Benny's later TV shows and Dennis's own radio and TV series. Bobby set up my meeting with Dennis for Thursday afternoon.

Two days later I was on the third floor of the Hyatt, knocking on the door I was told would produce Dennis Day, and it did. "David, come in. Bobby has told me about you; I've been looking forward to your arrival today."

He was attired conservatively in a dark blue suit, dress shirt open at the collar, and a face-wide, warm smile upon his face. His Hyatt suite was tidy except for a few leftover late-lunch items that he apologized for. "Set up your tape recorder and let her go whenever you're ready, David."

David: Everybody knows that you were on *The Jack Benny Program* for many years. How did you happen to get on his radio program?

Dennis: Well, prior to *The Jack Benny Program*, I went to Manhattan College. I graduated from college. I loved singing; I was president of the glee club. I had done a few amateur shows while I was in college. I won the contest for the Metropolitan Colleges of New York City, and I was on with Larry Clinton[73] about three or four times. I took an air check[74] of some of the songs I sang on there.

Then after I got out of college, I was going to go to law school, but I had an operation which kept me out of law school for a little while. In the meantime I went down and started singing and rehearsing and everything else, pounding the pavement trying to get a sustaining job on radio. I did; I got one with WHN in New York. There was no money, but it was experience.

Then, after a little while there, I went over to CBS, and I was on there for, oh, maybe about eight weeks. I was with Raymond Paige and Ray Block,[75] who was the conductor for Jackie Gleason for so long. I took several air checks, naturally, of everything that you would do on these shows.

So Kenny Baker[76] happened to leave the Benny show—seems there was an argument between him and Jack about a little thing that seems to come up a lot called money. Kenny thought he deserved more money, and he left the show and went with someone else. I think every singer in the United States who thought he had a chance was auditioning or at least sending records and everything else [to Benny]. Someone suggested to me that I should send one of my air checks to Jack's agent, which I did. I said, "Well, what have I got to lose?"

Well, by good fortune and good luck [Jack's wife] Mary Livingstone, God bless her, happened to hear it and liked it, and she took it to Jack in Chicago. She played it for him and said, "I think I like him; I think you should audition him." So he came into New York and I was asked to see someone. I didn't know who it was I was going to see. I walked into the room and I nearly fainted because there was Jack Benny, the number one giant in show business—in radio at that time and also motion pictures, he was very big. I walked in and he said, "Would you like to audition for me?" I said, "Well," I stammered, and I said, "Yes, when would you want me?" He said, "What about tomorrow?" I said, "Okay, fine."

So then I left and rushed over and got an accompanist and we rehearsed a few things and the following day I auditioned for Jack way up at Studio AH at NBC in Rockefeller Center. After singing for about twenty minutes, they asked me to take a rest. He was in the control booth way in the back, and I was up on the stage talking to my accompanist. And over the loud speaker after a little rest I heard, "Oh, Dennis." And I turned and said, "Yes, please." Jack told me months later that one of the deciding factors that he liked about me was the fact that I was so polite, [as shown when] he heard me say, "Yes, please."

After the audition was over, I waited around and heard nothing. I figured I had done my best and that was the end of it. About a week went by, maybe ten days, and all of a sudden I got a call to come down and record my voice from the old [*Jack Benny Program*] scripts that they had sent. I was to do the Kenny Baker part. Well, I recorded those, and I didn't hear anything. Another two weeks went by, and then I was asked to go out to California to audition for Jack and his producers.

So Jack gave me a round-trip ticket to go out on the Golden State Limited Train to Los Angeles. I did, and I auditioned for his writers and his producers, and they were non-committal. Jack was there and said, "Well, we still haven't made up our minds. There are a few other people we want to hear and see, but you stick around."

Now, they gave me no money; I had no money, you know. *[Laugh]* I was put up at the Hollywood Athletic Club, which is now the University of Judaism, I believe, on Sunset Boulevard—just about a couple of blocks from NBC, which has been torn down, incidentally. The NBC where I first started was torn down and is now the Home Savings and Loan; it's a savings and loan bank. So, anyway, I stayed at the Hollywood Athletic Club, and I had to send home to my mother and dad for some money, because I didn't have any money.

So then about a week, ten days went by and Jack went up to the World's Fair, which was up in San Francisco at the time, on Treasure Island. Then he came back, and just about a week before the show went on the air [for a new season], Jack signed me to a contract and I stayed with him, believe it or not, for twenty-five years. Incidentally, he took back the other half of the train ticket; he was no dope—he really wasn't. *[Laugh]*

David: I don't know if you happen to know of a singing cowboy of years past named Eddie Dean . . . .

Dennis: Oh, yes, yes.

David: He's a very good singer. I interviewed him some months back for a book that I've written on a history of the singing cowboys. Eddie told me that he auditioned for the "boy singer" role on *The Jack Benny Program* when Kenny Baker left and you beat him out. He said to me, "It worked out all right because Dennis was the one who should have gotten the part."

Dennis: That was very kind of him. It was a great break for me, you know, to come from nowhere, nobody, and to get a starting job at the top. I started at the top, really!

David: And you were very young at the time.

Dennis: Yeah, I was twenty-one. This was October of 1939 that I started and, my gosh, to start at the top, it was a great break, you know. Even though it was a five-year contract, there was a first-two-week option. I had to make good in the first two weeks. If I didn't, I was dropped. If I did, then I was picked up for the next eleven weeks. You see, in radio it was a thirteen-week cycle. The first year it was every thirteen weeks [that] I would be picked up. So at the end of the thirty-nine weeks, we had the summer hiatus, and they didn't know whether they were going to pick me up for the next year because it meant for the *full* year after that. Then Jack came to me and said that, yes, they had decided to keep me.

They still weren't too sure because I hadn't come on as strongly as they would have liked; that's why they brought in the character of my mother, Verna Felton,[77] because they knew I was pretty naïve and scared, you know, and not scrubbed behind the ears. Even though I was born and raised in New York, I think the biggest "hicks," in a sense, do come from New York because we feel that nothing else exists outside the city of New York, nothing west of the Hudson River. *[Laugh]*

I had never been away from New York. Yes, I'd been to Ireland with my aunt, God rest her. I went over to visit my grandparents. You see, both my parents came from the old country and my grandparents were still alive, and I went over to see them. That's the only place I had gone outside of the city of New York.

The Jack Benny Program is on the air! Jack Benny was Dennis Day's mentor and helped to get his career off the ground.

David: How long into the series, after you started, did you really get into the humorous Dennis Day character that developed over the years? Was that right at the beginning or did that grow over time?

Dennis: No, that was after the first year. You see, they had Verna Felton, who played the part of my mother. She was more or less the protector for me. Since I didn't have confidence yet, they didn't feel I had enough confidence, which I readily admit I didn't have the first year. I was just feeling my way and learning my trade and learning comedy and watching the master, Jack Benny, who *was* the master. But they used Vera Felton, you know, as a protective comic foil to aggravate Jack. I would say, "My mother. . . ." and Jack would say, "*Oooh*, your mother!" [as if he found her impossible and a shrew] She was always protecting her son.

David: Wasn't she always telling Jack, "Oh, shut up!"

Dennis: Yeah, "Oh, *shut up*, you!" She'd really put him down! *[Laugh]* Like for instance, Verna would say, "Now Dennis, straighten your tie" and "Here, let me fix it." Jack would then say to Verna, "You know, Mrs. Day, we're not on television." Then she'd say, "You're quite *fortunate*, Mr. Benny!" *[Laugh]* Right to him, a real putdown! It was after the first year [that my character developed]. The writers found that I could do dialects and [comic] things. I started coming out of my shell, and they started writing in things for me. I played the part during World War Two, of Rommel, [with German accent] "Here I am in a tank. Which way is Cairo?" *[Laugh]* They [the writers] gradually started to write all kinds of things for me. I did Jerry Colonna[78] [with Colonna's voice]. "What's the matter, Hope, you crazy or something?"

David: Yes, and I remember reading that one time as a gag, the whole *Jack Benny Program* was done as . . . .

Dennis: *The Bob Hope Show*, yes.

David: And then *The Bob Hope Show*, a few days later, did his show as *The Jack Benny Program*.

Dennis: When we did the Hope take-off, you know, I did the Jerry Colonna part. We were up in Fresno at an Army camp at that time. [After the show] all   the acquaintances of Jerry Colonna called his house—Jerry wasn't in town; he was in New York—and talked with his wife and said, "We just heard Jerry; he's up in Fresno." Well, they swore that Jerry was up in Fresno. *[Laugh]*

   I think one of the toughest things I ever did on radio was to do an imitation of someone and have them in my presence. As you know, Jack had Ronnie and Benita Colman on [his show]. He really started them in radio. Every star wanted to do the Benny show because they knew they would be treated like a star—that they would be the star and Jack would be the straight man for them—they'd get all the laughs.

Well, one of the particular things [on the show] was he [Ronald] was Benny's neighbor and that he hated Jack Benny, didn't want any part of him, and Jack was always trying to get an invitation to dinner or whatever. So [in the show's script] I got on one of the telephones in Jack's home and called Jack, and I pretended to be Ronald Colman. I

Dennis visits Jack Benny on one of his television programs and gets his "Bennys" confused.

said [using Colman's voice and English accent], "Ah, Jack, Benita and I would be extremely happy if you would please come over to dinner tonight. We'd love to see you." And Jack was so delighted; he was ecstatic, supposedly, in the script.

Well, I did that little impression at the rehearsal in front of Ronald Colman and Bonita, his wife. After it was over, Ronald turned to Benita and said [again using Colman's voice], "Wasn't that a wonderful imitation of Douglas Fairbanks, Jr.?" *[Both laugh]* I felt *that* small, but it was a lot of fun.

Then we used to do *The Fred Allen Show* and I'd do Titus Moody[79] [in Moody voice], "Howdy, Bub," the Parker Fennelly role. We used to have a great deal of fun doing satires of other shows. Of course, the thing between Fred Allen and Jack Benny, the so-called feud was not true; they were the best of friends. There was none of that at all. In fact, they'd call each other after the shows.

David: Did you ever do the Fred Allen voice?

Dennis: No, I never did.

David: You do so many voices so beautifully, and Fred Allen is such a type.

Dennis: With that nasal twang, yes. Those were really great days, the days of radio, because it was the theater of the mind. People were able to use their imagination a lot, where today with the boob tube everything is right there in front of you. Radio had such a stimulation for you [the listener]. On radio each person could imagine what the scene looked like or the person looked like, even if they had never seen a picture of them.

In the years that I was on with Jack Benny many people who hadn't seen pictures of me at all imagined that I was either tall, about six foot four with blond hair and a hayseed sticking out of my ears, or I was short, fat, and dumpy. Those were the two impressions that people had of what I looked like; that's what their imaginations did for them.

David: Could you tell me what the planning was for getting the show on the air? You had to get a new show on the air, live, each week.

Dennis: Well, Jack would discuss with the writers what he wanted; then they would meet. They would meet the following morning after a show and discuss [plans for the upcoming show]. Jack would have ideas, and they might have ideas. And then Jack would sit in with the writers; he didn't just farm them out and say, "Hey, you write this part; you write that." They all sat there and Jack would write with them.

David: It was a Sunday show.

Dennis: Yes, and they'd write and sometimes we'd rehearse on Wednesday, but normally it would be on Thursday. That was the first reading. After that they would have an idea where the laughs were and whether certain material was right or should be eliminated or changed. Jack was a great editor; that was the wonderful part about Jack; he was a genius in that respect. He knew what was right, what was good for Jack Benny and everyone in the cast. He knew intuitively what was right for him and for the show.

After the rehearsal, that Thursday rehearsal, we'd come in again on Saturday and read [the script] again once—it'd only take about an hour—and everything would have been tightened up and maybe some gags might have been eliminated and others substituted. The script was better; you better believe it that it was better.

Then we'd come in on Sunday and mike it, we'd rehearse it like a dress [rehearsal], more or less. We never did a dress rehearsal, really, because he didn't like to over rehearse comedy because it gets too pat and too static. He'd rather that you didn't really study your lines and have them down pat.

David: Did you do it three times live for the three time zones?

Dennis: No, we did it twice. We did it once for the East Coast and once for the West Coast. We did it at four o'clock which would be seven o'clock New York time and then we would do it at eight-thirty at night for the West Coast.

David: I read someplace that in one of the scripts it was supposedly contract time and that you and Benny had agreed to everything in the contract, but that you had one stipulation: you wanted to have one day off a week like most people; you wanted to have Sunday off. . . .

Dennis: *[Laugh]* Yes, that's exactly right; that was part of the script — which happened to be, of course, the day the program was on! *[Laugh]*

David: Was there in real life the feeling of "family" among the cast members that we, the listeners, felt?

Dennis: Oh, yes, exactly. I looked forward to it, and I think everyone else on the show looked forward to going to the rehearsals and going to the show itself. It was a charge, really! You really felt so great; you knew it was going to be a lot of fun. And Jack exuded all of that, you know. He was the greatest audience that there was in the world. If I looked at him and said something funny that was in the script—just my look or intonation or whatever it was—Jack would just break right up and fall down [laughing]. They used to talk about it in later days about George Burns; well, that was true. All George Burns had to say to Jack Benny was [in Burns' voice] "Jaaack" and Jack would fall on the floor laughing because he anticipated something hilarious was going to come.

David: *[Laugh]* I recently read a book entitled *The Jack Benny Show,* which you are undoubtedly familiar with.

Dennis: Yes, well, that is the best book that has been written to date; that's the one by Milt Josefsberg. [His book has] love and feeling for the show and really tells the inside story of the people who were associated with Jack.

David: That was my feeling as I read it. Josefsberg indicated in his book that the Dennis Day humor on the program was a little bit different, the way they developed your character. And he mentions this line that was typical of the type of humor they created for Dennis Day. Jack would say, "Well, Dennis, there may be something wrong with the wiring, maybe a short circuit. Did it give off sparks when you plugged it in?" Then you would say in a wide-eyed, naïve manner, "Oooh, plugged it *in!*" There was another situation he cites where you were at the hotel and went swimming in the pool and people laughed at you. Jack would say to you, "Did you have a funny pair of swim trunks on?" And you would say. . . .

Dennis: "Oooh, *trunks!*" *[Both laugh]*

David: Was this what you might classify as the Dennis Day type of humor on the show?

Dennis: Yeah, that's right. That's what Jack and the writers wrote for me. This is what they had: the naïveté, and kind of silly, not too bright—you know—nice but naïve.

David: But in the final analysis you always got the punch line on Jack.

Dennis: Right, yes! I always seemed to come out okay. There was an illogical logic to what I had to say.

David: *[Both laugh]* That's a good way to put it. How did you happen to get your own radio show when you were still the "boy singer" on *The Jack Benny Program*? *A Day in the Life of Dennis Day*[80] was your show that started in 1946.

Dennis: Well, the late Tom Harrington was with the Ted Bates Agency, and he had formerly been a producer for Young and Rubicam, an advertising agency of *The Jack Benny Program*. That was for several seasons before I came on the show. He had always been an admirer of mine, and when I got out of the Navy in 1946, after being in for two years, Tom signed me to a contract with Ted Bates, and they started to form a show which eventually became the Dennis Day radio show. He got the writers and everything else and that's how I happened to get my own radio show. I had that [show] for five years.

David: And Jack Benny didn't mind that you went off and had your own show?

Dennis: No, Jack was very good that way, you know. Of course, my five-year contract had run out with Jack Benny, and I was free to do my own show. I still stayed with Jack even though at the time Ted Bates and Tom Harrington felt that I should go off on my own and get away from Jack. I said, "No, Jack has been very wonderful to me; he gave me my start in show business and he helped me along and he could have let me go that first year when I hadn't really come up to the expectations that they had [for me]. But he stayed with me." And I stayed with Jack. Jack was very happy, and I was delighted too. So I did both shows. I could do my own show and *The Jack Benny Program*. Jack, many times, came on my radio show.

David: Oh, did he; I didn't know that. On the program you played a soda jerk who worked at . . . .

Dennis: Willoughby's Drug Store. We had Dink Trout and Bea Benaderet; they're both gone now. Barbara Eiler was my sweetheart; she was the daughter of Bea and Dink [within the scripts]. I was living at a boarding house.

David: Wasn't part of the plot that you just happened to have the same name as the "boy singer" on *The Jack Benny Program*?

Dennis: Yes, though we never did say on my own show that I was on the Benny show. But many times on the Benny show [when he would give me a hard time] I could say, "Hey, listen, I don't have to take this, Mr. Benny. You know, I've got my own show." But it's a strange thing on radio, especially on the Benny show, they [the audience] could separate the fact that you were a naïve, kind of silly kid, and yet after he [Jack] said, "Sing, kid!," you could sing a beautiful song. People could separate that fact. They'd never stop to think, "Well, my gosh, here he's got such a beautiful voice. He's studied; he must be a musician. He can't be that silly." But they separated that fact completely, which was beautiful.

David: Thank goodness! Luster Cream and Palmolive soap were your sponsors on your show.

Dennis: Right! Colgate-Palmolive.

David: And Ken Carson sang the commercials.

Dennis: Yes, that's right. Ken used to do our commercials. He used to be with The Sons of the Pioneers. . . .

This soap bar was a promotion for the fall premiere of Dennis's radio show,
A Day in the Life of Dennis Day.

David: And Garry Moore in later years. I was surprised, though, to discover that you had a "boy singer" on your own show.

Dennis: Yes. We had some good actors who were on the show. Hans Conried, who's played down here in Florida, was on the show.

David: I just talked with Hans Conried about a month ago.

Dennis: Did you? Hans used to be on with me because I did a lot of dialects on the show. Oh, Hans is great!

David: Was "Clancy Lowered the Boom" your biggest hit record?

Dennis: I think it was one of the biggest, yeah. I recorded that in 1947—that's thirty years ago—for RCA Victor.

David: I can remember when that came out; it was a favorite of mine.

Dennis: Another one was "Johnny Appleseed," which I did for Walt Disney. I was in the picture *Melody Time*[81] with Roy Rogers.

David: He did the "Pecos Bill" number.

Dennis: And I did "Johnny Appleseed," which was one of the favorites of Walt Disney before he passed away. Later he took it out of *Melody Time* and ran it as a featurette. Because RCA Victor no longer prints it, I rerecorded it for Buena Vista, which is Walt Disney's label, and I still get people who comment on it.

It's funny, that [film] had a great appeal not only to kids but also to many, many adults. Kids who are older men and women now say, "I grew up with it!" [In "old codger" character voice from film] *Go on out West there, Johnny. Why, you've got the breath and you've got the strength. You go out there and take your little book with ya, God's little book, and plant the apple seed. And all them settlers out thar, they'll say, "Bless ya, Johnny Appleseed.* And then I'd do Johnny's voice: *Who me? I can't go out there.* [Old codger] *Why sure you can, Johnny; you can show 'em. You*

Back stage at *The Dennis Day Show.* Charley Weaver is playing checkers with some young fans.

can do it! [Singing] There's apple dumplings, apple fritters . . . And then we would go on from there.

David: Oh, that's great! *Melody Time* was a wonderful film, and the Johnny Appleseed segment was a delight. I loved it and my kids loved it! Let's move on now to 1952 when you premiered your own TV show.

Dennis: Yes, it was called *The Dennis Day Show* and was sponsored by RCA Victor. I had that show right through the 1954 season. Cliff Arquette[82] was on there. [Doing Arquette's Charley Weaver voice] *That's my boy, heh, heh. I got a letter from Mama in Mount Idee. Says here, Dear Razor. Mama always said I was a sharp little fella'. Heh, heh. Things are fine in Mount Idee, she says. I just finished making your father's lunch, a mother-in-law sandwich: cold shoulder and tongue. Heh, heh. Elsie Crack stopped by the house today. She had her little son Gomar; Gomar Crack was with her. My, he's a cute boy, a bright boy. He can say Mama and Dada and wave bye-bye, which should help him a lot when he goes into the Army next week.*

David: *[Laugh]*

Dennis: *Well, I got to close now and go help your father. He just fainted and I brought him to; now he wants two more. Love, Mama.* Oh, yes. Those were great days.

David: Cliff Arquette was *so* great, especially as Charley Weaver.

Dennis: He was so unexpected, you know. You never knew what he was going to do or say. And I used to have so much fun when I'd dress up as Cliff [Charley]. He'd catch me, we'd face one another, and I'd think, oh, the goose is up, I'm dead! He'd look at me and then he'd say [Charley's voice] "Brother Gomar!"

David: *[Laugh]* I loved those shows! You were opposite *I Love Lucy* for a while, weren't you?

Dennis: Yes. That was the kiss of death!

David: And I watched *you*!

Dennis: You must have been the only one! *[Laugh]*

David: Because I thought it was a great show!

Dennis: Lucy was at the top of the heap at the time and continued that way because she was so great. Of course, I couldn't get a rating and that was the end of it; that was the demise of *The Dennis Day Show*.

David: That's too bad because it was a great series. Tell me about your personal life—I know you've got ten or eleven children.

Dennis: We have ten, my wife and I. We've got six boys and four girls. I've got four married; I still have six at home and six grandchildren.

David: And home for you now is. . . .

Dennis: Brentwood, California. It has been for the last thirty-seven years. My parents moved out there and my brothers and my sister all live in California now.

David: Tell me about this tour you are doing on the West Coast of Florida.

Dennis: Well, I played the condominium circuit the latter part of March this year in the Miami, Palm Beach, Fort Lauderdale areas, and now this is the first time on the West Coast of Florida—in the Sarasota area, St. Pete, and elsewhere—in mobile home parks and condominiums. Bobby Breen, who was in motion pictures when I was a little kid, he and his wife have this booking agency called Entertainment Plus, and they book people in here.

I understand the first of the year Gordon MacRae is coming in. Milton Berle will be coming in to play these condominiums and mobile homes. This is a whole new thing, you see, because you have a lot of retired people here who remember the Dennis Days and the Jack Bennys and the Milton Berles and the Gordon MacRaes. Norm Crosby will be coming down. They remember them and, also, they've got a lot of time on their hands and they would like to have a little live entertainment instead of just watching television, which can get a little bit tiring.

They've been marvelous audiences, really fantastic audiences. It's been a great pleasure and a great warm feeling for me to be here, especially at the Christmas season. You know, I run into so many people who are friends from New York, a lot of people I met when I was in the Navy and served with, people I've met throughout all the

As we were wrapping up our conversation, Dennis posed for me in his comic manner while doing his "Charley Weaver" voice.

years I was with Jack Benny, and they've been just marvelous audiences.

David: Thank you, Dennis Day.

Dennis: It's been my pleasure.

Dennis wished me an early "Merry Christmas" in an Irish brogue as I left. This man who was frequently billed as "America's favorite Irish Tenor" was indeed Leprechaun-like in a choirboy sort of way. Benny had it right: there was an overt naïveté about Dennis, but on closer inspection there could also be found an Irish rogue hiding under the choirboy disguise. He could verbalize a comic, stinging zinger at times—but only in a G-rated manner—and especially when embroiled in a dialect scene.

Dennis and I didn't talk about his limited exposure on the silver screen. As a result of his radio success, Dennis was cast in a few movie musicals of the 1940s and early fifties where his Irish tenor voice could shine. He first appeared on screen with Benny in *Buck Benny Rides Again*[83] in 1940. In 1943 he co-starred with Judy Canova in the bumpkin musical-comedy *Sleepy Lagoon*,[84] and he appeared with Anne Shirley in *Music in Manhattan*[85] in 1944. Later movie musicals included *I'll Get By*[86] with June Haver, *Golden Girl*[87] starring Mitzi Gaynor, and *The Girl Next Door*,[88] all in the early 1950s.

Dennis was sixty-one when we talked, and his glory years were pretty much behind him. As the years passed, he occasionally would show up on a television show or appear at local and state fairs and other regional venues. He was one of the stars of an animated television special entitled *The Stingiest Man in Town*[89] which was aired on the ABC network on December 23, 1978.

His recordings from the forties and fifties were repackaged when CD recordings arrived, and a new generation got to hear his versions of such Irish novelty tunes as "Clancy Lowered the Boom," and "McNamara's Band," but he could also charm the ladies with his tender romantic ballads such as "Mam'selle, " "Mona Lisa," and "My Wild Irish Rose."

His real name had been Owen Patrick McNulty, but he legally adopted Dennis Day as his professional name back in 1944 against his parents' wishes. He and his family were strict Irish-Catholics and very

Dennis did not have much of a movie career. *Golden Girl* is typical of
the few musical comedies in which he appeared.

conservative. (He was known to refuse any work that might be deemed
objectionable.) His marriage to Peggy Almquist in 1948 produced the
ten children he mentioned in our conversation and lasted until his death.
(As an aside, Dennis's brother James was married to film actress Ann Blyth.)

Dennis Day died on June 22, 1988, of amyotrophic lateral sclerosis,
commonly known as Lou Gehrig's disease. He was interred at Holy Cross

Cemetery in Culver City, California. Various publications over the years had listed his birth year as 1916, 1917, 1918, and Dennis had even told the *Entertainment New Service* writer Jack Hawn in 1985 that he had been born in 1921! (A little show business/leprechaun fib?) His tombstone states the following:

> Beloved Husband & Father
> Owen Patrick McNulty
> "Dennis Day"
> 1916-1988

Henry Denker

March 23, 1978

*"If you wait for inspiration to hit you,
you will die very old and very unhappy."*

Henry Denker has had seventeen of his novels—more than for any other author—selected for publication by *Reader's Digest Condensed Books*.

This is another one of those situations where time has dimmed the memory of how my conversation with writer Henry Denker came about. At first I thought I remembered that he was in Sarasota at the same time as Molly Picon, who was then performing Denker's play *The Second Time Around* at the Golden Apple Dinner Theatre, but, no, Henry Denker and I talked two months *after* that.

Anyway, I do remember that I got a phone call, I think from Roberta Turoff of the Golden Apple, telling me that Henry Denker was in town and that I might want to talk with him for my radio show or, maybe, from the standpoint of a famous, veteran novelist/playwright/screenwriter/radio scriptwriter talking with a younger, aspiring writer—me! I was then working on my second book.

Either way, the bottom line was, yes; I definitely wanted to talk with Henry Denker. I had not at that time read any of his novels, but I was very familiar with his hit Broadway play *A Case of Libel* based upon a section of Louis Nizer's book *My Life in Court*. (In fact, I took along my personal copy that I had had for many years and was hopeful that Mr. Denker would autograph it for me. He did.)

Prior to *A Case of Libel*, there was Mr. Denker's courtroom novel, *Time Limit!*, that he converted into a Broadway show in 1956 and later a movie with Karl Malden directing and starring Richard Widmark, Richard Basehart, Rip Torn, and Martin Balsam. Just a couple of years before we got together for our conversation, he wrote the screenplay for *Judgment: The Court Martial of Lt. William Calley* that Stanley Kramer produced for ABC in 1975. It might come as no surprise that Henry Denker is himself a lawyer, which probably explains his penchant for courtroom dramas. Another of his stories about courtrooms and lawyers is *Twilight of Honor*, a 1963 screenplay which was released by MGM and starred Richard Chamberlain, Nick Adams, and Claude Rains.

Henry Denker's most prodigious output, however, has been in the realm of novels, starting back around 1949 with *I'll Be Right Home, Ma* to *Cla$$ Action* in 2005, another story involving lawyers. Seventeen of his novels—more than for any other author—have been selected for publication by *Reader's Digest Condensed Books*. Well, you get the idea. Here was a man who had achieved success in a variety of literary arenas and had worked with some of the biggest names in Broadway and Hollywood, and I was eager to talk with him.

When I arrived at the appointed time, Mr. Denker was waiting for me, dressed in a conservative dark suit and dress shirt, the only acknowledgment of the warm Florida weather being the open collar where I felt sure a tie usually resided. He was a man obviously comfortable in his skin, relaxed, and upbeat. He seemed genuinely pleased to have this conversation with me, a feeling *I've* experienced over the years after spending a lot of time by myself finding the right words to put on the blank sheet of paper. It's good then to have someone eager to hear what you've come to know from that experience. And I was about to be an eager listener.

David: Henry Denker, it's a pleasure to meet and talk with you about your writing career.

Henry: David, it's a pleasure to be here. It's a pleasure to be in Sarasota, and I can speak as an expert because I just came from California where it is also very lovely, but it's nicer here I think.

David: You have written tense, probing dramas such as *Time Limit!*, which was on Broadway and was also a motion picture. You've written *A Case of Libel*, which falls into that same category and was a Broadway show and a TV special. Then you turned around and wrote light comedies with equal skill—such shows as *What Did We Do Wrong?*, which starred Paul Ford on Broadway, and *The Second Time Around*, which Molly Picon performed on Broadway and has been performing in dinner theaters around the country. You've written radio dramas— I'm giving your background for those few who may not be aware.

Henry: David, if you're going to say radio dramas, you'd better say over a thousand radio dramas.

David: You've done TV dramas; you've done screenplays of your own works and the works of others. You've written novels. Is this a skill that a writer can develop so that he can go from one area to another: from novel to plays to TV dramas to radio dramas?

Henry: Well, it's a two-fold thing. First of all, it's a necessity, and secondly it's a technique that you have to acquire. By necessity, I mean the following, David: Suppose I was just to write serious plays, and I get a very good idea for a comedy. If I don't write a comedy, I have to throw that idea away. Or if I have an idea that's too big to be encompassed on a stage—say an idea that's stretched over several years and a number of countries—that's the sort of thing you put into a novel or a screenplay. If I were just limited to stage plays, I'd have to throw that good idea away.

So what happens is the idea that you get picks the medium it should be told in. Sometimes you get an idea for a novel, sometimes your idea is for a play, sometimes the idea is not big enough for a play but is big enough for a ninety-minute television special. The idea selects where it should be told.

Now, having that happen to you, you then have to set about seriously—almost like a student in the beginning—learning the technique of that medium. If you've never written a screenplay before, you've got to get hold of a dozen good screenplays—and they're published in books; you can get collections of screenplays—and read the best screenplays and find out the way screenplays are written. You do that with each medium you get into.

In television it was a little bit easier because I was there at the very beginning. In fact, you are now talking to the man who wrote the first dramatic series in American television. If I tell you when that was, you won't believe it. It was 1939. It was a mystery show called *False Witness,* and it ran on NBC. The reason they had to take it off the air at that time was that it was pretty obvious that we were going to be involved with a war, and we needed civilian defense. In order to educate a large number of civil defense people in a hurry, they took all television off the air except for civilian defense instruction. Then they put television sets in local police stations and people were brought in to learn all about civilian defense by television. That's why that series went off the air. But that was the first dramatic series in the country.

David: But it's one thing to write a drama and an entirely different thing to write a comedy, and you've written both with great facility.

Henry: Well, you will notice that the comedies that I write are generally based on subjects that could be treated very seriously. For example, *What Did We Do Wrong?* came along at the time of this enormous conflict between the generations. That could have been treated very seriously and very heavily because the opening situation there was a boy at college who was arrested and thrown in jail for starting a riot. It could have been melodramatic. It just felt better to do it as a comedy.

The same thing [occurred] with *The Second Time Around.* You have a serious subject there, a subject that is now current in this country. There are several million elderly people who are living together unmarried because of social strictures, because of a tax situation in this country, because of a number of things that militate against people getting married. It's a serious problem. Right here in Florida you have more of it than any other place in the country, as a matter of fact.

That came up, by the way, because we had that problem in our family. A relative of mine, a man about seventy-two at the time, his wife died and he was alone. Every body would feel sorry for him and invite him to dinner once or twice, but then that sort of disappears. And he was, evidently, too alone.

One day we got a phone call from him saying that his phone number had been changed and that his address had been changed. So we thought that was reasonable: he'd moved from a bigger apartment to a smaller apartment. Then I called two or three days later and a woman answered the phone. I assumed it was an answering service; it turned out not to be an answering service. It turned out to be a woman he was living with. They subsequently did get married, but they lived together for about a year and a half because it was, as I say, under the pressures of the strange economic circumstances in which we live, the intelligent thing to do.

David: Do you find that it's more difficult to write, oh, dramas as opposed to comedies or vice versa, or do you just fall into the groove of which ever happens to be the one of the moment?

Henry: The story dictates what you're going to do. If you like the story enough, then it isn't really difficult at all. I don't mean that it's easy; it's never easy. I get up every morning at six o'clock, and I'm at the typewriter by six-thirty. I work four hours. Whether I'm doing a novel or a play—no matter what it is—I work four hours every morning before the phone starts to ring. In those four hours you can cover a good day's work. If you do that seven days a week, you find that it's such a habit that it's really enjoyable and not difficult in that sense.

Of course the actual writing, choosing your words, that's difficult; it always is, but that's part of the fun. It's as if you were playing tennis with somebody, and he was a pushover, you'd walk off the court and say, "Well, that was a waste of time." But if you were playing against somebody who was a very good player and he gave you a tough match, then you'd walk off saying, "Man, that was tennis!" It's the same thing with writing. If it's too easy, there's something wrong with it. It's got to be tough. Overcoming the tough part of it is what makes it enjoyable.

David: It just seems to me that comedy would take a particular quirk of mind—that you have to have that comic sense.

Henry: I just finished the first draft of a new novel which is, again, about a serious subject but is rather comic. In just the first couple of pages this character just took off by himself, and there was no problem with him after that. The problem was holding him back more than anything.

David: The character writes himself.

Henry: Yep, if the character starts off properly, you've got a momentum going that you just go along with, and the things that suggest themselves to you, as you go along, are really the enjoyable parts about it. That's one reason, David, that I never do a precise outline of something [that I'm working on]. I just want to know where it's going to end. If you do a precise outline, you're cutting off those things I call targets of opportunity.

By targets of opportunity in writing, I mean the amazing thing that happens: One day you get to the typewriter and something just strikes you. You never could have thought of it in advance; it just hits you at the typewriter. If you have too detailed an outline, those things are cut off; you can't use them; whereas, if you are moving in a general direction, at the end of the story the two characters are going to be in this particular relationship, and that's all you have to guide you, you then have opportunities to make these deviations that are really what the richness of writing consists of.

David: When you're starting a novel or a play, do you go to the typewriter immediately or do you work with pencil and paper?

Henry: I walk it around. About six months of my year is spent in New York City. That's where I live permanently. Then I spend several months in California and several months up in the mountains in the Adirondacks and about a month down here in Sarasota because my family has all moved down here. In New York we have Central Park right at our front door; that's where we live.

So if I have an idea, I just walk around Central Park several hours every afternoon. You see, I write in the morning and do my walking in the afternoon. I think of little things that add up to a story, and I make little notes and shove them in my pocket. When I get back, I throw all of those notes into a file, just helter-skelter; it doesn't matter what the order is or if an idea is at the beginning or one is the middle or the end of the story, it doesn't matter. Just keep throwing notes into a file for days and weeks and sometimes for months and sometimes for years, because you don't always get around to the idea when you'd like to because other things intervene.

And then when I feel it's right to go into that particular subject, I then open up that file. I've got all kinds of ideas in there: ideas for characters, ideas for little situations, plot ideas, geographical notions as to where the story should take place—a lot of ideas. Then I will sit down with a tape recorder, and I will just talk. I may talk for an hour, three hours, five hours. I just keep talking into a tape recorder, just sort of organizing all these facts that I've thrown into this file.

After a couple of days of that, I'll make a first try at writing. I'll sit down at the typewriter and dash off ten pages to see how it's going.

From that time on, I'll sit down every morning at the typewriter the first thing. Then several times a week I will replay that tape because of the things I might have forgotten—because there are a lot of ideas on that tape.

David: You won't necessarily transcribe what you said on the tape.

Henry: No, no, no. I like to play it because it has a different feeling when I *listen* to it than when I would read it on paper. That's about as much outlining as I do—walk it around to get the thoughts in fragments, [and then] you organize the fragments. You know generally, at that point, in what direction you're going, and then you should be ready to sit down and write. That doesn't mean the first ten pages or the first fifty pages are going to be good necessarily. You may throw them all out; you may throw out none of them. It depends.

David: How many drafts will you go through before you get to the final version?

Henry: That will also depend on how they come out. There are some scenes in a play you'll write once, and that's it, and you know it when you write it—that you can't improve on that. Then there are other scenes, trouble scenes, that you may write twenty-five times and then in rehearsal write another twenty-five times, looking for just how you solve that particular problem. Sometimes these problems never get solved; we should admit that too.

David: I think you have already answered this to an extent, but let me ask it anyway. Can a writer develop his writing skills or is he, to a certain extent, born with these skills within him that he can hone as he goes along?

Henry: I'm not a great believer in this word called "talent," because I don't think we're living in an age of talented people. I think we're living in an age of people who apply themselves and are, therefore, deemed to have talent. I think you can learn to write, and I think writing is very much like muscles—if you work at it every day. If you did calisthenics every day, at the end of six months your physique would be vastly improved.

The same thing with writing: if you write every day, the ability to use words will just get better and better, and it'll become easier and easier. It's a definite, distinct thing that you do; you do it intentionally. If you don't do it intentionally, if you wait for inspiration to hit you, you will die very old and very unhappy, I'm telling you now.

David: And poor.

A CASE OF LIBEL

A Play by Henry Denker

Based on the book, My Life in Court, *by Louis Nizer*

Random House

Henry: Absolutely!

David: How do you select your subject matter? For example, you wrote the play called *A Cast of Libel*, which is based on the book by Louis Nizer, the attorney, called *My Life in Court*. How did you come to select *A Case of Libel* as your subject?

Henry: There were two things involved in that, David. Number one was that case the play was based on was the case where Quentin Reynolds sued Westbrook Pegler for libel and is one of the classic cases of libel in our history. It so happened that years before I had worked with Quentin Reynolds. When he came back from World War Two, he was the narrator on a radio show that we were doing at the time, and I wrote all his copy, so I got to know him pretty well and admired him very much. He was a very nice man. In addition to being capable, he was *nice*, a real good human being.

I was always interested in that case while it was being tried in the courts; in fact, I went down there several times to sit in on it. I happen, by the way, to be an attorney; I haven't practiced in many years, but I'm an attorney in New York State. So I had a basic interest in that case, but the way I became involved in the play was as follows: a friend of my mine who is the sister-in-law of Louie Nizer lived out in Hollywood. When I was out there for a couple of days, she called me and said, "I'm going to leave a book at the hotel for you. It hasn't been published yet, but I want you to read it because I think you're going to find something there that you'll like."

So it was a Friday evening. I was taking a plane. I got on the plane and figured I'd fall asleep because it was what they call a red-eye special. It leaves LA at about eleven o'clock at night and gets to New York about six-thirty in the morning. There's a good reason why they call it the red-eye special. Most times I've been able to sleep on the plane, but this night I started to read the book, and the first case in the book was this one: Westbrook Pegler and Quentin Reynolds.

By the time I got to New York, which was six o'clock Saturday morning, I new I was going to do that [play]. In fact, I called Louie Nizer at ten o'clock that morning, and I said, "Louie, I'd like to come see you; let's make a deal and do this play." By Sunday it had been arranged that we were going to do that play. That's the way that one happened.

They don't all happen that way; they happen in lots of different ways. I find the best test of an idea for me is if the idea keeps coming back. In other words, you get an idea, you make a note and you put it away, you think about it a couple of weeks later or a couple of months later. If it keeps coming back, it's a pretty good idea. If it just disappears and remains on that little piece of paper, it's not strong enough to be worth all the time and effort.

David: You were associated for some ten years with one of the most respected radio series of all time, *The Greatest Story Ever Told.* How did you become attached to that program back around 1947?

Henry: In this business almost everything happens by accident, almost everything. I wrote and directed and produced that show for ten years and enjoyed every week of it because I found it a great experience. It started out, strangely enough, from a phone call that interrupted me at dinner. I was with a radio production company in those days in New York City called Trans American. I was doing three shows a week for them. In fact, I used to go from studio to studio to studio on Sunday. I had three shows on the air all at once: Ethel Barrymore and the *Radio Reader's Digest* and another show called *Keep Up with the World.* Therefore, I was working with these people seven days a week.

One evening in the middle of dinner I got a call, and they were in terrible trouble. The trouble was as follows: Fulton Oursler, who was also with the same company, had a title for a series. The title was *The Greatest Story Ever Told,* and he was one day going to do a book on it. They had been talking with various sponsors about this idea, and one sponsor, the Goodyear Tire and Rubber Company, said, "Hey, that sounds great! We'd like to hear that as an audition." [An audition] was a record of the show—what we now call a pilot on television; it was called an audition in those days.

This sponsor said, "I would like to not only hear it on an audition record, I will pay for it; I'll pay for the audition." Trans American had everything going for them except one thing: they didn't have a script. I guess they had oversold it a little because they had told the sponsor there was a script. So they said to me, "Come down immediately!" I rushed downtown; it was about eight o'clock when I got there. They said, "Here's the problem: we have to have a script by day after tomorrow. You've got to do it; you just have to do it; that's all there is to it."

So Fulton Oursler and I sat down for a couple of hours and talked over ideas and finally settled on one, "The Good Samaritan," as being the one we'd use as the illustration because the sponsor, I must say, was a man who was enormously public spirited, a man named Paul Litchfield, who was the chairman of the board of the Goodyear Tire Company.

Since "The Good Samaritan" had the whole concept of brotherhood built into it, it was the kind of thing he would like. So we decided on that, and I sat down and kept writing for about fourteen straight hours and finally came up with the half-hour script. Then they sent it to the advertising agency which sent it to Litchfield, and he liked it.

We then did the audition based on that. He [Litchfield] played it for his board of directors and said, "Gentlemen, I'm not asking you for your approval; I'm telling you this is what we're going to do." When we went on the air, people thought, well, a program like that, sort of public service, no commercials; it might last thirteen weeks. Nobody expected that it was going to last ten years, but it did. And "The Good Samaritan" show started every one of the ten years; we played that as the first show of every year.

By the way, Litchfield never had a commercial on that show. He said, "This is my way of sort of upgrading the neighborhood. This country was good to me, and I want to be good to this country." A most unusual man!

David: *The Greatest Story Ever Told* on radio had a full orchestra and chorus, I believe.

Henry: Oh, we had the biggest orchestra and chorus that anybody in the business ever had. We had a thirty-six piece orchestra for a dramatic show and an eighteen voice chorus. Nobody had ever heard of that before.

David: And it was also sort of revolutionary in that you had an actor who actually portrayed the voice of Christ.

Henry: David, that was the first time that was done, to have an actor impersonate Christ. In those days, you must remember, radio was in a situation that now, as we look back on it, we can hardly believe. For example, you never did a recorded show on the air. Everything was live! Even "The Good Samaritan," which we did eleven times on the air, was done live each time. Even though we had ten beautiful recordings, it was done live every time.

This was just an unusual show in an unusual time, that's all. In those days the idea of doing a religious show was so fraught with problems. We had a board of clergymen representing four faiths who passed on every script. We had them in the studio to make sure that nothing was done that was in bad taste. Technically, the way we did it, and I think you'll appreciate this, the Christ character was always in an isolation booth by himself, never with the rest of the company on stage. Also, there was always a touch of echo to give a sense of distance and perspective, to give sort of a heavenly aura to his voice, and always his voice was backed with music. You had to do all those things in order to make it acceptable.

One of the problems they have in motion pictures with the Christ character and the reason it never comes off, is that nowhere in the world can you find an actor who has within him all the things people endow Christ with, because each person has his own impression of what Christ looks like and sounds like. So you had to be extremely careful in the way you did this. We were fortunate in that we did it in a way that pleased a lot of people. In fact, we won more awards than any other program in the history of broadcasting.

David: It must have been intriguing for the sound effects men too because people didn't wear shoes in Biblical times like the shoes we wear today; everyone wore sandals, so they had to have a sandals' sound.

Henry: Sandal sounds scraping on sand most of the time. We had Camels galore [represented] with coconut shells.

David: Even a simple thing like doors opening and closing: no modern latches. . . .

Henry: No locks. Squeaks we had, and squeaks had to be unusual because now when you hear a squeak on a radio show, it's a squeak of a metal hinge, but they didn't have metal hinges in those days. So we had to have leather squeaking, not metal.

We had a lot of fun, and it was a tremendous challenge and everyone enjoyed it enormously, and we used to get stars coming in from Hollywood who would say they'd like to be on the show without getting any credit. You see, we never gave names of actors on the show. Nobody had any credit because the sponsor had no commercials. Mickey Rooney would come in and say, "Just let me be on there, that's all; I don't want any credit; I don't even want any publicity; just let me be on there. That happened very frequently, that people came in from the Coast to get on that show.

David: You wrote *Give Us Barabbas*, which appeared on the *Hallmark Hall of Fame* television series. I believe it was repeated four times over the years.

Henry: I think it's the only program that's been repeated that many times. They wanted to repeat it again and I wouldn't let them, and I'll tell you why. When that show was first done, television was at a certain stage in its development. Now the techniques are much better; therefore, to put a show on now that was recorded about twelve years ago, it's just not going to look as good. I said to them, "If you want to do it all over again, take the same script and just redo the whole production, fine, but don't repeat it anymore." I just don't want it to seem out of date because the story and what the story has to say is not out of date.

David: Tell me about the problems of writing for TV as compared to writing for the stage.

Henry: When you're writing for the stage, the problems come about when you have to battle with the director and the actors about certain things they say won't work and you say will work, and so on. With television it is the reverse. In television the author is almost always shut out. He writes a script and then it goes to a script editor and a producer and a director, and they sit down and butcher it up.

The reason I did the Hallmarks—and I've done a couple of those—with the Hallmarks you are with it all the time like a play. In other words, they make no changes unless you make the changes. In the average run of television shows that you see, including the specials that you see, they are run by producers and directors and script editors. The writer is almost never there. He can't protect his material; he can't explain his material to anybody.

I've had situations in the theater where just shear lack of understanding is the problem. And only the writer can solve it. In *A Case of Libel*, Van Heflin was playing Louis Nizer, the famous trial lawyer.

Quentin Reynolds, a noted War correspondent, came charging into his office declaring, "That son of a bitch Pegler lied about me in his columns and I want to sue the hell out of him!"

Heflin tries to calm down Reynolds who keeps insisting, "He lied about me and I can prove it. So sue the Bastard!"

Heflin points out that when you sue someone for libel, suddenly *you* become the defendant. "But *he* lied about *me!*" Reynolds keeps insisting.

Heflin has to explain, "When you sue for libel, the other side will try to prove your character is so low, your reputation so bad, that not even Pegler's lies can damage you. So you have no case."

"Let them attack my character! My reputation is terrific, clean!"

"It won't be when Pegler's lawyer gets through with you."

"Let them try!" Reynolds defies Nizer.

"Oh, yeah?" Nizer replied, "Let me show you what I would do if I had . . . . Jesus Christ. . . . on the witness stand."

Then I had Heflin go through the motions of sitting a non-existent Jesus in a chair like a witness. And he begins, "Sir, is it true that you are thirty-two years old and unemployed, just wander the countryside. . . . no, no, don't' try to explain. Just answer yes or no.! Thank you. And that you choose to mingle with winebibbers? Please, just answer yes or no! And, sir, isn't it also true you deliberately also seek out the company of sinners and prostitutes? Isn't it? Just answer yes or no! Thank you, sir. That is all."

Then Heflin turns to Reynolds and asks, "Well, Reynolds, how do you think you'd make out in that courtroom?"

That was the scene which troubled Heflin. The first time we did it in rehearsal, Heflin took me aside, "Henry, if I do that scene the audience will come up onstage and try to lynch me for attacking Jesus." But I reassured him, and he continued to rehearse the scene. But I could see he was still troubled.

It was the evening of our very first performance in Philadelphia, our world premiere, when Heflin declared to me and the director, "I'm not going to do it; I'm just not going to do that scene. I don't care what you say." So I said, "Van, let me make a deal with you. You do that tonight, just once, do it tonight, and if you don't get applause right in the middle of that scene, then I'll take it out tomorrow." He said, "Okay, I'll try it."

Well, he tried it. I must say in all fairness to him, he played it well, and sure enough, he got applause right at the end of that scene. There was no problem anymore. If I hadn't been there, if it had been like television, the star would have said, "Cut it out," and the director would have cut it out. It would have been gone, lost. That's the difference between the two kinds of writing.

David: You've written in so many different fields: novels, radio, television, and motion pictures, and for the stage, of course. I wonder if one gives you a personal pleasure over another, or do you get a deep sense of satisfaction out of each of them when they work?

Henry: Well, it's like children. You can have twelve kids and each one of them has certain values, and you like them for certain things. The same thing here: you have certain enjoyments out of a play. You drop into a theater and see it performed and you get a kick out of that. You walk onto a plane and someone is reading your book; you get a kick out of that. Each one has its own problems and its own satisfactions. I don't think there is any one that is better than another.

If you asked which I like the best, I like to write plays the best, but I don't like all the problems that go with them after you write them. With a book you don't have any trouble casting a book; you don't have any trouble finding a director for a book. You write the book and that's it!

But they have their pluses and minuses. As I said before, if you want to be a writer, you've got to do them all; otherwise, it's like using your right arm and never using your left. You've got to use all the muscles because otherwise you're going to have an off-balance body.

David: What are you working on right now?

Henry: I am reading the galleys of a new novel called *The Actress*, which is coming out in the fall, and on which I think we are going to announce a picture deal in about three weeks. I just came back from

California where we made a feature film and television deal on my most recent novel which is called *The Scofield Diagnosis*, which is a book about a woman doctor. While I was out in California, I wrote a first draft of a new novel, and I have another novel which tomorrow night I will go over with a doctor because it's a medical novel, and I want to have all the medical details exact. So I'm really involved with three novels at the same time.

David: And you can keep them all straight and all going and . . . .

Henry: Yeah, yeah. Your mind gets segmented; you get accustomed to all these things. What you can't do, I find, you can't write two things at once. In other words, it's one thing to read galleys on one book and be writing another book, but you couldn't be writing two books [at the same time], at least I can't write two books at the same time because there you do have a division. I think the creative part of you has to have a clear, direct channel to one thing and work on that only.

David: Thank you, Henry Denker, very much.

Henry: Thank you, David. Nice to be here and nice to talk to you.

Henry Denker was sixty-five at the time we talked, a time when many think about retirement—maybe not so much with writers. There's not much heavy lifting or outdoor work for writers, and the tools of the trade are a moveable feast. Henry continued his prolific ways.

He continued to turn out a novel each year and occasionally converted that novel into a screenplay or Broadway play, such as with *Horowitz and Mrs. Washington*, which came out as a novel in 1979 and progressed to Broadway in 1980 with Josh Logan directing and Sam Levene and Esther Rolle starring. He adapted his 1982 novel entitled *Outrage!* into a play and then a screenplay that was produced as a television movie for CBS in 1986 starring Robert Preston (his last role), Beau Bridges, Burgess Meredith, Linda Purl, Mel Ferrer, and Anthony Newley.

Henry mentioned in our conversation *The Scofield Diagnosis*, a story about a woman doctor. Doctors and medical topics have also been a frequent theme of his novels, turning up in such writings as *The Choice*

(1987), *A Gift of Life* (1989), and *Doctor on* Trial (1992), just to name three. His screenplay for *Love Leads the Way: A True Story* became a TV movie for Walt Disney Television in 1984. Based on a story by Jimmy Hawkins, the movie tells the story of a recently blinded man who becomes one of the first American users of a seeing-eye dog and has to fight to get the laws changed that forbid bringing such a dog into a restaurant, hotel, or other businesses.

And speaking of dogs and representing a change of pace in his subject matter, in 2001 Henry Denker published a novel entitled *Clarence,* which tells the story of a writer named Henry who feels victimized by the government and social movements that want to dominate his and our lives, dictate what we should say and do, where we may smoke or not smoke, etc. All of this is told from the point of view of the man's dog, a Golden Retriever named Clarence. One might call it a lighthearted fantasy of a dog and his man.

So Henry Denker has produced all of this and so much more over the last seventy-plus years. Now in his nineties, there seems to be little slackening of the literary juices that have made him one of the most prolific of American authors. Don't stop now, Henry. We're all looking forward to your next publication.

Phyllis Diller

March 27, 1978

"A lot of people think that I'm truly the harridan they see on stage."

The queen of the madcap comediennes, Phyllis Diller!

It was opening night for Phyllis Diller's week-long appearance at Le Club, a fancy-smancy nightclub in St. Petersburg that was part of a new luxury resort. There was the hope that high-end talent would lure a high-end clientele to this beautiful oasis on the West Coast of Florida. So far the plan was working beautifully. But then we're talking Phyllis Diller! She had been holding her own in the top nightclubs and comedy clubs all across the country since the 1950s, constantly playing to packed houses.

Early on she had created her stage character persona of the bizarrely dressed, wild-haired, eccentric housewife with a loud, cackling laugh who spun comic horror stories about daily life with her husband "Fang," all the while puffing on a long cigarette holder containing an unlit cigarette. In fact, she never smoked, and where her on-stage comic-harridan character came from is pretty much a mystery. It just evolved from the hidden pools of comic talent that bubbled up in her early life but didn't turn into a comic gusher until she reached her mid thirties.

She let go of her hope of being a concert pianist when she left her music studies at the Sherwood Music Conservatory in Chicago; went on to attend Northwestern University for a while; met her future husband, Sherwood Diller, at Bluffton College in Ohio; eloped with him in 1939; and became the housewife and mother (five kids) that she later made jest of. Her comic skits at PTA meetings and other social events led to her appearance as a contestant on the Groucho Marx show *You Bet Your Life* in 1950 and made her dream of a possible career as a standup comedienne. She studied acting and the comedy styles of the top male comics of the forties and fifties—there were no role models for a standup comedienne back then because there really weren't any. By the mid fifties she started getting exposure in comedy clubs of that era, and the rest, as they say, is history.

Phyllis's opening night show at Le Club was a comic hit. She covered all the usual comic territory: Fang ("His finest hour lasted a minute and a half."), the household miseries ("I'm eighteen years behind in my ironing."), on growing older ("You know you're old if your walker has an airbag."), the usual self-deprecating humor ("It's a good thing beauty is only skin deep, or I'd be rotten to the core."), and she riffed on her close friendship with Bob Hope (who had furthered her career through his films, television specials, and his frequent overseas shows for military personnel—where he took her along as "eye candy" for the troops).

After the laughter and applause and curtain calls ended, I was escorted backstage to her dressing room. She was already out of costume and makeup when I was ushered into the room. I hardly recognized her with her fright wig removed, wearing a robe, and her light gray hair pulled back close to her head. She rose from the easy chair she had been sitting in and extended her hand as we were introduced, and I was taken aback by how tiny she was (5 feet 1 inch). She may have been tiny, but she had *filled* the stage just a few moments before. Her voice was now soft and gentle, her manner quiet as she bid me sit down so that we could talk. Only infrequently in our conversation were there hints of the raucous onstage laugh that we are all so familiar with.

David: Phyllis Diller, I want to talk about some of the old days with you.

Phyllis: Okay.

David: Going back to the earliest old days for the two of us, you and I were born not too far from each other in the state of Ohio.

Phyllis: Where?

David: Well, you're from Lima, Ohio, and I am from a little, little place called Columbia Station, Ohio. You probably never heard of it.

Phyllis: I'm going to ask you one question: what's it near?

David: Elyria, Lorain, Ohio

Phyllis: I've heard of Elyria. Is that in the Eastern part of the state?

David: Yes. It's in the northeastern part of Ohio.

Phyllis: Well, you see I'm from the northwest part of Ohio, or I would have known about Columbia Station. We've had a lot of show business people from Ohio: Clark Gable, Dean Martin from Stubenville, Paul Lynde, Dody Goodman, Charley Weaver, Jonathan Winters, Jack Paar, Bob Hope—all the biggies! *[Laugh]*

David: So all the big stars are from Ohio!

Phyllis: Yes, and you and me. *[Laugh]*

David: You went from Lima, Ohio, to Ypsilanti, Michigan, and then you went out to Alameda, California. You'd been a housewife for a number of years, had five children, and then about 1955 you decided to take on a career, as of all things, a standup comedienne.

Phyllis: Well, I didn't decide that; my husband decided that. I had a husband by the name of Sherwood Diller, from another little Ohio town, Bluffton. There's a little college there, and that's where I met him, in college. He decided that I should be a comic. We had been married for fifteen years and had five children, and he got this idea, just out of the blue, I guess, and he wouldn't let go of the idea. He absolutely insisted that I become a comic, so there was nothing for me to do but to do it.

David: I read somewhere that you were what we might call a Laundromat comic to begin with.

Phyllis: Well, you know how writers are when they're writing a story about you. That comes out of a story written by Alex Haley in the old *Saturday Evening Post*. And it was a kind of telescoping of the fact that I was funny always: I was funny at the super market; I was funny at the grocery story, at the meat market, at the Laundromat, at the telephone company, at the PTA. In other words, he used the Laundromat to sort of put it all together and, do you know, that has stuck forever.

David: I believe you first played The Purple Onion in San Francisco.

Phyllis: That's true. And let me tell you who came out of The Purple Onion as their first job, the first place these people played was the Purple Onion: Jim Nabors; Ronnie Shell; the Kingston Trio; Smothers Brothers; Rod McKuen; the guy who created the [New} Christy Minstrels, Randy Sparks; Alan Sues, who played the sort of fey guy on *Laugh-In*; and Milt Kamen. Oh, there were just so many people who came out of that place. There was a six-year period when it was a hot bed of talent, that Purple Onion.

David: Did you play a lot of tiny little clubs and then suddenly get a break to play the Purple Onion?

Phyllis: No, it was a break-in spot. That's what they used to call a discovery club. We still have them. There's one in Hollywood and one in San Diego run by the same people, and they're called The Comedy Store. People can get up and do six minutes, five minutes, and they can get up every night if they want to. There are still places around. There used to be The Bitter End in the Village, and there used to be other places in the Village where you could do that.

David: Wasn't there The Hungry Eye?

Phyllis: No, that was in San Francisco, across the street from The Purple Onion. Out of that place came Mort Saul, Barbra Streisand played it very earlier in her career, as did Don Adams, The Limelighters, and others.

David: But did you perform before you played The Purple Onion?

Phyllis: Nope, that was my first job. Look, I lived in Alameda, which was close.

David: If I'm not mistaken, you played there for about eighty-nine weeks— something like that.

Phyllis: Yes, I was hired for a two-week fill-in for Milt Kamen whom they had just hired. He wanted to go back to New York; he was very home-sick—and he had an excuse to go back—he had something in radio; this was in the very early days of television. They allowed him to go back, and when he came back, I had my two weeks experience, and he had his two weeks, and we were both new. They wanted to keep the person who was going to make it [in show business]. They couldn't decide which of us to keep, so they kept us both—and broke all precedence by having two comics on the bill. Their policy had been to have a Black act, a self-contained act so that the musicians could have a break for union purposes, and a comic. In this case they had two comics, a self-contained act, and a Black act. It was way over their budget, actually.

LOVE

Phyllis Diller

Bob Hope frequently asked Phyllis to accompany him on shows overseas for the military.

David: And you both became stars, you and Milt Kamen.

Phyllis: Yes.

David: In 1959 or there about, a fellow by the name of Bob Hope saw you in a Washington, D.C., nightclub and had quite a big influence on your career.

Phyllis: Yes, but not until years later. He waited until I was quite a pro and then he started using me systematically and regularly on his huge NBC television shows. Then he co-starred me in three movies, for which I'm terribly grateful because it was a lot of fun making movies with Bob.[90]

David: Watching you tonight—and you were absolutely hilarious, and that's no surprise to anyone—I saw some Bob Hope influence in your act. I say that, of course, because he preceded you down the show business trail.

Phyllis: A long way, yes, because when I was a child, he was my idol. I used to sit by the radio with my ear glued to it, listening to him and adoring him. And actually having a good ear, I just simply absorbed that delivery, couldn't have been luckier because it's a wonderful delivery that he has.

David: Tonight, as I was watching you, I imagined Bob Hope sitting in a nightclub in Washington, DC, seeing this gal up on the stage who was then probably not well known—you were just breaking at that time—and his saying, "She's a female me!"

Phyllis: *[Laugh]* Well, I've been accused of that.

David: That's a compliment, by the way.

Phyllis: It's a great compliment, and I love it. He almost always says something about me in all of his shows; he always has a terrible crack about me, which I adore.

David: Your first movie break was a film called *Splendor in the Grass*.[91]

Phyllis: A terrific movie!

David: Yes! And you played a character called Texas Guinan.

Phyllis: Yes, but I was only on the screen for thirty seconds.

David: I'm curious as to how a raucous comedienne named Phyllis Diller ended up in *Splendor in the Grass*, a movie.

Phyllis: Oh, my dear, in those days—that was very early in my career—I was anything but raucous. I wasn't raucous at all; I was very timid, insecure. Texas Guinan was much more—I could do it now. I wasn't too good then; I didn't even do her very well because, you know, she was hostile and negative. Her whole thing was "Hello, Suckers!" [92] That was during the Depression, you know, and that went against my grain, actually, but I wanted the part bad. But I was really unable to carry that off. I looked good; they did me up to look so period.

David: How did you happen to get that role? You had done nothing in films; you were a nightclub performer. . .

Phyllis: Nothing! But I was beginning to be known. Look, I was the only female comic at the time; the only [female] standup comic in the world.

David: And why are there so few?

Phyllis: Because it is so difficult.

David: That's a good answer. You can almost name them on the fingers of one hand.

Phyllis: There're only three. There's Totie [Fields],[93] Joan Rivers,[94] and myself. Joan, of course, is very much into writing. She wants to be a director and a writer, which she is. I just saw her *Rabbit Test*, which is her second movie, and it's just marvelous. She has already written the third and gotten it financed. She's on her way and, I would imagine, not doing much of the other [standup]. [Standup] is in a whole other stratum in the entertainment world.

There's a new comic coming up by the name of Elayne Boosler[95] who, I'm sure, will make it. She's coming out of The Comedy Store that I spoke of before. I met her on a Dean Martin Roast. It was a feather in her cap to get that as an unknown.

David: You had two television series during the 1960s, but television never seemed to quite capture the Phyllis Diller that we see on the nightclub stage.[96]

Phyllis: No, it never did.

David: You were good, but what I see out on the nightclub stage. . .

Phyllis: . . . is just that much better. Well, it's very, very hard. Have you ever seen Don Rickles live?

David: No.

Phyllis: Well, there is a shining example of a man [who has had difficulty finding success on television]; this must be his sixth television series. This one comes the closest [to being a success], because it's a [Sgt.] Bilko type.[97] It comes the closest because he's all hostility.

He is so wonderful in person! I could see his show twice a night for a year, and every time I would laugh at the same lines! I've done it night after night; he's so funny! It's so difficult to get that kind of freedom [success] with the tube because it's just such a different medium, you know.

They've tried so hard to show a different side of me on television because the "hard side" is sometimes disliked by people, and they're aware of this. A lot of people think that I'm truly the harridan they see on stage, and therefore, they don't like that kind of a woman. They don't realize that that's an act.

So you have all of these problems: you don't want to be typecast, and yet you've got to be funny, you can't come out and be maudlin. If there is anything I can't stand it's people who throw kisses and beg for applause and do a sympathy act, you know. I'd rather be unknown, really!

David: In 1970 you did *Hello Dolly* on Broadway. At that time you are the top nightclub comedienne in the country, and you stopped playing nightclubs and for several months played Dolly Levi on Broadway. It seems a strange thing for you to do.

Phyllis: Oh, no. You do certain things simply for the "book." It looks good in the "book," really. It is simply a "legitimate" thing. You see, a lot of people have no respect for a nightclub comic. Nightclub comics know that, and they yearn for respect. They get the money and they get the laughs, but there isn't a human ego in the world that doesn't want respect. They call us "nightclub comics."

David: Yes, but *the* top nightclub comedienne in the country!

Phyllis: I know, but I'm considered a "nightclub comic," and, therefore, I'll take a Broadway show because it's considered "legitimate" where nightclub work isn't—although it is much more difficult. While I'm doing *Dolly* on Broadway, I'm going bankrupt. The money is here [in nightclubs].

I turned down *Mame* three times: once on Broadway, once the road show, and once at Caesar's Palace. In other words, it isn't that I couldn't play Broadway. You see, people don't think you can [do it] unless they see you do it. People have so little imagination, you know; it's too bad. People have a tendency—and this is very negative—to limit other people with their thinking.

David: Pigeon hole them.

Phyllis: Yes, pigeon hole. In Hollywood they call it typecasting.

David: You did *Hello Dolly* on Broadway, and that was a change of pace from your nightclub experience. You did several comedy movies with Bob Hope, and then all of a sudden you did a movie called *The Adding Machine* by Elmer Rice.[98]

Phyllis: Yes, a serious role.

David: A serious role, a shrewish wife, but not the shrewish wife Phyllis Diller plays on the nightclub stage.

Phyllis: Similar.

David: Yes, but not the same.

Phyllis: Oh, she was a terrible woman, that Mrs. Zero [the character Phyllis played in the film]. Wasn't that a wonderful name for her? She was a nothing! He was a nothing, and she was a nothing: Mr. and Mrs. Zero. That Elmer Rice, you just have to take your hat off to [him].

David: It's no secret that the movie was not a fantastic success. . .

Phyllis: No, but it's still a mystery why not. It's a mystery, [but] *you* don't know the mystery. It got caught in a tong war over at Universal Studios when they were going to fire everybody in the English office [writing department]. It was the last movie made under that regime, and for some reason they simply shelved the movie. That movie could be brought out anytime and publicized or even played. It never played [in many theaters]! How can you have a hit if you don't play it in a movie house?

David: I suspect that in time it's going to become a film that will be shown in university cinema classes.

Phyllis: Who knows? I don't know.

David: But why did you take that change-of-pace role?

Phyllis: You always want a challenge if you're alive. Listen, when I don't want a challenge, you'll find me in a home.

David: Well, that was certainly a challenge, and you met it.

Phyllis: You know it was directed by Charlie Chaplin's protégé, Jerome Epstein,[99] who had always worked with Chaplin as his protégé. And you noticed that Sidney Chaplin [Chaplin's son] was in it. He played God!

I met Charlie Chaplin, finally, and it was one of the great thrills of my life. I went to Switzerland to his home to the wedding of one of his daughters. One of my prized possessions is a picture of him and me together. I admired him. You see, I was around when he was the big comic in early movies, the little tramp.

Think of that, silent films. I saw the first color film; I remember the first talkie; I remember when there was no radio; I remember the first radios; they were usually Atwater Kents. You had to put earphones on [to listen to them]. Isn't this exciting? *[Laugh]*

David: How things do change with time! I read that at one time early on in your career—maybe you still do it—people would send you jokes, housewives would send you jokes that you would accept and send them—I don't know—ten dollars or some amount and say, "I'm going to use your joke in my act." Do you still do that?

Phyllis: I don't do it any more, but I did do that for years, and I have gotten a lot of wonderful jokes from people out there who wanted to become comedy writers. I'd say at least, oh, forty of those people are now working in Hollywood. I was their first sale, you see, so I helped people along, nurtured them.

David: You are now occasionally appearing with symphonies, playing the piano.

Phyllis: Yes, I did Sarasota. That's a marvelous hall over there, the Van Wezel [Performing Arts Hall]. It's a beautiful place and a wonderful symphony.

David: Again, is this just another way of stretching your talent?

Phyllis: Yes, it stretches me. It makes me work; it makes me work much harder. Look, what I do out here [standup comedy] is easy for me. But when I sit down at the piano, I'm working very hard and I'm pushing myself so that I don't get ready for the home. That's why I'm so thrilled when I'm allowed to do symphonies—because people respect symphony people; they don't respect saloon people. [100]

David: *[Laugh]* Well, lady, this is one fellow who does! I have not laughed as much and as loudly in many, many years as I did tonight. And I say that very seriously, very honestly.

Phyllis: Good! Well, you see, my goal in life is to be funny.

David: Well, you have succeeded admirably. Phyllis Diller, thank you so very much.

Phyllis: You made it very nostalgic; we went clear back to the horse and buggy days.

Phyllis Diller was sixty when we had our post-show conversation. She continued her hectic career full throttle for the next twenty-some years, eventually concentrating on the piano concert performances a little more heavily than the standup comedy appearances. She also did voice work for several animated films including *The Nutcracker Prince* (1990), *Happily Ever After* (1993), and most notably *A Bug's Life* (1998).

During these same years she appeared in large and small roles in a series of movies, mostly small budget, independent features that had limited release. These films, covering a bizarre range of subject matter, include *Pink Motel* (1982) with Phyllis and Slim Pickens playing a couple who run a cheap motel frequented by a wide assortment of weirdoes; *The Boneyard* (1991), a horror-comedy with Phyllis and Norman Fell playing two coroners who get involved with children who have been turned into zombies; and *The Aristocrats*, in which she was featured with many of her contemporary comics in a documentary film about, supposedly, the dirtiest joke ever told.

Phyllis never had another television series of her own, but she was a frequent guest on the small screen, showing up on *Tales from the Darkside*, for instance, or the long-running family drama *7th Heaven*, where she got tipsy preparing dinner for the family. Phyllis also put her voice to work on such animated television series as *Family Guy*, where she was the voice of Peter Griffin's mother, and *The Adventures of Jimmy Neutron: Boy Genius*, doing the voice for Jimmy's grandmother.

Ever on call, she was a panelist on *Hollywood Squares* and a judge on *Last Comic Standing*. In 2007 she guest starred on *Boston Legal* as herself. Then too Phyllis would make an occasional visit to the *Tonight* show with Jay Leno, doing a standup bit while sitting on the couch—all in a day's (or night's) work for the now comic legend.

These were the years that Phyllis also became an advocate for plastic surgery by candidly discussing the series of procedures that she had first undergone when she was fifty-five. As a result, she received numerous awards and acknowledgments from plastic surgeons and medical organizations.

And now, ladies and gentlemen, the BEAUTIFUL Phyllis Diller!

By the late nineties health problems began to plague Phyllis. In 1999 it was reported that she suffered a "serious heart attack" and was fitted with a pacemaker. After her release she returned to performing for a couple of years but at a lessened pace, and in 2002 she announced her retirement from the stage but said she would still do voice work and make occasional appearances on TV. Then in 2005 a bad fall in her Brentwood home caused her to be hospitalized again for tests. In the summer of 2007 *USA Today* reported that she had fractured her back and would have to cancel her appearance on Jay Leno's *Tonight* show where she had planned to celebrate her ninetieth birthday.

Despite these health scares, Phyllis was able to complete her autobiography, *Like a Lampshade in a Whorehouse: My Life in Comedy*, written with Richard Bushkin and published by Tarcher in 2005. This was not her first foray into writing; over her career she had published several books in the comic vein, most notably *The Joys of Aging—and How to Avoid Them* published by Doubleday in 1981.

Phyllis Diller, truly, has made her mark in show business, and with advancing years she has rightly received the accolades of her fans and peers. She was awarded her star on the Hollywood Walk of Fame back in 1993. Always a supporter of gay rights, Phyllis was honored by the mayor of San Francisco, Gavin Newsom, when he proclaimed February 5, 2006, "Phyllis Diller Day" in San Francisco. In 2006 a DVD tribute to Phyllis was released entitled *Goodnight, We Love You—The Life and Legend of Phyllis Diller* in which fellow comedians such as Roseanne Barr, David Brenner, Red Buttons, Don Rickles, Rip Taylor, Lily Tomlin, and others paid tribute to this female pathfinder in standup comedy and reflected on her considerable show business legacy. *Phyllis Diller: Not Just Another Pretty Face* was a 2007 DVD release that highlighted some of her best comic routines from over the years with (among others) her old friends Don Rickles and Dean Martin. There is even talk of a movie biography.

As of this writing Phyllis Diller is ninety-one years old and pretty much retired—and she's earned it!

Tony Dow & Jerry Mathers

February 28, 1978

"There haven't been any shows on TV that depicted what the adult world is like viewed from a child's eyes, and that's what Leave It To Beaver *was."*

Here are the *Leave It to Beaver* boys. Tony Dow as Wally and
Jerry Mathers as the Beaver.

When I first saw an episode of *Leave It to Beaver* sometime around 1957, it allowed me to become reacquainted with an old film friend, Hugh Beaumont, Beaver and Wally's dad in the series. I had enjoyed his work as an actor going back to the middle 1940s when I saw him in a brief series of detective films where he portrayed a private detective named Michael Shane. This was a three or four episode series produced by a poverty row studio called PRC, which stood for Producers Releasing Corporation. All of PRC's output was bottom-of-the-barrel B-picture fodder, each episode seemingly produced for about a hundred dollars and change.

But there was a charm about those little detective adventures that I enjoyed—and I particularly liked the flippant, hard-boiled-with-soft-edges persona of Beaumont as Michael Shane, Detective. He was in a lot of low budget, melodramatic potboilers of that era, and he wasn't always the gumshoe detective; occasionally, he would take on the sinister guise of a homicidal maniac to good effect—see *Bury Me Dead*[101] for his dark side. I was a tad disappointed to find him playing the somewhat bland, all-American dad in this gentle situation comedy—there wasn't much chance for snappy repartee with a satin-dressed floozy as he gun-whipped some thug in a bar—no, that went way back in Hugh Beaumont's résumé.

But I digress. *Leave It to Beaver* was a family situation comedy that seemed true to life in the close-knit-family times of the "togetherness" fifties when it premiered. The younger son, Beaver, was played by a boy named Jerry Mathers who I remembered seeing in an offbeat, quirky Alfred Hitchcock film, *The Trouble with Harry*,[102] a year or so before the TV series came on the air. I was struck by the boy's total naturalness in the film as the one who first discovers the body of Harry—in case you missed it, that's the trouble with Harry, he's dead. The "total naturalness" of little

Jerry, his "un-actorly" believability, made him outstanding in the film, and, later, outstanding in the *Beaver* series.

I had never seen Tony Dow before the show premiered, but here was another young actor who seemed "like the boy next door." There was, again, a "naturalness" that he exuded that made you, the viewer, feel that he was just like some of the guys you used to pal around with back in middle or high school.

This quality, this "ordinariness" that both boys displayed in their characters was no accident—it was exactly what the creators of the show were looking for, and they found it in Jerry and Tony and abetted it in carefully created dialogue, character development, and homespun subject matter. Here, presented from the boys' perspective, was a typical middle-class American family of the fifties and sixties involved in the daily experience of school, home chores, and playtime with other kids in the neighborhood—the good and not-so-good experiences of their everyday lives.

Inevitably the script would call for Beaver to get into a situation he couldn't handle by himself, so he'd go to his brother Wally for help and advice. If the two of them couldn't remedy the problem, they would go to the ultimate problem solvers, Mom and Dad. In the process they would learn some valuable lesson about life that they could carry with them from then on. If you lived through the middle-class world of the fifties as I did, that's the way life was supposed to be. And for some of us it was.

But it was now 1978, almost a decade and a half after the show's network demise, and *Leave It to Beaver* was still running in our Florida neighborhood on a daily basis, attesting to its broad general appeal that went far beyond generational appeal. I hadn't heard anything recently about Hugh Beaumont, Barbara Billingsley (who played the boys' mother), Tony, or Jerry for quite a few years. They seemed to disappear from my radar once the show folded. But that was to change.

I received a phone call from the Country Dinner Playhouse in St. Petersburg that Jerry Mathers and Tony Dow had gotten back together and would be appearing there in a comedy play. Would I like to meet and talk with them? "Yes, of course," was the answer to the question, and a date and time were set for me to get together with them in their dressing room before a performance.

I was met by the theater's PR lady and escorted through the lower caverns of the theater to where the dressing rooms were located. It turned out that they did indeed share a single dressing room for the show, and

A family portrait of the whole Cleaver family: Barbara Billingsley and
Hugh Beaumont as June and Ward Cleaver, Jerry Mathers as the Beaver,
and Tony Dow as big brother Wally.

they were waiting for me there. Their dark tanned features bespoke their
recent California leave taking, or else they had *really* soaked up some our
Florida sunshine in a hurry. The PR lady introduced us and then excused
herself, saying that she had to get back to the box office.

The Beaver boys, now grown adults, were both wearing dark slacks
and white shirts: Jerry a dress shirt open at the collar, Tony a polo-type
shirt. Their casual, laidback manner as we were introduced and then
made some brief small talk made me realize how close the TV characters

were to the real persons who had played the roles. Even their interaction here in the dressing room many years after the series was that of a grown up Wally and Beaver—and I don't say this negatively, only as an observation: Two fine boys were now two fine men.

David: Tony Dow and Jerry Mathers. Those two names should be very familiar to anyone who watched *Leave It to Beaver* on television. *Leave It to Beaver* started on TV back around 1957 and lasted until sometime into 1963. Let me take you fellows one at a time: Tony, how did you happen to be cast in the *Leave it to Beaver* series?

Tony: Well, it was kind of an accident—actually my whole starting in the business was an accident—but the actual *Beaver* part was just an interview that I went out on. My agent, as they do, had set up an appointment, and I went down and talked to them. What had happened was that they had made a pilot, and they had sold the pilot. The fellow who was to play the Wally character, which was my character, grew quite a bit during that period of time, so they needed to recast it, and I was fortunate enough to go to the interview and get the part.

Here are Tony and Jerry in their dressing room at the Country Dinner Playhouse at the time of our conversation in 1978.

David: Had you appeared in other shows previous to being cast in *Beaver?*

Tony: No. As a matter of fact, I had done one pilot for Columbia for a wildlife series; it was called *Johnny Wildlife.* The way I had gotten that was a friend of mine was an actor, and he thought he might get the part of the father if I went down with him because we kind of looked alike, and maybe as a package we'd work well together. And as ironic things go, he didn't get the part, and I did. But that was the only previous thing [I had done].

David: How old were you when you started *Leave It to Beaver?*

Tony: Twelve years old.

David: Jerry Mathers, the Beaver, how did you get cast in the show?

Jerry: I had been working as an actor since I was two, and they had a massive call for a series in Hollywood. There were about three thousand people on the original interview, and I went out. They just kept eliminating people, and I was the last person left after they eliminated everybody else.

David: That's a lot of competition. What was the secret quality that you had that caused you to be cast in the show?

Jerry: I really don't know; I guess they just liked me.

Tony: I remember the first time Joe Connelly and Bill Moser[103] saw Jerry. I guess, as the story goes, he was in a Little League game, a baseball game or something. What was it?

Jerry: Cub Scouts.

Tony: Oh, it was Cub Scouts. He had to go to a Cub Scouts meeting. He came in [for his interview] in his uniform, and he couldn't be bothered with these two producers that wanted to cast him in this TV series; he was late for his Cub Scout meeting. They liked that quality, I think.

David: Jerry, how old were you when you were cast as the Beaver?

Jerry: When I was actually cast—we did it about a year or eight, nine months before we actually started filming—I had just turned seven; when we actually started the series, I had just turned eight.

David: Hugh Beaumont and Barbara Billingsley were your mother and father on the program. I remember Hugh Beaumont from many years before that series when he played detectives in B movies; he was Michael Shayne, Detective, for one. I always enjoyed him in these detective roles, and then along came *Leave It to Beaver,* and there he was as your father. What's become of Hugh Beaumont?

Tony: Hugh is semi-retired. He's living in the valley in Topanga Canyon, and he's a really interesting fellow. He's a writer, he's a director, and he was a Methodist minister prior to becoming an actor. So he's pretty well versed, and he's done some writing; he wrote quite a few shows, and he directed some of our *Beaver* shows, as a matter of fact. About a year ago I did a stage play for him that he was directing. He, unfortunately, had a stroke about two and a half, three years ago, and he's recovering from that. It slowed him down a bit, but he's looking pretty good now.[104]

David: And Barbara Billingsley?

Jerry: Barbara is also basically retired. She married a doctor. In fact, she married him while on the series, and they both like to travel. So for the last several years they've been traveling all over the place. She just built a house in Malibu, and I think she's going to settle down a little bit more. It's on Malibu Beach and I think they're planning to live there now.

David: On the program it seemed to be a family. That was part of the magic of the *Leave It to Beaver* program; you really believed in the Cleaver family. What was your relationship to Hugh Beaumont and Barbara Billingsley.

Jerry: Basically, we were all really good friends. We were very close, but it was the kind of thing where we got there at eight in the morning and left at five. Although they were really close [to us], we were all

Here is another family portrait from several years later. Tony is a teenager and Jerry is approaching his teen years.

professional people, and they weren't so much like a family as they were really close friends.

Tony: Well, I remember Hugh giving me advice on a few problems that I might have had that I may not have talked to my folks about, but, generally speaking, Jerry is right; they were very good friends and really neat people. We were very close and we felt like a family, but it was an eight to five family, I guess.

David: *Leave It to Beaver* was and is considered one of the best of the family situation comedies. I think perhaps that's because of the sensitivity of the writing on the show and certainly the sensitivity of the actors who portrayed the characters. Could you as young kids have any idea of the quality that was going into that show or that it would have such a long-lasting appeal?

Tony: Well, I think it's difficult as a child, although I was eighteen when the show finished, so I was certainly quite aware at that point, I would hope. We were aware that there was an awful lot of quality just based on other shows at that same time. We shot a lot more film; we were a lot more conscientious; we had a lot more rehearsal time; the directors were selected a lot more carefully; and the coverage was a lot more selective as far as camera angles. They spent more money than the average show at that particular time. And, of course, the writers had, what did they have, sixteen kids, Jerry?

Jerry: Well, fifteen, I think—seven and eight between them.

Tony: Fifteen kids between them, so they had a pretty good ability to judge what family life was about and what kids would do. But the main thing that was interesting about the show, I think, was the point of view of the show: It was the adult world from a child's point of view, which philosophically is considerably different from a child's world from an adult point of view—which is all the other shows.

There haven't been any shows on TV that depicted what the adult world is like viewed from a child's eyes, and that's what *Leave It to Beaver* was. And that's why I think the show has a different feeling and maybe that special feeling because children can identify with that, they can pickup on that. It's not the type of thing where you sit back and say, "Oh, I see, that's from a child's point of view," but it's the type of thing, I think, that makes it so universally appealing.

David: Yes. I have a fourteen year old daughter now, and she has for the last several years watched the *Leave It to Beaver* reruns every afternoon that she can. It seems to be just as appealing for her as it was for the generation that preceded her that watched it.

Tony: Yeah, that's what's really neat, I think. We really enjoy that, and we enjoy the fact that people walk up and they feel like we're friends, you know. Of course, you get a certain amount of yelling at and people who . . . but, generally speaking, people feel that they know you, and they come up and they talk with you, and it's nice. They're friendly, and there's a warm kind of feeling, which we appreciate.

David: I recently talked with Luke Halpin who played the older boy on *Flipper* for a number of years. I asked him how the other kids his own age reacted to him when he was the star of the *Flipper* series. He told me there were some very mixed reactions. How did your peers, the kids that grew up with you, how did they react to your being the stars of a TV show?

Jerry: Well, basically, when I was on the show there was no real problem. Kids don't really spend that much time at home anyway. They got up and went to school at eight; we went to the set at eight. They got home at three, but we got home at five, so we'd go out and play after it was over. So there was no big difference there.

When I went into high school—which was just when the series ended—for about the first week I was a freshman and because a lot of the other people had come from schools where they had peer groups, I didn't know anybody. For about a week I had some problems. I went out for the football team and made a lot of friends there, and I never had any problems after that.

David: No one ever said, "Nan-na-na-na-na, you're the Beaver" in a taunting way?

Jerry: Not really. You get that every once in a while, but it's not that big a deal as long as you know how to handle people. I think a lot of it is just how you handle them. If you immediately show that that's going to hurt you—if they are out to hurt you—then they'll do it. But as long as you know how to handle people—you know, if they're obnoxious or aggressive—you can just put them in their place. If they're nervous or trying to be funny, you can make friends with them.

Tony: I had a group of friends that I kept pretty much throughout my childhood, as everybody does.

David: Were they actor friends?

Tony: No, I had a few friends or acquaintances that I knew [from the business], like I knew Paul Petersen, Micky Dolenz, and a couple of people like that, but not particularly close friends.[105]

David: Paul has written a rather bitter book about his experiences as a child actor.

Tony: He interviewed me, and, of course, I wasn't very bitter about things, and he kept trying [to get me to say something]. I kept saying, "You know, Paul, I never really felt that way." I understand his point of view, and I think it's a valid point of view, but I haven't read the book, so I can't comment on what he's actually written.

Hollywood sometimes has a tendency to take advantage of . . . but they take advantage of everybody. Every business takes advantage of everybody, so that's just, you know, what the hell. *[Laugh]* But, basically, I think it's how you relate to people. I don't enjoy people invading my privacy very much, if it's kind of a negative invasion. But if people are friendly and if people are genuinely interested, I can usually feel that and I enjoy it.

David: Did you feel that you missed something in your youth by being tied up working in a television series? Maybe you couldn't go out and play baseball because you had to learn your lines.

Tony: I think, as far as that goes, you probably get a lot more done because of working, because you meet a lot of interesting people, and you have more economic freedom, and you travel a lot. I found that I didn't miss anything except maybe playing on the football team in high school—where I would have had a bad knee for the rest of my life. *[Laugh]* Undoubtedly, there might be something down the line that I or we, whoever the child actor is, may have missed. But on the other hand, I guess you can't go through life and hit 'em all; you've got to miss something somewhere along the line. *[Laugh]*

David: How did you two get along on the set? Was there ever any sibling rivalry?

Jerry: Not really, because, basically, as I said, we were only there from about eight to five, so even if you've got rivalry, the next day you'd forgotten about it. We never had any problems that I can remember, to tell you the truth.

David: You two never fought much, did you?

Tony: No

Jerry: He was too much bigger than me. *[Laugh]*

Jerry: He never fights anyway, and I'm pretty passive myself.

David: What's the Beaver's first name; I can't remember it.

Jerry: Theodore.

David: The *Leave It to Beaver* series is a long time ago now. What have you been doing since then?

Tony: Well, let's see. When I finished the show, I did quite a bit of acting right after that for the next two or three years. I stayed very busy, and I did another television series called *Never Too Young*.[106] Then I got tangled up in the army. I was in the National Guard, so I couldn't work. What I thought would be about three years ended up to be almost six, because they make you very funny looking with the short hair and all that sort of stuff, and it's hard to work as an actor. So then I lived on a boat, and I did some painting and some sculpting, things like that all the time I was acting and going to school.

Then I started a painting contracting company. We did a lot of super graphics and interior paint design work. Then we got into general contracting, and I was a contractor for four years, designing and building, remodeling restaurants, commercial things. Then I got bugged with that one day and woke up and changed vocations, and here we are.

David: Back acting.

Tony: Right. And this is now like a full-time situation, where before I was working maybe three or four or five times a year. It's enough to get by economically sometimes, but it drives you crazy.

David: Yes, I would think the transition from producers and directors accepting you as a child actor to those same people accepting you as an adult actor could be quite rugged.

Tony: I guess. I don't understand where producers and people like that are [in their thinking]. There are an awful lot of good people around. I don't know, maybe sometimes that's a copout that there's a problem making the transition, or maybe there's some sort of psychological basis to it. Maybe people who are now producers and directors were our peers, and maybe they have some sort of hidden resentment, or maybe they don't think we are [still viable as actors]. I have no idea; it does seem to be a problem. It's too bad, because, like in any job, when you invest a certain amount of your time and your life and energy and you've got a certain knowledge, it's too bad that you can't continue to get better and use it.

David: Jerry, bring us up to date on your activities.

Jerry: Well, I went to college; I'm a graduate of the University of California at Berkeley. Then I went to work for a bank; I was a loan officer and operations officer with the bank for several years. Within the past year I have gone into real estate. While I was with the bank, it left me no free time to do other things except student films and things I could fit in on my vacation or weekends. With real estate I am still active in the real estate field, and I can be working here [on stage in St. Petersburg, Florida,] and still working in LA in my real estate. So that's what I'm doing right now.

David: One last question and I'll let you get ready for tonight's show—I know you haven't got much time. Are you married?

Jerry: Yes, I am. I met my wife while I was at Berkeley, and she's a student at the University of California and right now studying for a doctorate in linguistics. Her name is Diana.

David: Any children?

Jerry: No.

David: Tony.

Tony: I'm married, been married eight years. I have a son, Christopher, five years old. My wife's name is Carol; she's a travel agent. We live in the valley, got a dog and about five cats, and that's it, I guess.

David: Thank you very much, Tony Dow and Jerry Mathers.

Tony: Thank you.

Jerry: Thank you.

The journey through life, whether you're a former child actor in show business or a plumber, will have good times and bad, personal and professional ups and downs—and thus it was for the next thirty-plus years for Jerry and Tony. On the personal side, within the same year of our conversation, they both had life changing events: Jerry became a father for the first of three times with the birth of a son, Noah. In later years there would be two daughters added to the family: Mercedes in 1982 and Gretchen in 1985. Then, after fourteen years of marriage Jerry and his wife were divorced. Jerry would marry again and that marriage also would end in divorce.

Tony's marriage would end in the year we talked, and he would remarry in 1980 and the couple would eventually have one child. Tony revealed during the late 1980s that he had been diagnosed with Bipolar disorder and that he had struggled with depression for some years. He eventually starred in some self-help videos that chronicled his difficulties with the disorder in hopes that he might help others with the problem.

On the professional front they both flourished in the ensuing years. Tony made guest appearances on a number of television series (*Square Pegs, Quincy M.E., Knight Rider*), while Jerry concentrated on the real estate business. Then in 1983 they were approached about doing a television film entitled *Still the Beaver* that would chronicle the lives of Wally,

Theodore, and the whole gang from the original series as adults. In the story Beaver is divorced with two sons, Oliver and Kip, and moves back in with his mom, now widowed. Wally is now a lawyer (and actually handles Beaver's divorce), married, has a daughter (and eventually a son), and lives next door. The two-hour film ran in March of 1983 on the CBS television network to surprisingly good ratings.

And then that most rare of television happenings occurred, a series revival: The Disney Channel, using the TV movie *Still the Beaver* as a pilot, decided to create an all new series with most of the original cast from *Leave It to Beaver*. The *Still the Beaver* show premiered as a half-hour sitcom on the Disney Channel in 1985 and ran for a year. Then the series was picked up by TBS under a new title, *The New Leave It to Beaver*, and ran for another three years—until 1989—for a total of one hundred and two episodes.

In the years following that series Jerry and Tony continued their careers, mostly separately. Jerry proceeded to appear in a series of independent films: *Down the Drain* (1990), *Sexual Malice* (1994), *Playing Patti* (1998), *Better Luck Tomorrow* (2002), *Will to Power* (2008), and others in which he mostly played smaller roles. He also made appearances on a number of television series: *Vengeance Unlimited* (1999), *Diagnosis Murder* (1999), *The War at Home* (2005), and recurring spots on *The Tonight show* with Jay Leno, among others.

In 1998 Jerry published his autobiography entitled *And Jerry Mathers as "The Beaver"* which was published by Berkley Boulevard Books. Trying his luck in a new medium, between June and September of 2007 Jerry appeared in the hit Broadway musical, *Hairspray*, taking over the role of Wilbur Turnblad for a three-month run. From all accounts he was very successful in the role and had a ball.

Tony continued to appear as a guest actor in many television series over the next years (*Charles in Charge*, several episodes of *Freddy's Nightmares*, and a couple of episodes of *Diagnosis Murder*, among others. Tony also became a successful television director, directing episodes of such series as *The New Lassie; Harry and the Hendersons; Swamp Thing; Coach;* and *Honey, I Shrunk the Kids; Cover Me: Based on the True Life of an FBI Family;* and others. In the mid 1990s Tony became visual effects supervisor for the *Babylon 5* television series (1994) and then visual effects producer for the series *The Adventures of Captain Zoom in Outer Space* (1995), and *Doctor Who* (1996). He also held the title of producer for *It Came from Outer Space II* (1996).

Here we have part of the cast for *The New Leave It to Beaver.* Beaver now has two sons of his own, Oliver (John Snee) and Kipp (Kipp Marcus). Grandma (Barbara Billingsley) looks after her son and two grandsons in the series.

On October 3, 2007, the TV Land channel telecast a twenty-four-hour marathon of *Leave It to Beaver* episodes to celebrate the fiftieth anniversary of the show. The next morning the surviving stars of the show—Jerry, Tony, Barbara Billingsley, Ken Osmond (Eddie Haskell), and Frank Bank (Lumpy) appeared on *Good Morning America* on ABC to reminisce about success of the series and how it has affected their lives. It just goes on and on.

Incidentally, as of this writing Jerry Mathers is sixty and Tony Dow is sixty-three years of age, but in our memories they will always be young boys learning about life in a little situation comedy called *Leave It to Beaver.*

Tom Ewell

July 12, 1978

"I had twenty-seven failures before I had a success."

Tom Ewell exudes a sly smile in this publicity photo taken while he was working for Universal International Pictures in the early 1950s.

In the summer of 1978, Tom Ewell was touring with a stage comedy entitled *Never Too Late*, a warhorse of a show that Paul Ford had starred in on Broadway back in the early 1960s which later was made into a less-successful movie with Ford. Anyway, I was alerted by the Country Dinner Playhouse that Tom Ewell was coming to St. Petersburg with the show for one week.

I had long followed Ewell's acting career. He was a fine stage and screen actor with such credits as *The Seven Year Itch*, for which he had won a Tony Award on Broadway and then went to Hollywood to film the movie version with Marilyn Monroe with Billy Wilder directing—it doesn't get much better or more prestigious than that!

But Tom Ewell's career went back many years on stage and in films to some very humble beginnings in very small roles. He appeared on Broadway starting in 1934 in such plays as *They Shall Not Die*, *The First Legion*, *Geraniums in the Window*, and *Stage Door*—all with well-known casts but short runs. His most memorable role from these years of the middle-to-late thirties was the role of store clerk Cornelius Hackl in *The Merchant of Yonkers* (1938-39), which later became *The Matchmaker* and even later *Hello Dolly*. Tom's version, *The Merchant of Yonkers*, only ran thirty-nine performances. Perhaps Tom thought things would get better if he tried Hollywood.

He made his film debut in the Carole Lombard, Charles Laughton film *They Knew What They Wanted* (1940) based on the Broadway play by Sidney Howard (which many years later became the hit musical *The Most Happy Fella*). If you look quickly, you can see the unbilled Tom Ewell and Karl Mauldin as "ranch hands" in the engagement party scene. The film was prestigious even if the role was not. In 1941 Tom could next be

found at Republic Pictures—a low-budget studio noted for its westerns—
playing unbilled bit parts in a Don "Red" Barry western (*Desert Bandit*)
and Gene Autry's *Back in the Saddle*. Tom then had to put his career on
hold while serving four years in the Navy during World War Two.

But following the war, things got better for him, especially on Broadway where the roles better demonstrated his abilities, especially in comedy. By 1946 he was in the hit show *John Loves Mary*, and that led to
Hollywood again with an important co-starring role in the hilarious
Katharine Hepburn-Spencer Tracy film *Adam's Rib*[107] (1949), playing the
philandering husband that wife Judy Holliday tries to murder. Then there
were the popular *Up Front/Back at the Front*[108] comedies based on the Bill
Mauldin Willie and Joe cartoons from World War Two. These successes
led to *The Seven Year Itch* on Broadway and in films. From there his bi-
coastal career flourished pretty much for the next twenty years.

But now it was 1978, he was sixty-nine years old, and most of the
good leading roles were designed for younger actors. Tom hadn't been on
Broadway since 1965 and that was for only two performances of *Christmas in Las Vegas*. (Prior to that he was in *A Thurber Carnival* in 1960
which ran for 223 performances—okay, but not exactly a blockbuster.)

Now Tom was in a revival of *Never Too Late* on the dinner theater
circuit in St. Petersburg, Florida. The role was that of a sixty-year-old
husband who is told by his sweet wife that she is expecting a baby. Tom's
role called for him to be a selfish curmudgeon who is embarrassed and
dismayed at the prospect of becoming a father again at his advanced age.
The role was a natural for Tom because he could be something of a curmudgeon in real life, and he also had a reputation for being quite a pessi-
mist—not really called for much in the play, but nevertheless appropriate.

I went to see an evening performance of the show prior to talking
with Tom. For some reason he requested to meet with me prior to a
matinee performance, and for some reason long forgotten, I could not
stay for the matinee. So here it was one o'clock in the afternoon as I was
escorted to Mr. Ewell's dressing room for what I was told would have to
be a short chat. (Because I knew of his curmudgeonly ways, I was somewhat surprised that I was seeing him at all.)

He was already in partial costume (dress shirt open at the collar and
suit pants) and was about to apply makeup when he opened the door of
his dressing room and greeted me, I thought, rather jovially. We exchanged
the usual pleasantries, and he asked me to sit down in an easy chair next to

his makeup table. "Would you mind if I finished up putting on my makeup as we talk?" he asked politely. "I don't like to be rushed getting ready before a performance."

"That would be fine," I assured him, as I snapped on my recorder.

David: I understand that years ago you went to the University of Wisconsin with the intention of being a lawyer.

Tom: Well, no. With my *family's* intention of my being a lawyer.

David: And something happened along the way. . . .

Tom: Nothing happened. I knew what I wanted all along.

David: And you became an actor.

Tom: That's right. Well, something did happen. I was studying pre-law when one day they called from the local stock companies there, and one of the actors on Sunday morning had suddenly taken drunk, and they needed a replacement. They couldn't get anyone up from Chicago, where the casting was then, and they had to go on at three o'clock that afternoon to play a matinee, which was the opening show. They had a different show every week, and they always opened on Sunday with a three o'clock matinee. So they called me; I'd seen the show in New York the year before, and I went on and played it without a rehearsal, and that was the beginning of it all.

David: Without a rehearsal! My goodness!

Tom: Yes. I felt sorry for the audience not me. *[Laugh]*

David: Your interest then in theater expanded, of course, as you went along.

Tom: No, I'd always been interested in it, always knew what I wanted. When I graduated from high school, I wanted to go to New York to study at the American Academy of Dramatic Arts, but my family didn't see it that way. They wanted me to go into law because the family had been lawyers. I had every intention of following the theater as a career, right from the very beginning. Nothing ever changed my mind.

David: There's an old saying about Broadway, sort of a Catch 22—you can't get a job on Broadway unless you've had a job on Broadway. You, as a young actor struggling, got into a show called *They Shall Not Die* with Claude Rains and Ruth Gordon.

Tom: That was my first Broadway show up town. I had been in several off-Broadway shows, what they called Off-Broadway in those days, but that was the first official Broadway show.

David: So how did you get that first Broadway show?

Tom: Well, it wasn't talent. I didn't know for a long time how I got it. It was with the Theatre Guild; they were doing John Wexley's play. It was a play about the Scottsboro case that happened, I think, in Alabama, wasn't it? I remember they had a speech expert from, of all places, Louisville, Kentucky. He didn't know that I was from Owensberg, down river a hundred and twenty miles. He turned me down, said that my speech wasn't Southern enough. Phil Mueller said, "Aren't you from Kentucky?" I said, "Yes." He said, "Fire this speech expert and hire Tom."

I thought it was my personality, but years later I found out that the real reason was that I reminded him of Red Lewis, Sinclair Lewis. He was a close friend of Sinclair's, and I looked a great deal like he thought Sinclair looked as a youth, and he just decided to give me a chance. That's how I got my first opportunity.[109]

David: That was a drama of social protest at the time, and I believe that the show played in 1933 or '34. Was the show a big hit at the time?

Tom: No, the show was a failure. It was a beautiful play, really beautiful play, and Claude Rains gave one of the most stirring performances I will ever have seen. I can remember it vividly to this day, his closing summation of the speech to the jury about these boys down in Alabama. It was very stirring, very exciting, but the play lasted the period of the Theatre Guild subscriptions, which was about six weeks at that time. They lost money on it as they did a great many of their shows, but it was a beautiful show and tragic that it had that kind of a fate.

But a great many plays in the intervening years have had that fate too. I have known several plays that I've been in: *Ethan Frome*, for example, which Gilbert Gabriel of the *New York Journal American* called, "Absolutely top-drawer theater" and other people said that it was the best play of the season, was not a hit.[110] You just never know what will be hits.

David: But you've had your share of hits down through the years.

Tom: I've had more than my share of flops, shall we say.

David: *[Laugh]* But I think that's true of most Broadway actors. For every hit, you have three or four flops.

Tom: Well, I had more than that. I had twenty-seven failures before I had a success.

David: My goodness. That's a pretty good record.

Tom: I'd say it was a pretty bad record. It's all how you look at it.

David: Well, in the final outcome, you've done very well.

Tom: I can't complain.

David: *John Loves Mary*,[111] however, was one of the hits along the way. And I think that was one of the first Broadway shows that really established you, and I believe you won an award for that show.

Tom: I won several, yes. Yes, it did; it was a comedy and it was favorably received and comedies are always popular in the American theater, thank goodness, and I try to be a comedian. So as a result, that play provided me a wonderful part and Josh Logan, who directed it, helped me tremendously in my performance. It was a very flashy kind of part. As a result, it did win several awards. It won the Donaldson, and it won the Commedia, and I've forgotten what else, but it won two or three or four; I've forgotten which. You know, awards are fine, but they only bloom in the spring; in the fall they wither.

David: *Tunnel of Love* was another show you starred in on Broadway and then, I believe, it was shortly after that *Seven Year Itch* came along.

Tom: No, it was just the reverse. *Seven Year Itch* came first.

David: Now, *Seven Year Itch* was a blockbuster, really, on Broadway and, of course, went on to become the famous movie with Marilyn Monroe starring with you.

Tom: But, you know, it's an amazing thing. *Seven Year Itch*[112] ran three and a half years on Broadway, *Tunnel of Love*[113] ran over two years, and we think of them as hits, but they weren't really hits when they first opened. For example, there were seven critics on *The Seven Year Itch* and four gave it great notices and three hated it. On *Tunnel of Love* all seven hated it.

   Comedy is a strange thing, and a lot of times it doesn't get good notices. It's very, very seldom in my lifetime for a comedy to win unanimous critical approval. I think the reason for that is that most people think, and particularly critics think, that comedy is just to be laughed at. In other words, it isn't serious; it isn't important.

   But if you can make people cry, that's important. That's why I think drama always receives much more attention than comedy. They try to dissect it, [comedy] and they can't because what makes a laugh? Who knows? It just comes, effortless.

David: In recent years Neil Simon has had so many big hit comedies, and yet he hasn't been properly appreciated by the critics.

Tom: That's true. He won't be until he's dead. They all talk about George Kaufman now because George was the master. And yet Mr. Kaufman suffered his slings of outrageous fortune, the darts of the critics.[114]

David: I know some of the pit falls of *The Seven Year Itch* because I had the fortune or misfortune of directing it several years ago. I can well

This photo of Tom Ewell and Vanessa Brown is from the playbill of the Broadway production of *The Seven Year Itch*, for which Tom won the Tony Award.

appreciate how difficult that show was in many ways to pull off. It was a tricky show.

Tom: Well, it was; it was a very tricky show. When we first opened, our first performance was given in front of the backers. We had quite a few backers of that show because no one wanted to put money in it because it was the first play of George Axelrod, the playwright. And so they had a lot of trouble raising money. After that first showing—we had about two hundred and forty backers in the audience—they were all out in the lobby during intermission trying to sell their shares.

Huntington Hartford bought up quite a bit of the shares, and, of course, the show paid off something like forty to one—for every dollar you put in you got forty dollars. It made some people wealthy. Huntington didn't have to worry because the A&P markets do all right.[115] He was smart enough to see that the show would be a success. It *is* a difficult show [to perform].

David: You've got those flashbacks that are hard to pull off.

Tom: The trick to it, as we discovered after many weeks of working with it, is that the flashbacks have to happen in a man's mind. Well, to try to go from reality into what he's thinking about, has to be a combination of music and lights. It has to work in such a way that the minute they start to work [the music and lights] the next time, the audience is prepared to know that it is now fantasy and not reality. But it's very tricky to get those timings right.

David: Yes, it is. A good trivia question these days would be this: Who played the Marilyn Monroe part in *The Seven Year Itch* on the Broadway stage?

Tom: Well, I had about eight different girls that played it while I was playing it. But the one who started it, and the one who was the best of them all—although quite truthfully we didn't get along either professionally or socially, but she was the best—was a girl named Vanessa Brown. Vanessa was a very brilliant girl and was also one of the original Quiz Kids.[116]

She'd had a very difficult time because just before Hitler moved into Vienna, her family, who were very prominent there in the psychiatric field—both her mother and father were doctors—left and sent Vanessa to Paris to live, and she was only about two years old at the time. So they didn't get to see her again until she was five.

Between two and five I think Vanessa suffered a great deal from being amongst foster parents. Although she was tremendously brilliant, really—I think she was a Quiz Kid when she was seven in this country, fantastic mentality—she bore the scars of those early years of having been separated from her parents.

David: And then you went on to Hollywood to do the filmed version of *The Seven Year Itch*. Were you a shoo-in to get that part in the movie version? So many times they don't want the one who originated the role on Broadway.

Tom: No, no. Nobody wanted me. No, they didn't—quite seriously. My wife was one of the few people who wanted me to play it, and they announced several other [actors for the role]. As a matter of fact, they waited right up to the very last day that they had to decide before they finally signed me—they didn't know what else to do. Everybody was against me.

The only person who was really for me was Joe DiMag [DiMaggio]. He was married to Marilyn then, and she'd sent him to New York to

This, of course, is the iconic photo from *The Seven Year Itch* with Marilyn Monroe and Tom Ewell.

see the play. Joe recommended to Marilyn that she put her two cents in for me, which she did.

I think the deciding vote was cast by, of all people, Mrs. Samuel Goldwyn, who was very powerful at the time. She had many dinner parties, and she had seen me in New York. She was determined that I play the part. So Mrs. Goldwyn conducted a one-woman crusade for me to get the part. I never knew her very well. I did know her son, Sam Goldwyn, Jr., and he became a very good friend of mine. But his mother was the one who really swung the ballot box.

David: That's interesting. Billy Wilder, one of the top directors in Hollywood, directed *The Seven Year Itch*. A while back I read his autobiography and he comments on the making of *The Seven Year Itch* and that it was his first experience with Marilyn Monroe. Billy Wilder was not very kind in some of his comments about Miss Monroe and the fact that she frequently held up production on the film. Do you have any comments about working with Marilyn Monroe?

Tom: I did not read the book, and I never make any comments about anyone I've ever worked with. I don't believe in it; I prefer not to. I'll describe myself, I'll talk about myself, but [not] the people I have worked with—and a great many of them I have liked very much and a great many of them I have not liked at all. But I think that is a professionalism that happens between people. And also I think it is up to the audience and critics to comment upon personalities. I don't like to comment on them, no.

I know what you are going to ask: You are going to ask, "What are they really like?" Every one wants to know what they are really like. What is Woody Allen really like? What's Diane Keaton really like? What's Robert Redford really like? Well, they're like just exactly what you see. They can't hide their personalities. What they are is what you see.

There's not a single one of them that doesn't get mad. There is not a single one of them that doesn't have very charming moments. But whatever you see their personality to be and the facets of their personalities, if it seems real, then that's the person. There's no difference. I don't know of any monsters, and I don't know, really, of any angels in our business. I just prefer not to talk abut them, that's all. Let them talk about themselves. I'll sure talk about myself! *[Laugh]*

David: Okay, fair enough. During the late 1960s and early seventies I was suddenly not as aware of what Tom Ewell was doing in show business as I was during earlier years.

Tom: Well, there was a period in there, let's see, I did two plays in London, I think during that time, and I also toured fairly extensively across the country. I don't believe I appeared on Broadway—let me think, no; I wasn't on Broadway at that time. The last thing I did in New York was about 1966 or '67. Then I went to London and did two shows and then I did about five transcontinental tours.

David: And I believe you did some radio work in New York during that time.

Tom: Yes, we had our own radio show, my wife and myself, from our apartment in New York.

David: I thought I remembered that. Wasn't it a sort of Mr. and Mrs. type of show, over the breakfast table, *The Ewells*?

Tom: Yep, a morning show. But I believe we stopped that around '67 or '68.

David: How did you happen to get the role of Billy in the television series *Baretta*?

Tom: I don't know. Robert wanted me; no one else did.[117] That's the history of just about everyone in this business: No one else wants you except one person. It's just important that the one person who does want you has the clout to deliver. Robert wanted me to play it. I had never met him, but his wife turned out to be a great fan of mine, and she had recommended me.

David: You might be able to provide me with some insight on a book I'm working on right now that is tentatively going to be called *The Great Show Business Animals and Other Actors*.[118]

Tom: You won't sell many to actors, but the animals might buy them because of the billing.

Robert Blake (Baretta) and Fred the Cockatoo. A long search for a photo of
Tom and Fred was to no avail. If he could avoid it, Tom was not having his
photo taken with a child actor or an animal—a cockatoo in this case.

David: Could be. Certainly there's a facetiousness in the title. Lately I've
talked to many of the actors who have worked with animals in pictures and television. Of course, Fred the Cockatoo is now one of the
most popular animals—or in this case, birds—in show business, and I
wonder if you have any comments about working with Fred the cockatoo on the set.

Tom: Well, I don't think there is any actor in the world that likes to work
with an animal. Animals and cockatoos and other birds are not easy
to work with. You have to adjust yourself to them. You have to watch
them, and instead of concentrating on your own performance, you
have to concentrate on their performance because you can't use the
take you do until they get it right. This can be a very painful, long
process. Off stage they can be very friendly and wonderful—Fred
was very friendly; he only bit occasionally. As a result, I love to play
with them, but working with them, no.

I've never liked working with animals, and I've never liked working with children. Children are the same way. As Burt Lahr used to say, "Unless the kid's a heavy, you're dead working with children." They're not actors or performers; they're personalities, and you have to adjust your work to them rather than share it equally.

He [Fred] used to get a lot of fan mail. I used to read it because he wasn't paying too much attention to it. I remember he got several proposals for marriage.

David: Fred the Cockatoo?

Tom: Oh, yes, from other birds that wrote him. Then there was a bird who wrote him from someplace up in Maryland, some springs up in Maryland. He said, "I work for peanuts; how about you?"

David: *[Laugh]* I think you're pulling my leg.

Tom: No, I'm not. But the most touching letters that we got for Fred were from children. We got many letters from children for Fred. They were always the type of letter where the children felt close to Fred, and they would feel like he was their friend. A lot of children in this world don't think they have friends. They are either from large families or from families that didn't particularly want children but had them anyway.

I never realized how many lonely children there are in this world until I started to read some of Fred's mail. It was very touching. One little girl I remember particularly; I remember her letter very well. She said, "I cry myself to sleep every night because no one loves me. But when I watch you, I know that you do love me because I can see you look at me through the screen, and so that makes my life a little better." Letters like that touch you.

David: Very nice.

Tom: For that, I never mind working with an animal.

David: I'll include that story in my book. You know, I saw you in the play last night. It was an absolute delight to watch you on stage in *Never Too Late*. You have, as all actors do, little mannerisms, little things that you do that work particularly well for you on stage. You have a beautiful "take" that you do on stage, almost a Jack Benny take in a sense, only your own. That's the closest thing I can compare it to.

Tom: Well, I can't imagine anything better.

David: Are there performers over the years that have influenced you on the little devices that you use as an actor?

Tom: No, I never think of that, I never think of that.

David: Let me tell you, it was almost impossible to take my eyes off you when you were on stage.

Tom: Good! I believe in that! *[Laugh]* I thought only my wife did that, but I believe in that. [There was suddenly a knock at the dressing room door, and the stage manager called out "Half hour to curtain."] I'm terribly sorry. We're at half hour, and I have to get my thoughts together for the performance.

David: I certainly understand.

Tom: Thank you very much for coming. I've enjoyed it so much.

David: Thank you, Tom Ewell, very much.

I could certainly appreciate Tom's need to "get my thoughts together for the performance." As a theater director I had always insisted that backstage guests be asked to leave the performers at half-hour-before-curtain. It's then time for the actors to focus on their characters and the play. Tom Ewell was the type of old pro to treasure that time and to use it for full benefit in his performance.

I didn't hear much about Tom Ewell in the years that followed. He did some television work as a guest in several series. There were one-shot appearances on *Return of the Mod Squad* and *Taxi* in 1979, and a two-parter in the short-lived NBC cop series *Eischied* starring Joe Don Baker. Tom's most significant role during the early 1980s was four episodes on *Best of the*

West, a situation comedy series that was a spoof of every western film cliché imaginable. He played the town drunk, old Doc Jerome Kullens, in this ABC series which was shot down after twenty-two episodes.

In 1982 there was a *Trapper John, M.D.* episode and a character role in the Rodney Dangerfield film *Easy Money* in 1983. Tom's last role was in 1986: a *Murder, She Wrote* episode with Angela Lansbury—but that was long after he had pretty much retired earlier in the decade. He was plagued with various illnesses in these later years, and reports of a recurrent alcoholism problem had floated around for years.[119]

In rare interviews late in his life, Tom frequently stated his love for the theater as an actor's medium and his basic displeasure with working in films and television—the fact that films, he felt, were the domain of the director, and television was mostly the work of technicians. He did, however, state his pleasure working on the *Baretta* TV series with Robert Blake, saying it had given him greater pleasure than any project he had ever worked on; it had also provided him with his only Emmy Award nomination.

Of his films he said that they were for the most part nothing special with the noted exception of *The Seven Year Itch* with Marilyn Monroe, for which he had won a Golden Globe Award in 1956. Although he didn't want to talk with me about Marilyn back in 1978, when he did mention her in later interviews—and that was rarely—his comments were always positive in nature. He claimed that he never saw any of his films including *The Seven Year Itch,* that he could not bear to watch his own performances because he had an inferiority complex (You can see this in my conversation with him.) and over the years only caught snatches of his films and TV shows when his wife was watching television.

As the years passed, Tom Ewell seemed to slide off the radar into a self-prescribed oblivion, living in very quite retirement with his longtime wife Marjorie, whom he had married way back in 1948 and with whom he had had one son. Tom Ewell died on September 12, 1994, of undisclosed causes in Woodland Hills, California. He was eighty five.

Walter B. Gibson

September 26, 1977

"Who knows what evil lurks in the hearts of men?"

Walter Gibson and I are seen here with the Shadow at Orlandocon 1977.

My first book, *Who Was That Masked Man? The Story of the Lone Ranger*, had been published in 1976 and was the reason for my being invited to Orlandocon '77, which, as you might suspect, was held in Orlando, Florida, only a couple of hours from my home in Sarasota. The annual Orlandocon was primarily a tribute to the many newspaper comic artists who seemed to congregate in Florida, particularly in the Orlando area. Other participants of lesser emphasis at the Con included a writer (myself); an independent filmmaker (Harry Hurwitz); and an elderly, loquacious pulp fiction writer, ghost writer, and magician who stole the show—Walter B. Gibson. There were several other guests that year, but the mists of time have clouded my memory.

Walter, I was to learn, had just turned eighty a couple of weeks before I met him at Orlandocon, but he seemed to have the energy and stamina of someone at least half his age, which was about where I fell, agewise, at the time. He was heavyset but not overweight, of medium height, possessed of a ruddy appearance, and moved with surprising speed and grace for a man of his age—and he was constantly on the move.

Walter Gibson, I quickly discovered, was just *fun* to be around at the Con—and he seemed to be having as much fun being with us, a younger crowd in our twenties, thirties, and forties. We were curious and interested to learn of his experiences as the creator of the famous pulp, comic, film, and radio character, The Shadow, and of his friendship and ghostwriting time with The Great Houdini, the world-famous escape artist and magician. Our curiosity and interest in these areas and others seemed to spawn a youthful eagerness and enthusiasm in him to relate his adventures of those earlier years.

After being a participant in a couple of delightful, off-the-cuff, dining room talk-fests with Walter—where he would also usually mystify us with a bit of magic—I buttonholed him privately and asked if he, I, and a tape recorder might gather for a conversation that I could then take back to Sarasota for my radio program. Never one to miss an opportunity to reminisce about his fondly remembered years of yore, Walter quickly acquiesced to my request. The next morning we excused ourselves from the madding crowd and repaired to an office hideaway adjacent to where the Con was being held.

David: Walter Gibson, you've had such an interesting life. I appreciate the opportunity to talk with you today about some of your adventures. Let's start with how you happened to come up with the idea for *The Shadow?*

Walter: Well, it's a long story, but to put it briefly, I was doing magazine writing in the late 1920s, and at that time there were a tremendous number of magazines on the news stands. *Love Story* was selling one million a week, *Detective Story Magazine* was selling six-hundred thousand, and *Wild West Weekly* was selling a million. This was going on and on and the field was filled up with these and getting so competitive they thought they should try to bring in a new angle, and they thought of reviving some of the old type of characters that had existed years before but putting them out in magazine form.

Street & Smith, the publisher, was looking for a writer to write a pilot story about some unusual character, and we'd discussed it with editors and so forth. [Someone said,] "How about a mysterious character to be called 'The Shadow'?" Nobody had any idea of what he was to be except he was to fight crime which was very rampant in those days; that was the final days of prohibition. He could help people out of jams and things of that sort.

When I talked it over with the editor, he liked my concept of a weird, mysterious man coming in and suddenly taking a part in people's lives and having agents who worked for him. He said, "Go right ahead and write the story; it sounds good. Just keep it interesting, and if we like it, I'll give you an order for three more." They wanted to establish it as a quarterly magazine. Once you established a magazine on a recurrent basis like that, you could get second class mailing permits, and it was trademarked and established.

So I did the one and they liked it. They said to go on and do the others and get them in fairly soon. In fact, I started to do them rather rapidly because I wanted to get that assignment done and go on with something else. I adopted a pen name for it of Maxwell Grant.

David: Does that name have any particular significance?

Walter: It did in a very peculiar way. I was doing other writing, factual writing and news articles and some fiction, all under my own name. They wanted this to be established because it sounded as though Maxwell Grant was the one man who got the things directly from the Shadow's archives. We put that mysterioso thing at the front [of the story style]. I took two friends of mine, people who were interested in magic, and I wrote their first names and last. From Maxwell Holden I picked "Maxwell," and from a fellow named U. F. Grant I took "Grant" for the last name.

So, I've got the second story under way; in fact, it was even turned in when they called up and said, "Look, move on these things fast. Our first issue has sold out, and we're going to make a monthly out of it." So overnight I was pitched into a monthly. Instead of working one year on it, I was eighteen years doing nothing but turning out Shadow stories. I did other things too, but that was my major occupation.

David: How long would it take you to knock out a Shadow story?

Walter: I could turn one out in as fast as four days, but generally I would take five, more often six, and even up to eight or ten, though I'd take some breaks in between. I had to turn them out in between eight or ten days because I had to plot the next story. It started in 1931. In '32 they upped it to twice a month. By that time I was just turning them out; as soon as I was through with one, I'd start another.

They gave me a contract to do twenty-four stories in one year. That was to be one million four hundred and forty thousand words. I'd go into the office and talk with them about what would be our next story. I always did that first. That's why I could turn them out so fast. I plotted the stories so that every chapter was broken down, so that when I did the writing, I was never hung up.

David: You must not have had much time to do rewriting as you were going along.

Walter: I didn't do any rewriting. I left that to the editor. This was all first draft, but occasionally I would take a story, and if a chapter became too long, I would go back and condense three pages into two or do a little reshaping in process. If I had stopped and done rough drafts first, I would have fallen into the error that so many writers do. They suddenly feel as if they are doing some great literary work, and then they're really hung up. *[Laugh]*

David: Did you find that you'd go back and look at one of your manuscripts six or nine months later and say, "Gee, I don't remember that!"

Walter: Absolutely! I was my own best reader. See, I got ahead six months. When we were still on the monthly schedule, they had given me the contract for two a month, so I got ahead on that schedule. So I had the magazine actually six months ahead, twelve stories ahead. Frequently I would pick one up and it was like a new story to me. The other stories I had written in between time had crowded my mind out of the earlier one, you see.

David: To what do you attribute your ability to knock these things out just left and right? The words must come very easily to you.

Walter: Well, basically because I had been a news writer. For ten years I had been doing newspaper work and mostly in the form of feature articles. I had been writing for [Harry] Houdini;[120] I was writing for him at the time he died in 1926; that was five years before *The Shadow*. I wrote articles for Thurston the Magician.[121] The Ledger Syndicate in Philadelphia used to put me onto assignments. I'd go out and meet a man who was an expert in aerial surveying which was just starting, and I would write his story up. I did many interviews and things of that type.

The result was that I was very fast at descriptive writing. Stories of this sort with the Shadow moving in and out of people's affairs, fighting criminals and masterminds' plotting, I was able to treat in a semi-factual style. It was just like picking up the old newspaper work.

David: How many *Shadow* stories were there altogether?

Walter: I wrote two hundred and eighty-three. They're coming out now in paperback form, like pocketbooks.

David: Yes, I've seen them

Walter: They're hopping and skipping a little bit because the Shadow developed and got new agents as he went along, and, naturally, with so many stories, we're picking the ones that were sort of high marks. In other words, the twenty-four that we've done we're probably up to what would have been sixty in the original magazines.

David: Did you have a system for coming up with the characters you used in the stories?

Walter: There were hundreds of characters in The Shadow stories. During the first stories I started to keep an index file of all the characters, thinking they might come back into the stories. Well, pretty soon the thing just got tremendous because there were minor characters, lesser crooks, detectives that you would meet somewhere here and there. I found that was unnecessary, so I simply kept listings of the regular characters. We would have drawings made of them that would run in the magazine. A lot of them I would base on real-life characters whom I knew. For example, I had a reporter that was very much like a reporter I knew. There was always something generic with each one.

I found out one of my big problems was assigning names to characters. I'd have seven or eight new characters, and where was I going to get names? I couldn't just grab a name at random and then maybe get a real person's name who would say he didn't like it because now people were kidding him about it, and so forth.

So I would take a railroad timetable, a branch line, and take the names of the stations. For example, there's a branch line up in Massachusetts that left out of Wooster, Mass., and the first station was Chaffin, the next was Dawson, then there was Holden, then Brooks, Hubbardstun, and Gardener. Hubbardstun I cut down to Hubbard. If someone named Brooks said, "Hey, why did you put my name in and I was a crook?" I'd say, "You just happened to be station number three on this branch line."

Many of them [names] I got in Florida from the branch lines of the Seaboard and the Atlantic Coast Line. In those days, in the Thirties, there were all these little branch lines. I'd just pick up and go down and list them. It was easy to remember too. I learned all these little tricks.

What I was happy about was that once this writing got under way, it was absolutely successful. I was perfectly happy with it; it was my dish of tea. I would go into my office in New York and set up as many as three or four stories ahead, get the plots all okayed by the editor. We always talked about it with the business department because—a magazine of this sort, price wise, the sales on the stands—we didn't want to do anything that would disturb the way it was going.

Well, I'd get four ahead and then I could take off for Florida, come down to Orlando. I didn't have to worry for two months because I had my plots right with me. Even then I didn't have to go back to New York; I could send them in. Then I'd go up to Maine for the summer where I had a camp up there. I could bang them out up there.

John Nanovic, who was my editor, became the first editor of *The Shadow*. I came in and wrote the stories; he'd just come in as an editor at that time. Within three or four months we were the team; neither of us had seen the place the year before. We're suddenly top people! The general manager said each new magazine that came, like *Doc Savage*, he said give it to John Nanovic to edit. So John had me working full time; then he got Les Dent working full time. Other fellows—Frank Gruber, Steve Fisher, and all these other writers fed through this particular thing. John acted as coordinator.

The Shadow became a leading magazine for Street & Smith, but it never had as big a circulation as what I call the generic magazines like *Love Story* and *Western Story* and so forth. We did about three hundred thousand an issue. But what it did do was start other magazines of the type. So we had *Doc Savage* which was their adventure magazine. Then they had *The Avenger*. *The Avenger* was a cross between *Doc Savage* and *The Shadow*. They revived *Nick Carter* for a while and that came out as a magazine, and there were several others. So Street & Smith had at least a half-dozen magazines all of *The Shadow* type.

While Street & Smith was thinking of new ones for itself, all the rival companies came in. *The Shadow* hadn't been going more than six months before a magazine popped up called *The Phantom*. Then came *The Spider*, then came *Secret Agent X, Operator 5, The Green Lama*, all these things, and they began to dominate the field.

David: What happened that the pulps died out?

Walter: Several things happened with it. The main thing was the rise of the comics. Most of the pulp characters went into comics. I did *Shadow* comics, and we all rather liked that. The comics did not exactly bother the pulps too much, but what they did was capture a whole new audience. We figured that pulp readers ran from about sixteen years up. Oddly, some of the best selling in those days—I'm speaking now of the early Thirties—were around college campuses, groups like that.

Well, when the comics came along, they captured the twelve to sixteen group, maybe even younger, ten to sixteen. I'm not speaking of Mickey Mouse or such things; I mean comics that were written in the same vein as the pulp magazines. Well, here we had a whole new audience as big as our existing audience. They didn't steal too much from the pulps, but a lot of the readers who read comics kept on reading them as they got older and that increased their audience. So a publisher would say, "Well, look, if I can sell a million comics, and I can only sell two hundred thousand pulps, why not go in to comics?" So the trend became stronger for the comics.

Then the war came, and the war cut down on paper quotas. We had to change the size of all the pulps from the standard magazine size to what we call the digest size. So they lost a lot of their flair and flamboyance; they became more like such magazines now as *Ellery Queen* and *[Alfred] Hitchcock* and so forth. They were the new era of the pulps; the kind of things that go now.

Well, the comics kept on thriving, but the cutting of paper quotas—a comic only had forty-eight pages, but they [later] cut down to thirty-two and even less—meant they could print many more comics [compared to the higher-paged pulps]. Comics were very popular with the soldiers during the war. They'd pick up a bunch of comics; in fact, they were encouraged—I don't know if many people remember this—they were encouraged when sending packages to the soldiers to stuff them with comic magazines so that the package wouldn't break, and then they would read the magazines.

Soldiers out on drill could come in to the post or PX place and just pick up a couple of comics and read them and throw them aside when the bugle sounded. You couldn't do that with the pulp magazine; you'd have been so absorbed you'd have missed your drill. *[Laugh]*

David: The radio series began in1930. Were you associated with that?

Walter: To this degree: the radio series was started to promote the magazine. For the radio programs John Nanovic and I would suggest which stories would be good for them to use. They'd read the stories and adapt them as they saw fit. Well, Blue Coal who had a detective program wanted to have the Shadow as the announcer. He just announced [narrated] the program in a weird voice.[122] Street & Smith tried that for a while. But so many readers wrote in and said, "Give us *The Shadow* on radio," so we started a radio series based directly on my stories.

Lamont Cranston was the name I had given the Shadow. That was one of the characters in which he appeared; he was a master of disguise. In the magazine he appeared in various disguises or various forms. In this [the radio series] we took Lamont Cranston because we were able then to focus it on that one type of story, and we put Margo Lane in. In the magazine stories she appeared only occasionally. We kept Police Commissioner Weston, Joe Cardona the inspector, and Shrevvy the cab driver as running characters in every one of the stories.

If we'd gone into the twenty or thirty other characters we had [in the magazine] it would have confused listeners. They only had half an hour and you couldn't stop and explain who these people were. In my magazine stories, of course, if I reintroduced an agent, I would play him up.

David: Were you happy with the radio series?

Walter: Yes, but I didn't have too much to bother about with it. The editor coordinated it. When the radio [series] came in, that meant that every week the thing [the script written by the radio writers] had to be turned in to New York; generally the writers had to be in with the director [as the program was produced]. They would massacre the scripts when they would get them. The director would like one thing, and the sponsors, of course, were even in on it, so there was always something going on that way.

David: So the radio series was based on the stories you wrote.

Walter: That was announced; ["*The Shadow* is based on stories from *The Shadow Magazine.*"] that was one of the important [reasons] Street & Smith said go ahead [authorized the radio series].

David: There were a number of different actors who played the Shadow. Was there any particular one that you especially liked?

Walter: No, because they were all good. That was one thing about radio in those days. Most of the actors. . . . This is very interesting: I thought when I started writing pulp stories, writing for magazines, that this was merely a stepping stone to something better.

I never left it, because I had such a big turn out. Fellows like Frank Gruber[123] and two or three others who came in and wrote short stories didn't make enough in magazine work; they had to get other work besides or step up their production. They got into other things like movies. Once they were in the movies, they dropped that whole field [magazines].

Well, the same thing was true of radio. Don't forget radio was in its infancy; there were only a couple of dramatic shows existing, maybe all of a sudden another dramatic show would jump up; nobody knew how long it was going to last. And most of them [the actors] were thinking the same way. So if a fellow had the chance to play the Shadow for so many weeks, fine, he was available and played it. But then he might go on and go completely away from it.

David: Like Orson Welles.

Walter: Yes! Well, Orson Welles[124] only did it as a sideline. Orson Welles happened to be in New York with the Mercury Theatre. That was backed by John Houseman.[125] Incidentally, I had John Houseman's apartment in New York for a whole year when he was in Hollywood and I was knocking out the Shadows; this was at the time of World War Two—a very fine person.

Well, they had this Mercury Theatre thing and it was somewhat experimental and they were doing nicely with it, but the actors wanted some extra work. They decided to do something on radio. Of course,

Orson Welles, seen here during his early radio days, was the first actor to play
the Shadow/Lamont Cranston in the dramatic radio series.

people with that ability could get on the radio immediately. It just
happened that *The Shadow* came along then, so Orson Welles was
the first Shadow in the dramatic series. At the end of that year they
left.[126] Well, two men after that, [Bill] Johnstone[127] and [Bret]
Morrison,[128] were the ones that did most of the *Shadows*.

David: I think Brett Morrison is probably the most remembered of the
Shadow actors.

Walter: Yes, I think he is, yes.

David: Did you first write the line "Who knows what evil lurks in the
hearts of men" or was that strictly from the radio series?

Walter: No that really all stemmed from the magazine. That came under
what we call "blurbs." Every issue of the magazine would have some

little lead thing. For example, we would refer to the Shadow as "the knight of darkness" or "the cloaked Master," terms like that. In fact, just to give you one—this is amazing—when *Doc Savage* started as a magazine, we put an ad in *The Shadow* every issue, telling about this new magazine. In a full page it said at the top: "Superman." That's what they called Doc Savage, the Man of Bronze. They said he's a "Superman," but they didn't register it as a title. The word "Superman" got into vogue and, bang, that may be where *Superman* came from, which is perfectly legitimate. You know, like *Ripley's Believe It or Not*. He didn't invent the phrase "believe it or not"; that was a common-place phrase.

David: I understand that in your home you have eleven different typewriters and that there is paper either in the typewriter or next to it ready to go.

Walter: Well, that's true. Oddly, it should have been that way some years back when I was really banging them out. At that time I only had a few typewriters. The reason that this happened was that we happened to get a big house. My wife and I found an old house with a lot of extra rooms, and it was one of those things that needed a lot of repairs, so we lived in part of it, and during the last ten years we've been reshaping it.

I have one room where I have all the Shadow material and another room where I have quite a library of true crime and another room where I have magic, sleight-of-hand-type stuff and games, so I was able to departmentalize those [items]. I still usually only worked with a couple of typewriters, but you can't trade in typewriters for anything today. In the old days you could get a pretty good trade on a typewriter. Today you can get many typewriters at special bargain prices, at discounts, but you won't get any trade in. I finally said, "Why should I trade these typewriters in?"

So any time I needed a new typewriter, which I would occasionally, I would just leave the old one in a room where it is available. So if I do get an article on True Crime, I go into the True Crime room and there's a typewriter right there. So I do have half a dozen typewriters with things in process.

David: You are obviously very fascinated with magic and magicians. How did that come about?

Walter: I started with magic early and dabbled in it like most kids did about that time. It became very popular about the time of World War One. When I went to college at Colgate, I found out that the musical clubs would use a specialty act. I did some of my magic, and they liked it so well that I traveled with them as a magician.

When I got out of college, I was after newspaper work and did various jobs but, meanwhile, I would do private shows like club shows like a semi-pro. In fact, I had thoughts of getting up an act and going out with Chautauqua. At that time there were a lot of Chautauqua magicians.

Just by luck I landed newspaper work. When they found I knew magic, I began writing some articles on magic for the newspapers. That attracted the attention of the professional magicians, so I became the ghost writer for Thurston, Houdini, Blackstone,[129] and Dunninger.[130] All my life I've associated with all the magicians.

David: Well, I saw your tricks yesterday in the dining room, and you did them masterfully. *[Both laugh]* I understand that you were Houdini's ghost writer for a while, and I'm intrigued by that. What was the writing that Houdini was doing?

Walter: Houdini was quite a literary person. He wanted to be a magician, and he got into the escape work. That took so much of his time, and he was so famous for that, that instead of performing a lot of magic on the side and building big stage illusions like floating ladies and things, he began to study magic and had a tremendous collection of playbills and knew the generic things. He had a whole library and even had a man to keep the library in shape.

In the early twenties he took on a man name John Sergeant to work with him so that they could put out some books. For example, one of them was called *Miracle Mongers and Their Methods* in which they talked about people who had presumably been miracle men and so forth. Well, Sergeant died and he had another secretary named Teal. Teal was getting pretty old.

About that time I was doing articles on magic. This was about 1924 or '25. I had been writing a lot for Thurston the magician and later I wrote for Blackstone. Well, Houdini knew about this, and he was going to go on the road with a big show and he wanted to have a book to sell at the show. He wanted three books, in fact, that would be simple tricks that people could buy the book and learn about Houdini and then learn the tricks that were in the books. He gave me the order for the three books, and I'd finished one when he died in 1926. The second was a first draft ready to be okayed, and the third I had all outlined.

They never published those, but the Houdini estate paid me for the first book because it was done and then said instead of going on with the others, I could keep the three.

Houdini is seen here doing one of his famous escapes.

So the first book, which was on card tricks, I put out under my own name as *Popular Card Tricks* a year or two after Houdini had died. If he had lived, I would have gone on with it because he wanted to do a whole series of more sophisticated things. I think he would have been ready to retire in a few years, and I would have worked with him steadily.

I've always been unhappy that I missed that because he left a trunk filled with all kinds of notes that were to be used eventually in books. The lawyer gave them to me. The Houdini estate called me and we went through them and I wrote two books, one called *Houdini's Escapes* and the other *Houdini's Magic*. This was just before I started

The Shadow. I was working on the second one at the time I started *The Shadow.* I was finishing it up.

Those books went out of print for many years, but they've just been revived and they're out now. Those were authentic books from Houdini's own notes and, fortunately, they [the notes] were in pretty good shape. I had written so much on magic that I was able to fill in things. I don't know if they would have appeared in exactly that form if Houdini had lived, but I knew that they were the material he would have used in the books. So I went ahead and used my own judgment. The books really stand as a sort of a monument to Houdini.

David: Those books and the old pulps and comics have, with the recent nostalgia craze, become highly desired by collectors and have become pricey.

Walter: Yes. In 1927, right after Houdini died, I started a magazine called *Tales of Magic and Mystery.* While I was working on the three books for Houdini's show, I said to him, "Couldn't we do some newspaper articles?" He said he'd be glad to let me do them under my name but like interviews with him. I asked him about escapes where he had really gotten into trouble, almost lost his life, or something dangerous happened. So he made a list of them, and he sent me that list only a couple of months before he died. That's another story, but I can get to it later if you like.

So he sent me the list of these escapes, but before I had finished the article or sent it for approval, he died. We published it and syndicated it as Houdini's last interview. In this magazine called *Tales of Magic and Mystery* I built up those incidents as sort of a running account of Houdini; I had things from Thurston and other people, and we even had a couple of stories by Lovecraft, the famous science fiction writer, that landed in the magazine. It was a very picturesque magazine, but it didn't succeed. It did fairly well for a few months and then folded, as magazines did in those days.

You know, nostalgia has only begun to creep up on us during the last several years. Ten years ago you could buy almost any old pulp or comic for a couple of dollars maybe. To my amazement I find that among the rarities is *Tales of Magic and Mystery* and that thing is worth one hundred and twenty-five dollars! *[Laugh]*

David: That's so true. A Shadow novel now is worth quite a lot.

Walter: Twenty-five dollars is the lowest price.

David: A moment ago you referred to Houdini's death and said that you would tell me about it.

Walter: What happened was this: Houdini had a great physique, very husky. He never smoked, he never drank, and he prided himself on keeping physically trim. That, however, was a weakness. He overdid it too much. He just seemed tireless, and if he got tired, he'd just go the limit and then lie down and go to sleep.

He would grant anyone an interview at almost any time because he thrived on publicity. Where Thurston and these other magicians knew how to take it easy between times and were only available at certain times, Houdini would make himself available almost any time. Some students came down from McGill University and Houdini was showing them how he could throw his chest out and that you could punch him, and he wouldn't feel the punch.

When they did the punch, one of the other students thought that he was to punch him too, and Houdini didn't know that there was going to be another punch. It landed and hit him in the side when he was unready for it. It ruptured his appendix, but he didn't know it. He knew he had a pain there, but he was the kind of fellow who could stand any kind of pain.

The show was doing well, so he went right on with the show. If he had gone to a doctor, he would have been all right. He began to get a high fever and didn't attribute it to this. He got to Detroit and collapsed on the stage. When they got him to the hospital, it was too late. They operated, but peritonitis had set in and he died as a result.

Later, when they did a movie about Houdini's life,[131] they changed the whole thing. That wasn't dramatic enough to suit them. They had him die during an escape. But that was not correct. We're always running into famous incidents where some story has come up that has gotten popular belief, and you have a terrible time straightening people out on it.

David: I can't imagine you retired. Are you still writing?

This poster is typical of the type of publicity that Houdini used as he toured the country. The show was a combination of magic, escapes, and a debunking of mediums who claimed to be in touch with the dead and other scams.

Walter: Oh, yes, but I'm doing more factual things. I did a book for Doubleday on card magic. It's a book of about five hundred pages with about four hundred photographs of my own hands doing the tricks. I just finished another book for Doubleday called *An Encyclopedia of Close-Up Magic*. I did this one on general magic. It'll be a companion volume to the other book.

David: I'm told that you are eighty years old—obviously going on twenty-five.

Walter: *[Chuckle]* Last year when I was out at a pulp convention they said I was seventy-nine going on eighteen. I just got a birthday card from some of *The Shadow* fans whom I'd met at conventions. They sent me a card that looked like a book. When you opened it, signed on the left were signatures of about forty characters that had appeared in *The Shadow* magazine. The fans that sent it wrote their birthday greetings and signatures on the right.

But the cute thing was that there was a cat called "Washington Muse" from a Shadow story that was laid in Greenwich Village down by Washington Square. They had an alley there for carriages called Washington Mews. "Mews" means an alleyway. In the story a cat was found by the Shadow in that area, so they named the cat "Washington Mews." Well, the birthday card had a little paw mark from "Washington Mews" among these various signatures. *[Both laugh]*

David: Thank you, Walter Gibson alias Maxwell Grant. Say hello to the Shadow when you see him.

Walter: Thank you, David.

And that was the last I ever saw of Walter B. Gibson. We did correspond by mail a few times over the next year or so because it had been suggested that the Orlandocon photo of the two of us might have nostalgia value to Lone Ranger and Shadow collectors; therefore, we agreed to sign a slew of the photos and, gratifyingly, quite a few were sold.

Over time I learned through an acquaintance that Walter had been married since 1949 to a lady named Pearl Litzka Raymond, that it had been an extremely happy union, and that she was devoted to Walter. Litzka, as she was commonly called, shared his interest in magic since her previous husband had been "The Great Raymond," a well-known magician.

Occasionally, over the next few years, I would read of his appearance at a nostalgia or magic convention in one part of the country or another, so I knew he was around and about telling the good folks of his lifelong experiences. We should all be so fortunate as to have such an audience when we reach our "golden" years and have stories to tell.

Walter Brown Gibson died on December 6, 1985, in Kingston, New York. I remember coming upon his obituary in my local paper and pausing for several minutes to remember my brief encounter with him in 1977. As is so often the case, it didn't seem possible that it could have been eight years previous. The obit mentioned, of course, his creation of the Shadow and how the character had gone on to be a world-wide phenomenon. And there were the other career highlights one would expect. No cause was given for his death—just "natural causes," I guess, for someone who lives to be eighty-eight years of age. Perhaps the Shadow knows, I thought.

Myrna Loy

November 1, 1977

"I was pretty much just playing myself in The Thin Man *series."*

Myrna Loy was one of Hollywood's most glamorous stars during its Golden Age.

When a Hollywood legend comes to town, attention must be paid, to paraphrase Willy Lohman. And I was paying *close* attention to the fact that a screen legend from Hollywood's Golden Age, Myrna Loy, was coming to St. Petersburg, Florida. She was about to star on stage in British playwright Alan Ayckbourn's comedy *Relatively Speaking* as staged by the Country Dinner Playhouse.

Myrna Loy was the actress eventually labeled "the perfect wife" by Hollywood who started in silent pictures, helped usher in the sound era with a bit part in Al Jolson's *The Jazz Singer*, and went on to become one of the brightest stars in Hollywood, perhaps reaching the pinnacle of her career in *The Best Years of Our Lives,* one of the most highly acclaimed films of all time. Could it be that our Nora Charles of *The Thin Man* films had hit the dinner theater circuit at this late hour in her long and illustrious career?

Yes, it was true, but dinner theater seemed a somewhat unlikely venue for the sophisticated, urbane, witty, and wry actress who had co-starred with most Hollywood leading men of the twenties, thirties, forties, and fifties (Maurice Chevalier, Clark Gable, Spencer Tracy, Gary Cooper, Leslie Howard, Tyrone Power, and William Powell just to name a few). Back in 1936 she was crowned "Queen of the Movies," and Clark Gable was crowned "King" in a national poll. Well, unlikely venue or not, I wanted to talk with her and, fortunately, it was quickly and easily arranged.

While doing a little research prior to the show's opening, I got a better understanding of why, perhaps, she had chosen to do the play in a dinner theater setting in Florida. It seemed that she had long had the desire to perform the show and had even gone to London when it was first playing there in the 1960s to discuss the possibility with the playwright and producers. In studying the feasibility of bringing the show to America, there was some worry that the show "wouldn't travel well," meaning that maybe the farcical, "silly ass" British humor of the piece might fall flat with American audiences. Perhaps wisely wary, Myrna Loy at that time demurred doing the play. Nevertheless, *Relatively Speaking* crossed the ocean in the mid sixties and played fleetingly Off Broadway in New York and was not financially successful. But still Myrna Loy wanted to do the show and where better and at least risk than in a dinner theater in the hinterlands of Florida.

I was told that Ms. Loy would prefer to meet with me in her dressing room after the Saturday night performance. I attended the dinner and performance that evening, and as I viewed the proceedings, I could empathize with Myrna Loy's fascination with the play and the role she was playing so delightfully, but I could also appreciate that the play *was* very "British" for an American audience. But the Florida dinner theater audience loved her nevertheless, perhaps because she was still our charming Myrna from all those Hollywood screenings—even if they weren't thirsty for a cup of English tea.

After the show I was taken backstage to Ms. Loy's tiny dressing room. She greeted me warmly and graciously as one would expect the "Queen of Hollywood" to do, even though her official reign had ended many years previously. I had been entranced by her throaty but lilting voice for the previous two hours, and close-up it was even more seductive—no wonder those leading men sought her company in films.

I found that I couldn't be an overly-familiar young whippersnapper in her presence and call her "Myrna." Yes, she *was* a legend, and "Ms. Loy" was as familiar as I wished to be in her presence. To follow the format of this writing endeavor, however, we will use "Myrna."

David: Near the beginning of your career, back in silent pictures even, you got typed in films in which you played oriental villainesses and vamps.

Myrna: I did get typed. Well, I was a dancer, and I think that that had something to do with it, and then I played a rather exotic part in a picture that Mrs. Rudolph Valentino made, Adrian designed the clothes, and I think that was what did it. Then my first talkie was with an accent—*The Desert Song*—and I played Azuri[132] who spoke with a kind of northern French accent. It was really absurd. I loved [those kinds of roles.] I did *The Mask of Fu Manchu* at MGM. I played the daughter of Fu Manchu.[133] *[Laugh]* It was a great experience for me.

David: You *did* get out of that type casting. . .

Myrna: Eventually. I did other things. I also played white women who were not very nice and stole other women's husbands and that kind of thing. *[Laugh]* Of course, with *The Thin Man* that changed everything, and they never put me back in those kinds of roles.

Myrna Loy as the exotic daughter of Fu Manchu.

David: It's interesting that you could do the daughter of Fu Manchu, and then you could get out of that kind of role and go into the sophisticated, witty role that you are known for in *The Thin Man* series,[134] Nora Charles. That's quite a leap

Myrna: Yes, I suppose it is, but actually I was pretty much just playing myself in *The Thin Man* series. I mean, it wasn't much of a stretch as the other was.

David: Was *The Thin Man* series planned as a series?

Myrna: No, it was not. W. S. Van Dyke was the director, and he hasn't had enough attention as a director, *wonderful* director.[135] He had directed me in two films, and so he asked if I might play this role [Nora]. It was just such a success! It was actually a B picture; it was a low-budget picture, and it was just such a fantastic success. Of course, it was a wonderful script. The original story was by Hammett, Dashiell Hammett.[136] Of course, the screenplay was written by Albert Hackett and Frances Goodrich. Their later play was *[The Diary of] Anne Frank.*

David: Yes, as a matter of fact, that's a show I directed some years back.

Myrna: Did you?

David: *The Thin Man* films with William Powell were certainly marked by sophistication and wit. They seemed to be saying, "You see, marriage can be fun." You and William Powell as Nora and Nick Charles seemed to be having great fun in all those films. Was it as much fun to work on them as it appears when we watch them?

Myrna: Oh, yes, of course. It was marvelous fun. As it turned out we did only six over a period of ten years. We did a lot of other pictures together, though.

David: William Powell was such a fine actor. Can you just comment on him, about working with him on *The Thin Man* series and other films?

Myrna Loy poses with her *Thin Man* costars William Powell and Asta.

Myrna: He's still with us, fortunately. He lives in Palm Springs and doesn't allow any publicity about himself any more, so everyone thinks he's dead.[137] I have a terrible time telling everyone that he is still handsome with his white hair and white mustache. He's a man with enormous grace. He's a great friend of mine. I don't get to see him very often, but we correspond from time to time, and I talk to him on the phone.

David: He's one of the few actors who just retired and stayed that way. James Cagney is another one.[138] Hasn't William Powell had quite a bit of illness over the years?

Myrna: No, he hasn't. He was ill almost forty years ago and hasn't had a reoccurrence.[139]

David: Oh, really. I'm pleased to hear that.

Myrna: He did a very good thing. They asked him if he would write something about his illness which was—I'm not joking when I say it—was almost forty years ago. He did, and people read [and remembered] only the first paragraph in which he said that he had had cancer. The result of that was that they didn't read or remember the whole story, so the impression was given that he was ill.

No, he stopped [working] because he'd had a very long career. He was working with Ronald Colman in *Romola* [1924] when I was [dancing] at Grauman's Egyptian Theatre. He was a big star before I even got started. He worked with Richard Barthelmess in *The Bright Shawl* [1923]; he played villains a lot.

David: Yes, I think before *The Thin Man* films he was known primarily for his villain roles—more than for heroic roles

Myrna: He did play one detective before *The Thin Man*; he played Philo Vance in *The Kennel Murder Case* [1933].[140]

David: *The Thin Man*'s Nick and Nora Charles had Asta, a little wire-haired terrier who became a very famous dog as a result of the series. Do you remember any anecdotes regarding Asta that I might use in

Nora Charles and Asta are all dressed up and ready to go out.

my upcoming *Great Show Business Animals* book?

Myrna: We couldn't be friendly with Asta because he was a trained dog, and he had to respond to his master. You couldn't interfere with that control, so we could never play with him. The trainer was a wonderful man and was very good to his animals. He was Rudd Weatherwax, the same man who owned and trained Lassie. Asta did everything for a little squeaky mouse. I'd squeak the mouse and put it in my pocket, then he'd do anything he was told to do if he thought he was going to get the mouse; he never did get the mouse. He'd get a cracker or something. He was a wonderful dog.

David: Did they use the same dog in all of *The Thin Man* films?

Myrna: No, because he was getting along [in age]. *[Laugh]* His name was Skippy and he was a beautiful animal, but the others were very cute too. Nobody ever knew that there was a change in dogs. They never advertised that.

David: No, they never comment on that. I found out there were a lot of doubles for most of the star animals, dogs and horses especially. You think there is only one animal, and there are really a lot of them. In 1939 *Another Thin Man,* the third in the series, was released. It was in this film that Nick, Jr. was introduced. You and Nick had a child. I was wondering . . .

Myrna: And then he disappeared. *[Laugh]*

David: Yes! I was wondering why they added the child.

Myrna: Well, I thought it would be fun, but Bill thought it was a terrible idea. He said, "Why, the little so-and-so will be in preparatory school in the next film and then he'll be in college, and what does that make me?" He was very funny about it.

David: He already had a dog to contend with; now he had a kid. *[Laugh]*

Myrna: So, he figured it would age us too much. Oh, he really didn't; he was only joking, but as it turned out the producer decided to drop Nick, Jr. Someone would say [in the script], "Where is little Nicky?" And we would say he was off to school some place; you never saw him again.

David: So the original reason was just to have the boy in only one picture?

Myrna: Well, they ended the second picture *[After the Thin Man]* with Nick saying to Nora, "What are you doing?" She says, "I'm knitting something." And then she says, "You certainly are a bad detective." I guess they felt they had to follow it up [in the next film]. It was the script writer that really got us into that problem. [141] *[Laugh]*

David: If you could magically return to the Hollywood of the 1930s and forties, and you could star with any leading man of that era, who would he be?

The witty, sophisticated, and stylish Mr. and Mrs. Nick Charles (Myrna Loy and William Powell) take Asta out for a walk in this MGM studio publicity shot.

Myrna: That would be a very difficult question to answer.

David: I know. It's a terrible question to ask. Would there be maybe two or three that you might use in an answer?

Myrna: No, they were all my friends. They were all such extraordinary men; I can't make a choice.

David: I can't lure you into that question.

Myrna: I mean I'm not like that; I'm very catholic in my taste. I mean, I have no favorite colors, etc.; I love everything.

David: You were with MGM in the peak years of the thirties and forties when they had under contract, as they said, "More stars than there are in the heavens," or something like that.

Myrna: They had a lot at the other studios too.

David: Yes, but I think MGM was considered *the* studio to work at. At that time did you realize that it was a special era in filmmaking or was it just a job, a nice job?

Myrna: Oh, no, we knew it was exciting; we knew we were creating things, of course. I think a lot of it was due to the publicity we got; there was a tremendous amount of publicity. The kids today don't get it; I mean they are absolutely on their own, or they have to hire a press agent, and if they do, it doesn't last long. It's very expensive.

They don't have anything like the attention that we had. And we had writers writing for us that the studio had under contract, so there were some advantages to being under contract. There were some disadvantages too, but there were great advantages because you had a whole studio behind you.

David: Today in motion pictures there are no studios that maintain a stable of actors on a long-term contract, so actors have to "freelance." You've worked both ways, really. You were under contract at MGM for many years, and since then you've worked in individual films as a freelance performer. Do you have any feelings about which system is better for the actor?

Myrna: Oh, I think it depends on the time. As you are being built up, I think the [studio] system is much better. I think a lot of it depends on what time it is in the person's life and career. I was freelancing when I did *The Best Years of Our Lives*.[142] I had left MGM by that time. There comes a time when you are in a situation like that when you feel that you must go out on your own, and there is a lot of other talent around that you want to be with. I mean, I worked with Cary Grant after that; I did *Blandings.*[143] I did two pictures with Cary; I would never have been able to work with him at MGM. So it's a question as to which is better; I was very glad I was there [MGM] for the years that I was there.

David: As a leading actress for so many years, I was just wondering who you like to see. Who are your favorite actors or actresses today? Can you mention a few?

Myrna: Oh, my, lots of them, yes. I think Jack Nicholson is fantastic, Robert De Niro. I was stunned at the performance he gave in *The Last Tycoon* [1976]. He literally was Irving Thalberg. These are extraordinary, very talented people. And the girls; oh the girls are marvelous. I love Jane, Jane Fonda; she's an extraordinary actress. And [Barbra] Streisand, of course.

David: You recently worked with Burt Reynolds in his film called *The End.*[144] How was he to work with?

Myrna: Well, I'm mad about him, he's a marvelous man. It was a very short role; most of the roles in that film are, you know. It's an odyssey of his life. It's an interesting picture, very strange, very serious, and terribly funny, hilarious! If I can be so bold, I think it will turn out that way; it has to. I find him talented, gifted, *very* gifted. Pat O'Brien and I play his father and mother, you know. It is for a very brief moment. His mother and father are rather awful people. They're sort of *nouveau riche.* His mother is a television addict. *[Laugh]*

David: You must have had fun with the role.

Myrna: Oh, yes. I've always liked him; I always knew he had a great sense of humor from the first time I saw that centerfold or whatever you call it, in *Cosmopolitan.* *[Laughs]* Everybody was so shocked; they said, "How dare he do that." I thought, well, he's funny; he knows what he's doing. He is charming—and a good director.[145]

David: Where do you make your home these days when you're not performing around the country?

Myrna: In Manhattan.

David: Did you live in Los Angeles during your most active film years? I assume you didn't fly back and forth from New York when you were making pictures there.

Myrna: Like they do now. No, I lived there, of course. I moved there when I was very young. I went to school there. Oh, yes. I lived there, but it has gotten so big, such a cumbersome place now. It used to be a nice Spanish town with pepper trees.

David: I mentioned before that Jimmy Cagney retired from acting and, of course, William Powell did many years ago. . .

Myrna: Not very many of them did.

David: No, that's right.

Myrna: Most of them die with their boots on.

David: I just wondered if you have any intentions of retiring on us.

Myrna: No, no. I wouldn't be here [in St. Petersburg] if I were going to be doing that. I came here because I wanted to do this play, *Relatively Speaking* by Alan Ayckbourn; I've wanted to do it for a long time. They wanted me to do it years ago, as a matter of fact, when Alan Ayckbourn first wrote it—it was his first play—and they were afraid that he was so English that audiences wouldn't understand him in this country. The title of the play has very little to do with what the play is about. I wanted to do it.

David: It's a very fine show; I certainly enjoyed it. Where do you go from here—back to Manhattan?

Myrna: Well, yes, of course. I'm going to stop on my way and see some friends in North Carolina for Thanksgiving, and then I'll go home.

David: Well, thank you very much, Myrna Loy. It's been a pleasure.

Myrna: Thank you.

It was quite late by the time we finished talking, and she had a matinee the next day. (The stage manager had knocked on the door midway during our conversation to say that Ms. Loy's car and driver would be waiting at the back of the theater for her.) As I packed my tape recorder, she prepared to go back to her motel. I helped her into a cloth coat made of nubby, light-blue material and of indeterminate age—a very unNora-like cloak, I thought. Together we walked through the hushed darkness of the now vacant dinner theater and out into the rainy, chilly night. A rental car and sleepy driver were waiting to whisk her back to the motel.

She seemed very happy to be still working at her craft at age seventy-two, even in a small dinner-theater on the West Coast of Florida; she certainly didn't appear to be doing it because she needed the money. Who was I to question her reasons? But I felt Asta would have been very out of place in this late-night scene.

Despite her fame and long career before the public, I was surprised to discover that she had not made her stage debut until 1960 when she starred in a summer stock production of *The Marriage Go-Round* with French star Claude Dauphin. She explained her late arrival on the stage by stating, "I felt I had a lot to learn." She followed up that stage work by going on a nation tour of Neil Simon's *Barefoot in the Park*, playing the show-stealing mother role.

It was only five years before our conversation that she had made her Broadway debut in a revival of Clare Boothe Luce's vitriolic comedy *The Women*, again playing a shrewd mother, as she had done in *Barefoot* and so many times on the screen—remember her motherhood and brood in *Cheaper by the Dozen* with Clifton Webb?[146]

Myrna Loy's screen fame as "The Perfect Wife" and in mother roles was not played out so successfully in real life. She was married four times (Arthur Hornblow, Jr., a movie producer; John D. Hertz, Jr., an auto-rental and advertising executive; Gene Markey, a producer-screenwriter; and Howland H. Sargeant, a producer and, at the time, Assistant Secretary of State for Public Affairs). All four marriages ended in divorce, and she had no children. She commented on this predicament: "Some perfect wife I am. I've been married four times, divorced four times, have no children, and can't boil an egg."

Despite her comments to me about not retiring, her failing health forced the issue. Myrna Loy played her final role in a 1981 television movie entitled *Summer Solstice* in which she starred with Henry Fonda. It was the story of an elderly couple who quietly reminisce about their half-century of marriage—again she was the perfect wife. It turned out to be the final screen appearances of both Ms. Loy and Henry Fonda.

And now with legendary fame and advancing age, the accolades were forthcoming. In 1980 the National Board of Review of Motion Pictures presented her with its first David Wark Griffith award "in grateful recognition of her outstanding contribution to the art of screen acting." There was a Carnegie Hall tribute to Myrna Loy in 1985 that was packed with Hollywood stars and lifelong fans. Mistress of ceremonies Lauren Bacall said that she admired Ms. Loy "as a person, an actress, and a face, but also as a woman aware of what went on in the country and the world." In 1987 she published her autobiography entitled *Myrna Loy: Being and Becoming.* She was a recipient of the prestigious Lifetime Achievement Award from the Kennedy Center in 1988. A further tribute was a Turner Pictures documentary in 1990 entitled *Myrna Loy: So Nice to Come Home To* written, produced, and directed by esteemed film historian, author, and critic Richard Schickel.

At the annual Academy Awards ceremony in 1991, she was awarded an honorary Oscar for "extraordinary qualities, both onscreen and off, with appreciation for a lifetime's worth of indelible performances." In frail health and unable to attend the ceremony, she spoke by satellite from her Manhattan apartment. She kept it brief but expressed her appreciation: "You've made me very happy. Thank you very much."

Less than two years later, on December 14, 1993, Myrna Loy died at Lennox Hill Hospital in Manhattan. She had been a breast cancer survivor for many years, following mastectomies in 1975 and 1979. Her longtime friend Sherlee Lantz stated that she died in surgery after a long illness. She was cremated, and her ashes were interred at Forestvale Cemetery in Helena, Montana, her adopted home town where she had spent her youth. Myrna Loy was eighty-eight years old.

Jock Mahoney

June 23, 1977

*"Every boy, no matter how old you get,
wants to play Tarzan."*

Jock Mahoney's first starring role was in the *Range Rider* television series produced by Gene Autry's Flying A Productions.

I was talking with a friend in the crowed dealers' room at the 1977 Houstoncon film festival and not paying enough attention to the activity around me. As I finished the conversation, I turned and walked into an oak tree—well, it seemed like an oak tree. It was a fifty-eight-year-old gentleman, six feet four inches tall with appropriate bulk to match. His name was Jock Mahoney, a guest star at the festival, and a man I wanted to talk with.

I had been a fan of Mr. Mahoney since my youthful journeys to the Saturday matinee movies where I frequently thrilled to the adventures of the Durango Kid played by Charles Starrett. It became puzzling for me in the late forties and early fifties as Charlie Starrett grew older in his bland role of "Steve" but seemed to become more and more youthful and athletic in his screen action as his masked alter ego "Durango."

The mystery was eventually solved when I realized that Starrett was being doubled as Durango by a young guy who otherwise was usually one of the "henchies" in the background stirring up trouble for the old rancher or was playing that "nice-looking young fellow" who is in love with the rancher's daughter and shows up fairly inconspicuously in a couple of scenes. Interestingly, that henchie or young fellow was never seen when the action reached a fever pitch—he was in Durango Kid garb and the black mask, routing the bad guys for Starrett. This young actor's name was Jacques O'Mahoney, but he was then usually billed as Jack Mahoney— but everybody called him Jock or Jocko.

I found out years later that Jock had been born in Chicago but early on moved to Davenport, Iowa, and later attended the University of Iowa. When the Second World War came along, he joined the Marine Corps, becoming a pilot and flying instructor. After the war he moved to Los Angeles and started work as a horse breeder, which somehow led to movie

Jocko as the Durango Kid makes one of his giant leaps to thwart
the bad guy at right.

stunt work and doubling actors such as Gregory Peck and Errol Flynn.
The famous scene in Flynn's *The Adventures of Don Juan* where he leaps
from a high staircase was performed by Jock. It was commonly acknowledged that he was the only stuntman in Hollywood who would dare such
a leap, and he reportedly demanded and got a thousand dollars for the
stunt. And the rest, as they say, is show business history.

I had come to the 1977 Houstoncon festival to talk with several of
the guest stars for my radio show and for some writing I was planning.
When I walked into the oak tree known as Jocko, he caught me with his
right arm, clutched me to his huge frame and proclaimed in a loud voice,
"I told you we must stop meeting like this; people will talk!"

The nearby festival-goers laughed, and Jocko guffawed louder than
all of them. He loved this sort of prank.

When he released me from his hold—I felt like Fay Wray escaping
King Kong—I broached the possibility of our meeting again, despite his
recent protestations, to talk about his long career in pictures and television. "Sure, whenever you want. I'm going to be here all weekend."
Well, that was easy.

Late that afternoon Jock met with festival fans in a meeting room where he talked a bit about his career and did a Q&A with those in attendance. He was light hearted, friendly, and very articulate—all of which made me more eager than ever to have a one-on-one with him. At the end of the session, I cornered him as the last stragglers were leaving the room and asked if we could set a time for our get together with my recorder. "Let's do it tomorrow in the dining room at around one o'clock. You'll see me there; just come on over when you get there."

When one o'clock rolled around the next day, I found Jocko in the dining room at a table deep in a conversation with husband and wife fans who were accompanied by their little girl on the opposite side of the table, eating messily some sort of kid's desert. (Yes, I have a thing about kids being around when I'm trying to do an interview—kids and animals; you know the old W. C. Fields shibboleth.) This was not going to be easy, I immediately deduced, but put a smile on my face and sidled over to the table.

Jocko greeted me warmly, introduced me to the couple and their little girl who, despite her struggle with the desert, seemed passive and shy, which I took as a good sign. They were just finishing lunch and asked if I wanted to order anything. I passed and protested that I had had a big breakfast and couldn't eat a thing. Jocko said, "Well, let's get going. Turn on your tape machine." With that the couple asked if they could stay and listen if they were very quiet. Well, that wasn't the way I envisioned it, but, "Yeah, sure." The little girl smiled and licked her fingers.

David: You started your acting career primarily as a stuntman for Charles "Durango Kid" Starrett, Errol Flynn, and Randolph Scott, among , many others.

Jock: I started acting in 1946 when I got out of the Marine Corps, and I was awful—seriously! A man told me he would give me parts in two Charlie Starrett pictures if I would teach a man how to ride. I said, "How much time do I have?" He said, "A week."

I said, "You want me to teach a man how to ride a horse in a week?" He said, "He doesn't have to do anything, Jocko; he just has to look good."

So I put him on bareback from sunup to sundown, and the last two days he was in the saddle, for a solid week. He was rubbed raw, but he looked like he could ride a horse and that was all that was necessary—and I got the two parts.

David: You did a couple of *Three Stooges* shorts early in your career.

Jock: I did five or six *Three Stooges* comedies. I was a blacksmith and a guardsman, and a couple of them were westerns. They're tough to work with. *[Laugh]* It's hard to keep a straight face; you've got to be straight, but they can do anything they want to do. I think they had the oldest contract at Columbia Studios. They made pictures for twenty-some odd years. They were inveterate gamblers and, boy, the horses had better come in or they were down in the dumps. They didn't like to lose. They were fun, and they were funny, and I loved them! As a matter of fact, when I went out to the Motion Picture Home when I had my stroke, Larry [Fine] was there. We visited back and forth. He never got out; he died there.

David: So you had a couple of bit parts in *Durango Kid* pictures, played straight man with the Three Stooges, and became a stuntman. How does one become a stuntman?

Jock: When you're not good enough to be an actor—which I found out I wasn't after two quick pictures for Starrett—then you stay in the business any way you can. I was a swimmer; I was a trampoline man; I did flying trapeze; I worked high bar; I was a tumbler; and I had ridden horses all my life, motorcycles, automobiles; I was a pilot, so all I had to do was learn fights and learn motion picture technique to become a stuntman, but I was so self-conscious and so inhibited.

They called me one day and said, "Hey, we need a fellow to double Charlie Starrett." I said, "Pinhead doubles Charlie Starrett. What's he doing?" They said, "Well, he doesn't want to do it anymore." I asked, "How much does it pay?" They said, "Two hundred and fifty bucks." Two hundred and fifty bucks in 1946 was a lot of money! That was manna from heaven; that was pure gravy and frosting on the cake! I said, "Okay, let me call Pinhead and if it's okay with him, then I'll go to work."

I called Pinhead and he said, "Hey, if you want it, you got it." So I called them back and went to work doubling Charlie Starrett. That put a lot a beans on the table; Charlie was awful good to me and we're pretty good friends. Then I started doubling Errol Flynn, Sonny Tufts, and Randolph Scott and doing parts and bigger parts and bigger parts and, finally, I started out on my own as an actor.

David: Is being a stuntman really dangerous work?

Jock: If you are very athletic and you know your abilities and you know when to say no, it's not dangerous. There was a young man here in Houston that jumped out of the top of the Astrodome—a hundred and eighty-five feet, I think it was, or something close to that—into a big air cushion. If he didn't spot himself correctly on that hundred and eighty-five-foot jump or there was wind blowing and he didn't take that into account, he could miss that mat completely.

Yes, you can get killed; you can get killed very handily, very readily, very easily. I've had my nose broken four times; my left shoulder was broken here in the Houston Fat Stock Show and it's still in two pieces; my left elbow broken; my chest crushed three times. But on a thirty-year period, that's not a bad score. The things that hurt you are usually the stunts that you've done nine million times before, but this particular time you don't check out where you're going, what ground you're going to cover and make sure that all the rocks and Coke bottles have been removed.

One time I dove out of a buckboard down a hill, landed, and rolled over just as I got to the camera. I thought that we had really cleaned out the area, but just underneath a tuft of grass that was hanging over was a Coke bottle, and it found my right kneecap and split it open. That's how you usually get hurt. The difficult stunts you plan and plan and plan.

David: Gene Autry's Flying A Productions produced your first television series, *Range Rider*.[147] How did Gene happen to tap you for that role?

Jock: Because I had worked with Gene Autry on quite a few of his pictures, and he evidently liked my work as a heavy or as a leading man—Gene Autry's the only leading man in any of his shows, so mostly heavy. In doing fights with Gene, he liked the way I did my action scenes, so when he decided on doing *Range Rider*, he chose me and Dick Jones. He wanted more of an American name for Dick Jones, so he named him Dick *West*. *[Both laugh]*

David: As a matter of fact, I mention that in *The Singing Cowboys*, a book I have coming out in about a year. . .

Jock: Which you didn't put me in, you rat! *[Laughs]*

David: Yes, I did! I've got a picture of Gene clobbering you in a movie called *Cow Town*. *[Both laugh]* You worked for Gene Autry for a

Jock costarred with former child actor Dick Jones in the western TV series *Range Rider*.

number of years. What was it like working for him?

Jock: He was a star, and I was just coming along in the business. Dick Jones's and my relationship with Gene was always very pleasant, very nice. He was very helpful, and he was a gentleman. There is a little story, though, that you might enjoy. We were in Los Angeles at the Sheriff's Rodeo at the Coliseum, and Gene was introduced and he rode out on the track, and his horse did a side pass, which takes quite a bit of time. Somewhere between the quarter mark and the halfway mark they decided that Gene was taking too much time, and they introduced the Ranger Rider and Dick West.

Now, you have to understand that you don't step on your boss's introduction! *[Laugh]* But we were introduced and we had to go. So Dick and I do a fast run up to the quarter mark, wheel our horses, doff our hats to the crowd, and start making our dash up to the halfway mark. When we got to Gene Autry, whose horse was still doing the side pass between the quarter mark and the halfway mark, we put our hats over our hearts and said, "Hi, boss," and went on. *[Both laugh]* Oh, well, those things happen, I guess. But he was a good sport about it; he knew we had to do it.

David: When you became the star of the *Range Rider* series, did you then, in fact, have a stuntman for yourself?

Jock: Yes. I've always had a stuntman, but he never did any of my work. He got paid for everything I did because having been a stuntman, I didn't want to cut a stuntman out of a job, and I never did. Stuntmen have been paid for every stunt I ever did, but I've always done my own work.

David: Why, I ask naively?

Jock: What the hell, who could do it better!

David: That's true! In other words, you had to have a stuntman?

Jock: No. I didn't have to have a stuntman, but I have a tremendous respect for stuntmen. I was doing a picture at Universal called *Slim Carter.*[148] They called up a young stuntman we hadn't used before and told him, "Come on out; you've got to double Mahoney." He was a very handy, young, athletic cowboy type. He came to the set and he was scared pea green. He got hold of me and took me aside and said, "God damn it, Jocko, if you can't do it, I know sure as hell I can't do it. What is it?" *[Both Laugh]*

Dick Bartlett was directing the picture, and Dick was a good friend of mine. The deal was that I had to fall off a horse. We put the young man up on the horse and I said, "Do a stirrup fall out to the right." So he did a stirrup fall out to the right. Dick said, "Well, I don't care for that." I said, "Do a fall over the left shoulder of the horse," so he did a fall over the left should of the horse. Dick said, "I don't particularly care for that." So I said, "Do a fall over the back right hip of the horse," and he did a fall over the back right hip of the horse. Dick said, "I don't particularly care for that either."

I said, "Well, hell, there's no other way to fall off the horse unless you're going to get athletic or tricky." He said, "Okay, you do the fall over the left front shoulder of the horse; that'll look all right." So the young man's job was done, and he picked up three times a hundred and fifty dollars. I did the shot for the show [filming]. Some directors are pretty nice about that.

David: You wore moccasins instead of cowboy boots while doing *Ranger Rider.*

Jock: I wore moccasins because I was six-foot-four and Dickie Jones was short. As you know, the camera has to keep everybody in perspective. If I towered over Dickie, we would look like Mutt and Jeff. It's hard for the cameraman to hold the two of you in the same frame and it's hard to light. Dickie with his boots on and me with moccasins kept us closer to nearly the same height. That's why I wore moccasins, plus the fact that if you are going to do action of any kind, you get out of boots and you put on tennis shoes.

David: And there was a lot of action in that series!

Jock: You know, when you are doing seventy-nine half-hour shows, you've got to think up different things that you can do to keep it interesting. One time up at Big Bear we rode our horses up to where we were to talk with an Indian girl. I always rode on the right, Dickie was on the left, and the girl was to the left of Dickie when we stopped. So as we're talking to the girl, our horses side by side, I swung around to where I'm sitting on Dickie's horse's rump and we're back to back, Okay? When the dialogue was finished, we each put a leg over, hit the ground together, and walked over to the girl. It was a silly little thing, but I always wanted to do a back to back and couldn't figure how in hell to make it work—and it worked that time.

David: It was fun watching *Range Rider* for unusual little touches like that—and they came frequently.

Jock: One time we had a new director and, boom, we come riding in on the horses. Dickie dismounted with a normal dismount. Sometimes, if my horse was too close to his horse, I'd just throw my left leg over the horse and slid off the right side of the horse. In that way I didn't hold anything up, and I didn't get wedged between the two horses and have to fight and elbow them apart, making it look clumsy. So I did that as we rode up to the house and went inside.

The director said, "Cut! Do it again." The assistant director said, "Excuse me, sir, but that looked all right to me. What was wrong?" The director said in a whisper, "That goddamned Mahoney doesn't know how to get off a horse; he got off the wrong side." The assistant told him, "You better get used to it or you're going to be in a hell of a lot of trouble because Mahoney gets off over the head, over the ass, over the left, over the right. He's liable to get on or off any way under the sun!" *[Both laugh]*

David: In one of the *Range Rider* films we saw yesterday here at HoustonCon, you jumped onto the horse from what is usually considered to be the wrong side.

Jock: With a particular horse it doesn't make any difference. If the horse isn't trained to handle that, you not only confuse the hell out of him, but he's liable to kick you or shy away from you.

David: You must have loved doing that series. You were really in your element doing those stunts.

Jock: Oh, I was. I was a natural athlete anyhow; I was born a natural athlete. My judgment was good on distances and all that sort of thing. God did it all; I enhanced it a little bit. As I said before, I learned to fence and did tumbling and high bar and flying rings and flying trapeze, trampoline, and everything. I got a national championship in swimming and a state championship in diving. I was a fencing instructor in college. So, I did it all! *Range Rider* gave me a chance to do all my good things. If you can do those things, do 'em!

David: But does that lead to directors expecting ever more difficult and perhaps dangerous stunts from you?

Jock: When *Range Rider* first started, one of the first things I had to do was jump off a rock, taking a man off a horse. I picked out a rock and took the director out and I said, "I'll come off this rock that's about ten feet high; I'll just dive off and it's nice and sandy where I'll land. It's no problem." He said, "That's too damned high; we're not going to let you do that, you'll hurt yourself. Pick out a rock five feet high and come off of that."

Well, five feet high is just about the same height as the horse and the guy, but I had to do what the director told me. Dissolve. After about twenty shows or so, the director goes out and picks out a rock. He says, "Jocko, I found a rock for you. You've got to bulldog a guy, taking him off his horse." That rock was another five feet higher than the ten-foot one I had selected back in the earlier show, and there was no place to go, just rocks down where I was to fall. I said, "You're crazy; I'm not going to come off there!" He said, "Well, hell, you did it in so and so's picture; you can do it in mine!" *[Laugh]*

David: After twenty shows, the expectation was much higher!

Jock: We were out at an old movie location ranch which is now a cemetery about five miles from Burbank, and I was doubling Charlie Starrett in a Durango Kid picture. They had a Brahma bull there that was six feet tall at the hump and the rest of him was commensurate. He was in an open trailer, and when they brought him out, he came along like a whole parade. I watched this bull as they took him alongside the road where there was a bank of earth. He ran his horn into the bank, just straight in, and threw dirt all over his back—and I watched the power.

I had read the script, and I knew what they wanted me to do: they wanted me to bulldog this bull so that it wouldn't chase and hurt a little girl. I walked over to the wrangler and asked, "What would happen if I dropped onto this bull's head and neck?" He said, "Well, he might keep on running and not even know you're aboard, or he could lay his horns back and we could pick you up in three pieces, or he could throw you and we could pick you up in Burbank!" *[Both laugh]*

I said to the wrangler, "Would you mind telling that to the director?" I brought the director over so that he could see the bull. The wrangler reiterated what he had told me and finished by saying, "Jocko's supposed to bulldog him!" The director looked at the bull again and then at me and said, "Well, there's no way Jocko can bulldog this bull, so you might as well forget that. We'll rope him!"

The old bull didn't like to run but we started him on a hill, and he ran down the hill. I tried to rope him three times and I got one loop right over the top of him, but the last minute he ducked right under it. I said, "Rocky Shahan is an expert roper, a much better roper than I am. We'll let him get in the clothes [Durango's] and do it, and we won't hold up the production." So Rocky got into the clothes, got on to the horse, and we ran the bull down the hill.

By this time the bull knew what we were up to. Rocky was a damned good roper, but he couldn't get a rope on that old bull either. Do you know what we finally did? They took the shot where I just got the rope over the bull's head, then they cut to the little girl, then they cut back again and the rope's *on* the bull. *[Both laugh]* Charlie [as Durango] was on the horse by that point, and it looked as if he had done the bulldogging and saved the little girl. By this time the bull was so tired he didn't care. *[Both laugh]* Discretion is the better part of valor!

David: You played Yancy Derringer on CBS television for one season, 1958-59, thirty-four episodes, and then the popular series was gone.

Jock: Because CBS wanted twenty-five per cent of us, and we wouldn't give it to them for free, so we lost our timeslot. We had a contract with Johnson's Wax; they wanted thirty-six more episodes, but CBS was too big to fight. They screwed us out of our eyeteeth. I went to

Jock played Yancy Derringer, a New Orleans gambler who sometimes
sidelined as a special agent.

Honolulu on vacation for about a month with my wife Maggie and
when I came back and called Richard Sale [creator and writer of *Yancy
Derringer*[149]] and said, "Hey, let's get it on and start getting stories so
we're not behind on stories and shooting like we were last year." He
said, "We don't have a show." I said, "What do you mean we don't
have a show. We had a big party; Johnson's Wax sent us a telegram

that said 'Love the association; there will be thirty-six more next year. God bless and good luck.'"

CBS said they wanted twenty-five per cent of our show. Well, three of us owned the show outright, so we said, "No, we're doing fine." Long story short: we lost our timeslot, and that was end of *Yancy Derringer*. The same thing happened to *Tightrope*,[150] same reason. Incidentally, are you on CBS?

David: No. There is a CBS outlet in Sarasota, but I'm not with it. *[Both laugh]* Was that during the reign of James Aubrey at CBS?

Jock: Yes, sir!

David: After he left CBS he then went on to ruin MGM.

Jock: Every time I was in New York and walked into the CBS office, Jim made sure there were a couple of other people there because he was afraid I was going to sue him.

David: Or worse?

Jock: No, no.

David: Everybody wants to grow up to be Tarzan, and you did it.

Jock: I was very lucky. At forty-two years of age, after I'd played the part of Corey Banton, the bad guy, in *Tarzan the Magnificent*[151] with Gordon Scott as Tarzan, Gordon blew his contract and went to Italy to become an actor. That left Tarzan open and, luckily, Sy Weintraub, the producer, came to me and said, "Jocko, do you want to play Tarzan?"

I went home that night and talked to Barbara Hale and Bill Williams, who are two of my closest friends, and my doctor, Dwain Travis, who is a very close friend of mine. My wife Maggie and I had them all over to our house. I asked them, "What do you think about my playing Tarzan?" Everybody put their two cents in. So I went back and talked with Sy Weintraub the next day.

For half an hour I gave him all the reasons why I should not be Tarzan. To enumerate a few reasons: I was the *Range Rider*; most of

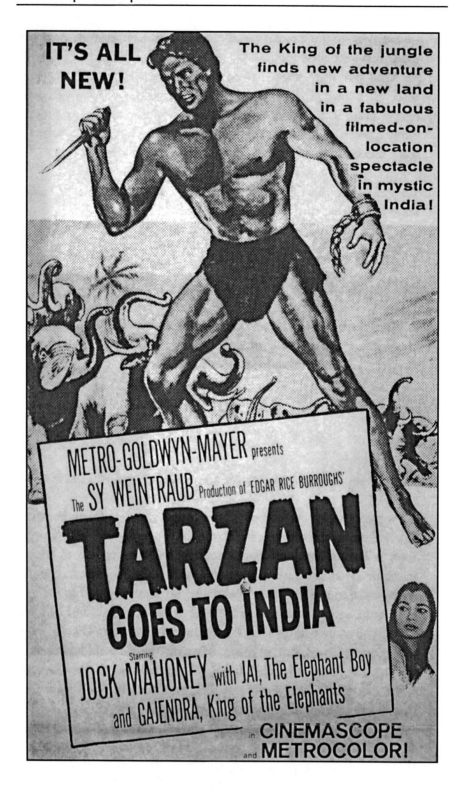

the films I had made were in the western field; I had the western flavor. Would they [the audience] accept a man known as a cowboy to be Tarzan? I had done the *Yancy Derringer* show. Would that be a detriment to the audience accepting me as Tarzan? So after a half hour and my enumerating all of the ramifications and complications, he said, "Do you want to play Tarzan?" And I said, "Yeah." So I first played Tarzan in *Tarzan Goes to India*[152] in India.

David: You were—take this now in the right way, please—an entirely different looking Tarzan in physique. You were willowy where most of them had been muscle-bound-type actors.

Jock: Normally I weigh two hundred pounds; I'm much heavier than that now. At forty-two I weighted about two hundred pounds, and I was slender. The producer said, "Jocko, start getting into shape." Thirty days before I left for London on my way to India I went on a regimen and workout schedule with the high bars and parallel bars and the trampoline. I took my chest up to a fifty and my waist down to a thirty-one, thirty-two, and I put on twenty pounds. So I weighed two hundred and twenty pounds when I played Tarzan.

David: You're so tall and with it spread over your body, it didn't look as if you weighed that much. There was a cat-like quality in your movements that I don't remember seeing in any of the other Tarzans. I don't have anywhere for you do go with that comment; it's just a personal observation.

Jock: Well, just watch it, fella'. Don't get too personal! *[Both laugh]* Thank you. That's a very nice compliment.

David: There was talk at that time that we were going to see a new type of Tarzan in that he was going to be articulate. There wasn't going to be "Me Tarzan, you Jane" any more. Was that a conscious thing they really talked about, or did they just say, "Well, that's been done; let's try something new"?

Jock: Well, I read all the Tarzan books; I also read a dozen or so of the *John Carter on Mars* books, science fiction books that Edgar Rice Burroughs had written, in order to get the flavor of what the man was talking about.

Tarzan was an erudite gentleman, tremendously wealthy, preferred the green jungle to the concrete asphalt jungle where people are backbiting and selfish and not to be trusted. He preferred the animals that are true to their nature to self-serving politicians and that ilk. As I said, he was an erudite gentleman; he spoke English, French, German, Spanish, half a dozen different African tribal dialects. So he could speak, speak very well.

David: The two Tarzan films that you did, *Tarzan Goes to India* in 1962 and *Tarzan's Three Challenges* in 1963, were shot abroad in India and Thailand, I believe.

Jock: Yep.

David: Tell me about working on location in countries that are not quite as advanced as ours and some of the problems that you ran into.

Jock: I loved working in India. We had problems with food, water, generators, lights, and elephants. Problems with fourteen different dialects—nobody understanding anybody—while we had four, five, six hundred people at a time working on the dam in one shot and working on the elephant drive in another. I loved it! I loved the Indian people; I loved being there, and I would like to go back sometime.

David: I understand you had some problems with the sound and a lot of dubbing had to be done.

Jock: That was generator problems. As you know, we shoot twenty-four frames a second, which is normal. The sound was out of sync, out of phase, and it was just too fast. So we went to London and lip-synced the whole damned picture. The same thing happened in Thailand with *Tarzan's Three Challenges*.

David: There was a talented boy in *Tarzan Goes to India*.

Jock: His name was Jai. I had been his constant big buddy. He was poor and his dad was always running off with his money and betting it on the horses and all that sort of thing. I would loan him money, and he would pay it back; he was very good about it. We were good friends, literally.

We were nearing the end of the filming when all of a sudden he realized that it was the last scene in the picture that we were doing—he realized that I was actually leaving, going back to the United States. So the tears that you see in *Tarzan Goes to India* are real tears. I'm a sentimentalist, so when he cried, I damned near cried. He was a beautiful little boy and I loved him.

David: In westerns you had to deal with horses and Brahma bulls while doing stunts. As Tarzan, at forty-two years of age, you had to deal with wild animals of the jungle. Did you let a stuntman double you in the Tarzan pictures?

Jock: In *Tarzan Goes to India* during the scene when the leopard was in my arms and I went to the ground and rolled over twice, that was not me; that was a double. There was a tiger at the zoo that we were originally going to use, but then the producer and the director and I got into a hassle. They brought the tiger out, and without any anesthetic they started to sow the tiger's mouth together so that it couldn't open it and bite me.

I didn't know what to do. So I said, "That isn't the problem; the problem is if the tiger hits you with its paw when it's claws are extended, he can rake you like four or five butcher knives. His strength alone can break the neck of an ox." So they said they'd pull the claws of the tiger. Now this is in India and they'd already sown the tiger's mouth up. It was a big tiger and he hated me! If you turned the tiger loose with a man, he'd kill the man—even if he is Tarzan! It was the end of the day, so we went home for the night, and they were going to pull the tiger's claws in the morning.

We had an English crew, and an English crew has a shop steward that says what they will do and not do. The shop steward went to Mr. Weintraub and said, "If you put that tiger within twenty miles of Mr. Mahoney, we will block the picture in England and all the other countries associated with England—the RSPCA and the ASPCA in America—which meant that nobody would come to see the picture.

So the big cat was gone the following morning, and they brought in the little cat. All the passes that were done with the little cat, the leopard, I did. When it came to picking the cat up, we, the producer, director and I, had another altercation—and I don't have these alter-

cations; I'd never had altercations in my life with producers and directors—but it just so happened that when it came time to pick up the
leopard, I told them what they could do with their picture—oh, it
was ridiculous—and they had a stuntman do it.

David: And then there were the elephants.

Jock had to contend with an elephant herd in *Tarzan Goes to India.*

Jock: The elephants were not a big problem, but they were big! When they first arrived on the set, the crew would walk way around to give the elephants plenty of room. After we'd been working with them for three weeks, the next thing you know the guys are pushing the elephants around, "Move over, move over. Come on, get over there!" It was just wild!

All you have to do is be around something for a short length of time and the next thing you know, you're pushing elephants around—which is kind of ridiculous because they are so big! I can reach eight feet up, and the elephant I rode was eleven feet tall at the shoulder; that's big! Well, I got a nosebleed every time I got on it! *[Both laugh]*

David: What were the living conditions like in India when you made the film?

Jock: My accommodations included several large rooms and a bathroom. There were fans in the ceiling because it was hot, and there was no air conditioning. Trees grew up right outside my hotel window. There was no glass in the window, just iron bars. The cast and crew made me a birthday cake, very garish, very beautiful for my birthday. I said I'd save the birthday cake because my wife was coming over in two days, and I wanted her to see what these nice people had done for me. I went to bed that night in my bed that had mosquito netting all around it.

In the middle of the night I heard the damnedest caterwauling I'd ever heard in my life. I found the switch for the light, turned it on, and there were five of the biggest rats you ever saw in your life fighting over my cake. When the light went on, I yelled and the rats went out through my bathroom, out the windows and into the trees. They ate my soap continuously. They'd eat anything! I didn't want the rats back in my bedroom, so I took the cake and threw it out the bathroom window, so my wife never did get to see the cake. But it's a beautiful, wonderful, strange country.

David: Well, rats were the least of your problems making *Tarzan's Three Challenges*[153] in Thailand.

Jock: In Thailand I got sick. I swam in the klongs which are the open sewers of Bangkok, big canals. I had to swim in the klongs and let a speedboat run over the top of me. It was supposed to knock me out and cut me up—but it didn't; I got away! *[Laugh]* In swimming you do get water in your mouth and you swallow some of it. About a month later I came down with dengue fever, ended up with interstitial pneumonia, and amoebic dysentery.

Anyway, I lost forty pounds. I went from two-twenty to a hundred and eighty pounds. I ran a fever between a hundred and five and a hundred and six for eight or nine days. They got me up out of the hospital and took me to location; I was passing out fifteen, twenty times a day. They wouldn't let me walk alone unless I was in a scene, and that's when I did all the fight stuff with Woody Strode on the net and running all over the mountains and jumping off the bridge and hanging by one leg.

David: You went through Tarzan's three challenges and several more of your own!

Jock: I was so skinny that my diaper kept falling off. *[Both laugh]* But that's the truth! I was skinny and sick. It took me a year and a half to get over that and put my weight back on. Making motion pictures is very easy! *[Both laugh]*

David: There were a number of what appeared to be harrowing scenes that comprised the three challenges. Was there any one scene that was particularly hazardous or tricky to accomplish?

Jock: That would be the scene in *Tarzan's Three Challenges* where I leaped off a bridge that was a hundred and fifty feet high tied to Woody Strode with ropes around our feet. We were to fight hanging in the air and then eventually fall into the water below. We did the first thirty feet off the bridge and the last thirty feet. In other words, we dove off the bridge and went thirty feet into a net. For the last thirty feet we dove out as far as we could and the ropes caught our feet and swung us in a big arc. In the meantime we tied two dummies together for the long shot of the entire hundred and fifty feet, and when they reached the end of the ropes, they disintegrated; they exploded; there was nothing left of them.

Woody was scared to death of the water. I never could find out why; he must have had some traumatic experience with water. He was scared to death to drop into that stream. When we did it, he dropped in and swam to the shore and just lay there for about a half

hour. He was traumatic about the water; evidently something had happened to him to make him that way. He was a beautiful man; I loved him, and I loved working with him. Any time the good Lord sees fit, we'll work together again.

David: A few years ago I saw a photo of you and all the other surviving actors who played Tarzan in films, going all the way back to silent film days. Most of them had lost their Tarzan physiques, and they were joking about it in the caption, standing there in their loincloths. Are you friends with any of the other Tarzan actors?

Jock: Buster Crabbe was born on the same day that I was, just a few years earlier than I. He is such a gentleman. He keeps himself in such good physical shape—mental as well. He's one of my favorite people. Ron Ely is a very close friend of my wife and me. I'm looking forward to seeing *Doc Savage* that Ron did. I did a number of the Tarzan episodes with Ron Ely down in Mexico where they shot that television series. Ron did all this own action, and I did all my own action, so we loved to get together and beat the hell out of each other. I loved playing baddies, which I always did with Ron. You get rid of all your aggressions; you get to hit him, spit on him, get to do all the things a dirty little kid would do, and then you get paid for it. *[Both laugh]*

When my wife and I came back from the islands, we lived with Ron for about two months. When I would phone to the house when I was out and everybody would be gone, the message service would pick it up and say, "Who is calling?" I'd say, "Well, tell him the *real* Tarzan!" *[Both laugh]*

David: You're in the movies, and I understand that you're something of a movie buff. What's your favorite of all time?

Jock: *Patton* is a movie I thoroughly enjoyed. On the other end of the spectrum, *Robin Hood*, starring a man I used to double and had great respect for, Errol Flynn. There are so many [movies] that I have so thoroughly enjoyed because in the old days you used to go to a movie and when you walked out, you walked out about a foot above the ground because you felt great, and you felt like you could whip all of your problems as insurmountable as they seemed. When you walk out of today's movies, you kind of walk under the rug and down the gutter. It's totally different today.

David: What is the favorite role that you've played?

Jock: I thoroughly enjoyed playing the Range Rider because I was young and I loved action and still do. I loved Yancy Derringer because he was more dressed up, more couth, and we had excellent stories and some action. Every boy, no matter how old you get, wants to play Tarzan. Fortunately, I got the chance when I was forty-two. I can't say that I had a favorite role; I enjoyed doing all three.

David: I'm told that you've been ill in recent years.

Jock: Two and a half years ago I had a stroke;[154] I'm fifty-eight years old. The whole right side of my body and the left side of my face went numb. I'm about three-quarters recovered from it now. Life has been so good to me, and God as been good to me. I have no complaints. As a stuntman, He always seemed to give me that extra foot that I needed, that extra six inches of grab I needed, and that extra bit of muscle I needed to get out of trouble. Believe me, as a stuntman you can get into a hell of a lot of trouble that you're not contemplating. Just a hair's difference in a car skid or a motorcycle skid—you might have zigged when you should have zagged. There is so much trouble that you can get into that it's frightening. But that's part of the fun!

David: Thank you, Jock Mahoney.

Jock: God bless you, and you take care.

By this time the dining room was pretty much deserted. The other tables had been cleared, and I became aware that only our table still contained the lunch dishes that the waiters had discretely ignored, realizing that I was doing an interview with one of the guest stars. The husband and wife fans had listened intently and quietly as Jocko and I conversed. Even their little girl had shown an abundance of patience and quietness. I switched off my recorder, thanked Jocko profusely and excused myself. Sometimes things go better than you expect.

Jock Mahoney had impressed me with his outgoing, likeable personality, his sense of humor, and his intellect. This big bear of a man was just fun to be around, and we had the chance to chat a couple of more times before I left Houston and headed back to my home in Sarasota.

Time passed and the next year, 1978, brought me into the position of Director of the Sarasota Visual and Performing Arts Center, a federally-

Jock is talking with parents and students his first evening at the VPA center in Sarasota, Florida.

funded magnet school within the Sarasota public school system. Students with a penchant for the arts from all over the county could enroll in the program and be transported to the VPA campus for classes by trained teachers in the various arts areas covered. Part of the funding provided for professional "guest artists" to be brought to the campus to work with the students, usually for a week of classes. One of the first people I invited to work with the students was Jock Mahoney.

When I phoned Jock, he was immediately intrigued with the idea of meeting and working with the students and agreed to a week of daily classes to commence upon his arrival in two weeks. The first evening in Sarasota I invited the students and their parents to come to the campus to see *Tarzan's Three Challenges* and to meet our guest artist. Jocko loved mingling with the parents and kids, explaining how some of the stunts were done in the Tarzan film they had just viewed, schmoozing that his stepdaughter Sally Field[155] had been *The Flying Nun*, discussing the positives and negatives of a life in the arts—in short, Jocko was an immediate hit.

During the week he met with the students and their teachers and talked about film and television acting, what a professional actor's life is like, and the "business" of being an actor—the waiting on tables time before, hopefully, the big break. Later in the week he discussed his work as a stuntman, brought out mats, and put the students through some simple stunt exercises—staging a fight scene for the camera, taking a fall—business that any working actor might have to contend with. It turned out to be a mutual love fest between Jocko and the students.

One of the evenings during his stay he came home with me for dinner. At that time my wife Nancy and I had two riding horses, a half Arab we called Shada and a red dun horse I called Red Ryder. After dinner Jocko asked to see the horses. Walking out to the barn in the early evening darkness, he said, "Why don't we take a short ride in the pasture?" A chance to ride with one of the best horsemen in films or otherwise? "You bet. That's a great idea!" So we saddled up and rode for about a half hour, slowly because Jock was still not totally recovered from the stroke he had suffered a few years back.

Then he was off to California and home and a new job he told me about just before his departure. Director John Derek had contacted him about being the stunt coordinator for the John and Bo Derek re-imagining of *Tarzan, the Ape Man*[156] with Bo as Jane and an unknown, Miles O'Keeffe, as Tarzan. Jock would soon be leaving for Sri Lanka

Time for a little clowning around at the VPA TV studio. Jock conducts the
recorded background music prior to meeting with students.

where most of the filming was to be done. He was excited about the
venture and confided to me that it might be the start of a new career for
him.

As is well documented, the production was fraught with problems
from the start. At some point mid production, the filming sight became
a land of discontent for most of the people involved—and then there
were rumors of money problems. Before the end of filming, Jocko, an
extremely unhappy jungle camper, flew home, reportedly unpaid.

The tagline for the movie was "Unlike any other *Tarzan* you've ever
seen." And that was certainly a correct statement! The film became almost a total disaster. One reviewer commented, "Even people who love
bad movies won't like this one." Leonard Maltin in his annual *Movie
Guide* stated that the film "nearly forced the editors of the book to devise
a rating lower than BOMB." When the annual Golden Raspberry Awards
came out for the year, Bo Derek won for "Worst Actress." The film was
also nominated for "Worst Picture," "Worst Screenplay," "Worst Actor"
(Richard Harris as Jane's father), "Worst Director" (John Derek), and
"Worst New Star" (Miles O'Keeffe). The only good news was that the
film grossed more than $36,500,000 in the United States alone.

I didn't see Jocko again until the 1982 Memphis Film Festival where he was a guest star and I was promoting one of my books. When I asked him about *Tarzan the Ape Man*, he sighed, shrugged, and said, "I'd rather not talk about it." For Jocko not to talk about something said a lot. During the early 1980s he made a few "guest star" appearances on such shows as *B.J. and the Bear* and Lee Majors' series, *The Fall Guy*.

In 1983 we were both at the Charlotte Western Film Fair, a yearly event that many of the old-time cowboy stars attended. Jocko was still wearing the handsome white beard he had had when he visited the arts center and was still the devil-may-care joker and raconteur, always a funny story to tell or film anecdote to recall for those who clustered around him. It was good to see him again, but that was the last time I would see Jocko.

Occasionally over the next few years I would get word of some activity that Jocko was involved in. In 1985 he was a guest at a conference at the University of Iowa, his old stamping grounds. Jock and his third wife, Autumn, whom he had married in 1967, moved to Poulsbo, Washington, at some point during the eighties. Then on December 12, 1989, there was the news account that Jock Mahoney had been involved in a car accident in Bremerton, Washington, and had been taken to the Harrison Memorial Hospital, but there was little information about how seriously he was hurt. Two days later it was announced that Jock Mahoney had died, apparently from a stroke which followed the car accident. Jock was only seventy years old.

Virginia Mayo

July 13, 1990

"Let me be candid, if I may . . ."

Virginia Mayo is seen here in a typical glamorous publicity photo from her years under contract to Samuel Goldwyn and later Warner Brothers.

When it was announced in the spring of 1990 that Virginia Mayo would be a guest at the Raleigh Western Film Fair in July, there was great enthusiasm among the usual assemblage of Western film fans who looked forward to the festival each year. Most often the Film Fair was held in Charlotte, but this year Raleigh was hosting and a major star of the golden age of movies, Virginia Mayo, was to be on hand.[157] And it was unusual for a star of Mayo's magnitude to appear at a *Western* film festival—Western film festivals weren't considered as classy as such other festivals as the Sundance one in Utah or Colorado's Telluride Film Festival where new (and mostly independent) films were previewed and examined by film aficionados, critics, and distributors in hopes that a cinematic gem might be uncovered, bought up, and in a few months show up at a local multiplex—and make millions.

No, at the Western film festivals it was a time to look back and to re-appreciate Western films that you might have originally seen thirty, forty, or maybe even fifty years previously when you were a front-row buckaroo at the local double-feature Bijou and thrilled to the on-screen adventures of Gene Autry, Roy Rogers, Hopalong Cassidy, *or* Kirk Douglas, Joel McCrea, and Alan Ladd—these last three leading-men being screen cowboys who tangled with this feisty blond, Virginia Mayo, while she was trying to defend her cattle ranch or getting her herd ready for the long drive. During her more than fifty-year career, Virginia Mayo had ridden those dusty western trails in about a dozen "oaters," as *Variety* often liked to call them.

I got a call from one of the organizers of the Western Film Fair in mid June asking if I would host a couple of the Western star panels that were held at each festival. I had been hosting such panels for almost a decade and enjoyed the opportunity to meet the guests in a more personal way and have the chance to ask them the questions that I'd been storing up, in many cases, since I first saw them on the silver screen so many years before. Where else are you going to have the opportunity to meet and interact with such cowboy film legends as Lash LaRue, Sunset Carson, Rod Cameron, Dale Robertson, Jock Mahoney and their sidekick buddies Pat Buttram, "Arkansas" Slim Andrews, Dub "Cannonball" Taylor, Richard "Chito" Martin and Dick Jones? These guys were some of the few Western film performers who were still alive, for crying out loud.

I said I would be happy to host and moderate a couple of the panels and that I would be particularly interested in doing the Virginia Mayo panel. "That's not going to be a panel, David," I was told. "We want that to be a one-on-one with you serving as the host." Great! That's just what I had hoped for. Now, if Virginia Mayo will just show up! Since, to the best of our knowledge, she had never been to any film festival before, there was a lot of speculation that she might change her mind and cancel; also, she hadn't made many public appearances in recent years, and, you know, she might decide that spending a long weekend with a lot of cowboy fans was not her cup of tea.

When Ken Taylor[158] and I arrived in Raleigh on Wednesday evening for the Western Film Fair that would start the next morning, Virginia Mayo had not yet arrived, but we were told that she had boarded the plane in Los Angeles, so her arrival was definite and imminent. We checked into the festival hotel, got the schedule of upcoming events, and adjourned to the dealers' room to see what western film memorabilia might be there that we couldn't live without. Later that evening Virginia Mayo swept into the hotel, escorted by festival representatives, and was ushered to her suite before just about anyone at the festival could clap an eye on her—but that would change the next day.

These Western film festivals usually start slowly on Thursday morning with fans rambling in with their luggage and coolers, greeting friends they haven't seen since the previous festival, paying the registration fee for their name tags, getting their event programs, and then, later, registering for their rooms at the hotel, in this case the Mission Valley Inn. You could hear bits and snippets of conversation regarding Virginia and the other guest stars who were scheduled to attend the festival—who actually made it and who couldn't for one reason or another. Virginia was the biggest name among the guests (although MacDonald Carey and Lash LaRue were pretty big), and everyone was delighted to hear that she and the others had arrived the night before or would be arriving that day.

By late morning Virginia was around and about the hotel lobby, speaking her mind, we would quickly learn, as only Ms. Mayo could. Arriving at the dealers' room, she cheerily noted that she couldn't imagine why anyone would want that junk (photos, lobby cards, posters) from the old cowboy movies—even while noting that a vintage Tom Mix one-sheet was selling for several hundred dollars and a set of John Wayne (Lone Star Pictures) lobby cards was going for even more.

A little later she settled into a chair at the autograph table and proceeded to question why anyone would want an autograph—hers or anybody else's—but she was agreeable to signing anything that was put in front of her—mostly vintage photographs and lobby cards from her long career in films. This *was* Virginia Mayo; she wasn't being nasty, she was just stating her personal opinion—totally unwary (or uncaring) as to how it would play to the festival fans. The candid Ms. Mayo was soon the talk of the festival.

When the notice was posted of the one-on-one panel that I was to moderate the next day, festival friends began to buttonhole me with amusing cautions: "You're going to have your hands full tomorrow with Vir-

Virginia Mayo and I are at the start of our conversation at the Raleigh Western Film Fair.

ginia Mayo." "Don't cross her, David, or her sharp tongue will slice you up and spit you out!" "Good luck, David, you're going to need it with her!" It wasn't that the festival fans didn't like Virginia Mayo—on the contrary, they *loved* her candidness—and were anticipating that Virginia and I would have a lively conversation when we met in front of the festival audience. Needless to say, there was a full house in the panel room the next afternoon when our conversation began.

And the next hour and a half was a delight for me and for festival attendees—and maybe even for Virginia Mayo.

David: I'm happy to greet all of you here and to introduce you to our guest star this afternoon. I would like you all to meet Virginia Mayo.

[Applause]

Virginia: Hello, everybody.

David: Well, we are so happy to have you here in Raleigh; so many people have been looking forward to your visit.

Virginia: I'm happy to be here in Raleigh.

David: I think the question that we always like to ask early on is how did you get into the business of show?

Virginia: Well, as a child all I wanted in my life, even as a little girl, was to be in show biz. When the kids would say, "Come on, Virginia, let's go play ball," I'd say, "No, let's play show." It was just something that was ingrained in me. And I was very lucky because my aunt had a dramatic school and my mother sent me to the school when I was very young so that I could learn how to get up in front of people and dance and sing. She thought this was good to be able to do these things in the Muny Opera.

I went to her school from about the time I was seven or eight and learned elocution, singing and dancing, just everything to do with show biz, so I just naturally gravitated to that by way of her guidance. I started dancing lessons and excelling in that, so I got in the Muny

Opera which is a big thing in St. Louis, a big ten-thousand-seat out-door theater, and I became a dancer in the Muny Opera.

From there [a few years later] I joined an act, a comedy horse act that traveled around in vaudeville. I joined that act and stayed with them for four and a half years before eventually going to New York and being seen by Sam Goldwyn in a Billy Rose review.

David: Let me stop you for a moment, if I may. I'm intrigued by this horse act you were involved in. I know you joined the act, "Pansy the Horse," in 1937 and that you took your stage name "Mayo" from your brother-in-law, Andy Mayo, whose act it was. That sounds so bizarre; could you tell us a little bit more about that?

Virginia: Back in the late thirties and early forties there were movies that played with five acts of vaudeville. Perhaps some of you remember that. You'd go to a movie and then there'd be appearances on the stage by acts. Well, this act was two men inside of a horse skin.

The horse was very cute looking; it had a face that was very horsy/human looking, and the eyes would look around at the audience. It was a "standard" act, which meant it was very well accepted everywhere and played for years and years and years. We played all over the United States with this act, and we played New York: the Radio City Music Hall, the Roxy, the Strand—all these theaters in New York are big theaters. We toured around the East mostly, Chicago, those areas.

David: And you performed the act in 1940 on Broadway in Eddie Cantor's show *Banjo Eyes*. Was there music in the act?

Virginia: Part of it was music. Part of it was my coming out at the beginning and telling the audience about my wonderful horse Pansy who was a marvelous horse and could do lots of tricks and stuff. Then I would introduce the horse and they would come out and do tricks that I would ask them to do. It was very funny, a very funny act. We got lots of laughs, and it was really fun to do.

David: So you eventually ended up in New York with Billy Rose and his Diamond Horseshoe Review. Billy Rose was one of the top showmen around at that time.

Virginia: Absolutely! He certainly was.

David: How did you get with Billy Rose?

Virginia: Well, Billy Rose was doing a new show at the Diamond Horse-shoe called *Mrs. Astor's Pet Horse*; it was sort of a book show, almost like a Broadway musical. My partners met with Billy Rose before he met me and he said, "I don't think I need the girl." And my partners said, "Well, we don't know about that; we can't separate the act." So Billy said, "Okay, I'll meet with her."

So he met with me and he liked me very much, and he built a place in the show for me that was absolutely wonderful; he showcased me. I had a singing role, a dancing role; I did part of the act. And it was so good, this showcase at Billy Rose's Horseshoe, that I got lots of offers to go to Hollywood. So I really owe my career to Billy Rose.

David: Billy Rose was no dummy; he always appreciated a beautiful woman.

Virginia: Oh, thanks. It was really great the way I was showcased by Billy Rose.

David: And that was where Goldwyn saw you?

Virginia: He came down to see the show, saw me in the show, and wanted to sign me to a contract.

David: And that's how you got to Hollywood.

Virginia: That's how I got it.

David: Did he really say those Goldwynisms that he is credited for— "Include me out," "Our comedies are not to be laughed at," "If Roosevelt were alive today he'd turn over in his grave," and all that sort of thing?

Virginia: Oh, yes, yes; he was funny!

David: *Jack London;*[159] was one of your first films.

Virginia: That was the first really good part I had. I was supposed to play the lead in *Up in Arms,*[160] the picture that first introduced Danny Kaye. They tested me for it, but I'd get in front of the camera and freeze. I was scared of the camera. I didn't get the part I was supposed to do in *Up In Arms.* So Samuel Goldwyn said, "You have to be a Goldwyn Girl and learn how to be in front of the camera."

He put me in as a Goldwyn Girl in *Up In Arms,* which really made me very unhappy because I was scheduled to play the lead. Here I was relegated to the chorus. I thought that was awful. Nevertheless, I did it and then got a part in *Jack London,* which was filming on the lot. I got a part in that which was a very good part. I also got another part in an RKO film that was being done, so I got a good lot of experience.

David: You met someone who became a very important person in your life in *Jack London.*

Virginia: Yes, I met Michael O'Shea, who became my husband. He played Jack London in the film. By then Samuel Goldwyn was producing *The Princess and the Pirate,*[161] the picture he was going to do next. So I tested for that, and I was very good in the test and got the part.

David: I read that it was in *The Princess and the Pirate* that you, working with Bob Hope, began to feel comfortable in front of the camera. And that you credited him for some of that.

Virginia: Well, no. In order to do Jack London I had to have gotten rid of that fear, which I did. But working with Bob [was] such a delight; you couldn't help but have fun.

David: Any anecdotes come to mind from working with him?

Virginia: *[Laughing]* Oh, many. Right before the camera would be ready to roll he'd make some kind of a joke, so I couldn't stop laughing when the camera was starting to do the scene. He was always joking.

David: You worked with so many of the top leading men throughout your career, so, of course, I'm going to ask you about some of them and your remembrances of working with them. I believe you worked with Danny Kaye in four films.

Virginia: Yes. When I was doing *The Best Years of Our Lives*[162] and *The Secret Life of Walter Mitty*,[163] I had to do them simultaneously. One day I'd go to this picture and the next time I'd come back to Danny Kaye. Well, one day I was doing a very difficult scene in *The Best Years of Our Lives*. We were filming in a very tight area; it was supposed to be a lady's room where Teresa Wright and I were discussing something. So we're trying to do the scene and the camera is here and there are mirrors all around. You can imagine that filming with mirrors is very difficult. The director is squeezed in with us and we're trying to do the scene. I'm trying to get it all in my head because it's very difficult; it's my scene and I have lots of props to work with. I look up and there's Danny Kaye! He's sitting up on the top of the set [on the catwalk] making faces at me. *[Laugh]* It didn't throw me; well, for a minute it did, but he just wanted to see what I was doing.

David: But you were an old pro in films by that time.

Virginia: By that time I was. We'd done *Wonder Man*,[164] *Kid from Brooklyn*,[165] and *Walter Mitty*.

David: Wonderful movies!

Virginia: Yes, they were.

David: Let's talk about James Cagney, *White Heat*.[166]

Virginia: That was a wonderful picture. I think Jimmy should have won an Oscar for that.

David: At the time it came out, it was admired, but as the years passed it became more and more admired.

Virginia Mayo and Cagney in *White Heat*.

Virginia: You know, back in those days there were a lot of gangster pictures and they would never think of giving an Oscar to anybody for a gangster picture. It had to be *Mrs. Miniver* or [*The Life of*] *Emile Zola*, you know, some kind of film that supposedly had "substance." But I think when you review his acting in that picture you see how really great he was, one of his great performances; he should have won an Oscar.

David: The prison scene where Cagney goes berserk is a true classic scene if there ever was one. You weren't in that scene, but would you have any idea how many times that was shot to get that take?

Virginia: Once! When I see that scene I get chills up and down my spine.

David: You worked with him several times, not only in gangster pictures like *White Heat*, but also *Starlift*[167] and . . . .

Virginia: *West Point Story*.[168] Jimmy wanted me in that. You know, working with Jimmy, he was very anti-social in a way. We wouldn't have any conversations on the set. He would just be in his dressing room most of the time. But when he came out on the set, we all knew who the king was because he was so magnetic when he'd start acting. I mean, we would react to him because he was so dynamic. It wasn't difficult because fire crackers were going off with Jimmy, and you just

Virginia with Gordon MacRae, James Cagney, and Gene Nelson in a scene from *West Point Story*.

had to react and say your lines. He was the impetus to the scene, gave it lots of guts.

David: Those were very contrasting movies, *White Heat*, a heavy gangster movie rather brutal, and *West Point Story*, a musical which really showed off his song and dance ability. It must have been a ball working with Cagney on those song and dance numbers.

Virginia: Well, it was fun. Of course, Jimmy was a great dancer; we all know that. When I rehearsed the one special number we had together, I rehearsed with a girl, and he rehearsed with a girl; we didn't rehearse together. Then when Jimmy came to work with me on the set, I towered over him. You see, he was a very short person. It didn't matter in the dramatic scenes, but when we were doing a dance number it made a lot of difference. I looked like a giant next to Jimmy. *[Laugh]* But it was a darling number[169] and anything that he did was great.

David: Over the years we've heard about another of your leading men who wasn't very tall but who, apparently, was self-conscious about it, Alan Ladd. Was Cagney self-conscious about his height?

Virginia: Oh, no, heavens no. I don't think it ever even struck his mind. He was such a great actor, so full of spit and vinegar. He could make a scene beautiful just by his attitude, his toughness. Alan was a much different guy. He was sensitive and sweet; he didn't have that dynamic appeal that Jimmy had.

David: There was a gentleness about the Alan Ladd character on screen, we might say. Certainly in those days actors were particular types very often, and Alan Ladd had an "Alan Ladd character" that he played so beautifully, probably never better than in *Shane*, but certainly in *The Iron Mistress*[170] he was very, very appealing and you, of course, co-starred with him in that.

Virginia: When we did *The Iron Mistress*—it was such a lovely picture— and I played a real mean woman; I was awfully mean to Alan Ladd in that. At one point he was in love with me and he wanted me to marry

Virginia is seen here with Alan Ladd in the Warner Brothers production of
The Iron Mistress.

him, and I thought he was beneath me—my station in life. I wasn't
going to marry him; he was just a farmer. I told him, "Maybe we will
later on." And then I went off and married somebody else, someone
with stature and social position. Then he comes and sees me and I tell
him, "Oh, I'm married!" The look on his face was so sad and heart-
broken; I couldn't get over it, it was so beautiful. His eyes were so
beautiful and sad when I told him that I'd married. I always remember that expression on his face.

David: He was wonderful with facial expressions on the screen that would
show what he was feeling.

Virginia: I don't think I've worked with a better actor, facially, than Alan.
He had very expressive eyes and he really expressed emotion beautifully.

David: A very melodious voice too. What was he like off camera?

Virginia: Very friendly, very nice, always inviting you to come into his dressing room. Most actors wouldn't do that; they like to go to their dressing room and be alone, but Alan would play records and maybe we'd talk a little; he was really terrific. He was very shy, however, very shy.

David: Many of us have read his biography by Barbara Linet. Certainly most of us who followed his career saw that it was on a downward spiral those last few years, as was his personal life.

Virginia: Yes, it was. I don't know exactly what went on between him and his family. I know that Sue [his agent and wife]was sometimes hard on him; she would berate him in front of people, which was not the right thing to do, but that's husbands and wives; they can do what they please, you know how it is.

I think he may have needed psychological help. But I wasn't that close to the family so I couldn't intrude on them. I would read about his having trouble, you know. I just never thought I could be forward enough to say, "Why don't you see a psychiatrist." You don't even say that to your best friend. I think he needed some help and maybe he could have survived his problems.

David: In his later years there was a sadness about him, even on the screen in some of those later films, particularly in *The Carpetbaggers*,[171] where he seemed to be almost playing himself.

Virginia: Well, it was a very sad story.[172]

David: Let's move on to some of the other actors you've worked with. How about the man who became president, Mr. Reagan?

Virginia: I don't think he's sad at all. *[Laugh]* I think he's rolling in dough right now, very happy! *[Laugh]* He was wonderful, very much a gentleman and nice to work with. He was great on the set, knew his lines. He was always ready with a joke, fun to be with. When we made *The Girl from Jones Beach*,[173] we had a lot of fun.

After the picture we went to take some photos at the beach for publicity purposes; Ronnie and Eddie Bracken, Dona Drake; we all went down to the beach. We were playing leapfrog, and I'm jumping over Ronald Reagan's back, and people were photographing it. And that picture is still circulating around—me doing a leapfrog over Ronnie Reagan! *[Laugh]* He was just getting divorced [from Jane Wyman], and he may have been unhappy about that—I'm sure he was—but he never discussed it. He was very professional, always.

David: From everything I've read about him during his Hollywood years— except when he was talking about business—he seemed to be a rather carefree person

Virginia: Well, he's got that wonderful personality, you know, gracious, charming. I mean, he's Mr. Charm all over *and* Mr. Nice Guy! There's just not a better description for him, because that's what he is. He made it to President by way of his charm.

David: Well, I think most of us have enjoyed Ronald Reagan as an actor and as a President over the years.

Virginia: Well, I have to say something. Just last week I went to see Ronald Reagan at his office. He invited me and Eddie Bracken to come up and have a little get together. This was in Century City in Los Angeles. He was telling us that an intruder got into his house in Bel Air.

David: Yes, I just read about it.

Virginia: Well, evidently this guy had it in for him and had been writing letters threatening Reagan. This man was going to choke President Reagan because he didn't have any weapon. This is what Ronnie said, that he was going to choke him. It was a good thing they got him; Ronnie would have been defenseless.

David: Did he seem disturbed by this occurrence?

Virginia: No, he was just sitting there just as charming as ever, talking about this guy that was going to choke him. *[Laughter]*

David: He never let things really bother him too much.

Virginia: They don't seem to. When I would watch him as President talk on television, I thought he must have a double personality or something. Because he was always laughing and waving as he got in the helicopter, you know, nothing seemed to bother him.

David: Well, he was the first President we've had in a long time who really seemed to enjoy the job. He wasn't in agony over day-to-day situations; he just enjoyed the job. It was fun to be President.

Virginia: I guess so—a good acting job!

David: Kirk Douglas, there's a very different type of actor.

Virginia: Yes, he's too intense for me.

David: I don't think that you're the only one to find him that way.

Virginia: Oh, really? Someone else has spoken out, huh?

David: Well, the comment has been made.

Virginia: Let me be candid, if I may. He's so difficult; I wasn't friendly with him. He was just self-centered, I think, too much so. I didn't care for him too much.

David: A contrast perhaps to Kirk Douglas, Joel McCrea.

Virginia: Wonderful guy, really wonderful, very easy to act with, nice person, what a friendly person. I mean you'd have lunch with him and have a million laughs because he was always telling a great joke or great story or reminiscing about his past, very wonderful person.

David: You did *Colorado Territory*[174] with him. That was with Raul Walsh directing and *White Heat* was directed by Raul Walsh too. Let me skip off Joel McCrea for a moment because I want to touch on Raul Walsh, a director who did so many fine films. You worked with him in at least two.

Virginia: I did four pictures with him altogether. Well, he was my favorite director because we just hit it off working together. I find him to be a very gutsy kind of guy; basics, he was down to basics all the time. He would make jokes; I was always laughing at his jokes because he was hilarious.

He would say to me, "Okay now, Virginia—you know, he had one eye and a patch and he'd roll his cigarettes like this [demonstrates and continues in Raul-like voice]—Okay now, Virginia, you run around this barn here, and you run around it as fast as you can run, like you just had a free beer around the corner." *[Laughter]* He seemed to like me because I liked that gutsy approach to movies; we got along great!

David: Back to Joel McCrea. *Colorado Territory* is a fine Western. I wish it had not been made in black and white.

Virginia: I do too. The studio was trying to save money or something. It should have been in color.

David: There weren't many interior studio shots in the picture. You must have spent a lot of time on location.

Virginia: Yes, when we made *Colorado Territory* most of it was on location in Gallop, New Mexico.

David: Did you like working on location?

Virginia: It's a lot more difficult to do a scene outdoors because the sound is not as contained. The winds and all kinds of scenery seem to tear you apart. It's much easier to work inside where there are no distractions. Nature is a beautiful distraction; to work opposite nature is tough. Joel McCrea's my neighbor. He has a big ranch that he bought in the thirties.

David: Does he still have that ranch?

Virginia: He has part of it; he sold most of it for millions and millions of dollars. He is a very wealthy man, and he's a *real* cowboy. I mean, he really had a ranch with cattle and everything. He'd ride over [his] range, and it was like a symphony to see this man ride—a beautiful rider.

David: He was probably as much a rancher as he was an actor.

Virginia: That's right, absolutely.

Man in audience: Since you're a neighbor of Joel McCrea, would you encourage him to come to the Western Film Fair when you get back?

Virginia: He advised me not to come! *[Laughter]* You're not getting him here.

David: Well, I'm glad you didn't follow his advice, we all are. You've made comedies, you've made dramas, musical comedies, westerns— all types of films. If the studio called you today and said they wanted you for a picture, what genre of film would you like it to be?

Virginia: Well, they wanted me to do a picture once with a comedian and I didn't think the part was very good and I didn't want to do it. I said to the head of the studio, "I don't want to do this picture because it's not worthy of my talents, but if you let me do musicals in the future, I'll do it." They wanted me in the picture because of my name value at the time. He said, "Yes, okay, we'll do it; we'll put you in musicals." So they kept their promise, and I did the picture.

David: Was that *Always Leave Them Laughing* with Milton Berle?[175]

Virginia: Yes. He's a very funny man; I just didn't want to work with him. *[Laugh]* I guess I thought it was sort of a comedown. I mean, come on, I shouldn't have been too egotistical about it. I should have done it without even fussing. So from then on I did some really good musicals.

David: So are you saying that of all the different types of films you love musicals the most?

Virginia: I think so. I love the dancing parts.

David: Well, you certainly were excellent in them and popular in them— films like *She's Working Her Way through College.*[176]

Virginia: With our friend Ronald Reagan.

David: You were a product of the studio system, going out there with Samuel Goldwyn, being under contract to him, and then eventually going under contract to Warner Brothers. I've talked with performers who say, "The studio system was the greatest thing that ever was." And I've talked with actors who say, "Thank God we don't have that any more." What is your feeling about it?

Virginia: Well, I think it was a good thing, especially for women, because women need special care in order to maintain a career. If a woman is freelancing, she gets pushed around a lot. For instance, the vehicles of today are all man vehicles, you know, nothing for women. Very seldom do you find anything for women. Maybe *Pretty Woman*, the movie that is out now, is one vehicle for a woman, but most of them are all men oriented, written for men.

David: A movie like *Steel Magnolias* is very rare.

Virginia: Yes, very rare. Back in the old days women were equal with men in the pictures. They'd always have great roles for women. Nowadays, you have to scrounge around to find five women to nominate for Oscars. They nominate and give some woman an Oscar and you never hear of her after that. Can you name the last five years of Oscar winning women?

David: Jessica Tandy, but after that it gets dim.[177] *[Laugh]*

Virginia: And she's ninety! *[Laughter]*

David: Yes, it took her a long time to get that Oscar!

Virginia: Maybe there's still a chance for me someday. *[Laugh]*

David: But the studio system. . . .

Virginia: Yes, I liked it. Maybe the studio system wasn't for a man like Kirk Douglas, who wanted to produce his own movies and was grumpy about the whole thing anyway.

David: Well, certainly it seems that the majority of the people who worked under the studio system liked it. They weren't making ten million dollars a movie, but they were probably turning out better movies in those days.

Virginia: I think so.

Michael O'Shea circa 1940s.

David: Let's go back to Michael O'Shea. He was an actor that I enjoyed so much through the years.[178]

Virginia: Wasn't he wonderful? He was great!

David: You were married to him for a very long time, and you met him on one of your first movies, *Jack London*.

Virginia: He was underrated all the time; he never really worked hard at a career. He thought anybody could do it. But they can't, you know. It takes a special talent to be Spencer Tracy or Michael O'Shea. Acting is a very difficult art and it doesn't come off easy for everybody. He never pushed himself; he never got a special agent. He just had some average guy to handle him, and he didn't make a big enough career for himself—but then he subjugated himself to me. We would go on publicity tours for the studio where he didn't work then. He was always pushing me, pushing me to the fore, and my career was first. It's kind of rare to have a man do that; most wouldn't stand for it.

David: He was so natural on the screen; as you say, it seemed effortless and there was a charm there that he didn't have to work at.

Virginia: No, he didn't. We did a lot of plays in the sixties and seventies, and I really learned a lot from him. It was just something that he had, a quality in his personality. He'd be on the stage doing nothing and everybody would be looking at him. They wouldn't be looking at me or the other actors; they would be watching him because he would do funny little things that were nothing, just nothing! But the audience was riveted on him.

I remember one man said to him as we came out of the stage door one night, "Oh, Michael O'Shea, you're a whole show all by yourself." And it was true, he was! He could even ad-lib much funnier than the script and occasionally he would do that. I remember one play where every evening when we came to a certain scene he would have tears coming down his face. I could never do that; I couldn't cry every night at a certain place. He did it! And he never even worked hard at the scene; it just happened. He was a fabulous actor.

David: He worked in a television series *It's a Great Life* very successfully. Why have you never gotten involved in television?

Virginia: I don't know. I did a pilot for a TV show, but they didn't buy it. They bought Donna Reed instead. But that's the only chance I ever had to be in a TV show.

David: That's surprising! Because with the type of background you had in motion pictures it would seem that you would be a natural in television.

Virginia: Well, I don't know. I guest starred a lot of times, but I never did a series.

David: Well, that should change; you should do a series.

Virginia: Oh, I'd like to, but everything's Angela Lansbury. *[Laughter]* They've run that thing into the ground! *[Laughter]*

David: Well, Angela's talking about quitting *Murder She Wrote*. As we got into the sixties and seventies you moved on to, as you said a few moments ago, performing on stage, stock shows, and doing dinner theaters around the country. After years of working in the studios of Hollywood, did you like that or not?

Virginia: Well, coming from the stage, it wasn't difficult—only learning those plays. They'd say, "This is the play that we want you to do." And then I'd have to learn the whole thing. Well, I want to tell you that it's a very difficult thing to learn a whole play. I'd get panicky when I'd start to learn it. I'd say, "I can't do it! I can't do it! This whole play; I can't do it!" And I would panic for weeks on end trying to learn this play. But eventually you get it and then you rehearse and then it's okay. You do it over and over. But it is really panic time when you start to learn a play, I want to tell you.

David: Your early experience on the stage was more in the line of short musical comedy acts.

Virginia: Yes, the horse act was very short. But I liked the comedies working with Mike because he was so funny. Then I did another show that he wasn't in, but it was a very good show called *Barefoot in the Park*, a wonderfully written show. So it was fun; we had a very good cast.

David: All right. Let's open it up for the audience and let them ask some questions.

Lady in Audience: At a recent film festival Gregory Peck named you as one of his three favorite leading ladies and elaborated on that. I'm wondering if he is one of your favorite leading men.

Virginia: What did he say?

Lady in audience: He said you were beautiful to work with, that you were gracious, and he just had loads of fun working with you on [*Captain Horatio*] *Hornblower*.[179]

Virginia: Oh, really! Well, I thought he was wonderful. I tell you, Gregory Peck is fantastic, a wonderful talent, and so charming. He's one of the nicest men you can meet. He and Ronald Reagan, they are equal in their kindness and generosity. I think Gregory Peck is by far a better actor, but he studied a lot harder than Ronald Reagan did. He would go to a coach and she would write down things that he should think about when he is acting. This coach was wonderful, the best there was, and I know Gregory Peck went to her for [guidance on] all the scripts. If the director isn't good, you want to have guidance from somebody else so that you are sure you are doing right.

Man in audience: Did Raul Walsh direct *Hornblower*?

Virginia: Yes, he did.

Lady in audience: That was the one in which he [Peck] had great things to say about you. Was that the only film that you and Peck appeared in?

Virginia: Yes, that's right. He was wonderful, I must say, a fine gentleman.

David: You commented on him along with Ronald Reagan a few moments ago as being two very charming men. They certainly are different in their politics.

Virginia: Absolutely. They're complete opposites. Gregory Peck is very liberal and Ronald Reagan is very . . . Republican. *[Laughter]* I'm a Republican; I mean I'm for him! I don't go for these liberal theories.

Lady in audience: You worked with Steve Cochran a lot.

Virginia: Yes. Steve was one of my very good friends. Steve was like a Marlon Brando-type person. You know, he did what he wanted to do when he wanted to do it, and he wasn't disciplined at all; he was kind of wild. We were very good friends because we were under contract to Sam Goldwyn at the same time. Steve was what Marlon Brando *thought* he was.[180] *[Laughter]*

David: Wasn't he in *She's Back on Broadway* with you?

Virginia: Yes, he was the leading man in that. He was also in *A Song is Born* and he was in *White Heat* with me and *Best Years of Our Lives*. There were a lot of films where Steve and I worked together. He would always confide in me; we were that close. We were like buddies. We didn't have any romance of any kind because, I don't know, I didn't go for him that way. He was a strange man. At the end he had a boat. He went out and took all these women on his boat. He supposedly was screen testing them for something *[Audience laughter]*—some silly thing like that. He took these women out on his boat, and he proceeded to have a heart attack [sic].[181] They didn't know how to get the boat back to shore, so he died.

Man in audience: Could you talk a bit about another of your leading men, Clint Walker?

Virginia: Clint Walker was the biggest man I ever saw, a giant! *[Laughter]* The picture I did with Clint we went to Utah—Kanab.[182] We had Brian Keith in that picture, and Brian Keith was the complete opposite of Clint Walker. He was relaxed; he'd sit in the studio car that brought us to location and drink beer all day, just lounging around. Clint Walker was up [Virginia demonstrating] exercising and picking up logs—a health nut! *[Audience laughter]* [He] wouldn't drink or smoke or swear or anything. But Clint was a wonderful person, a really terrific guy, but he was new and I don't think show business is really what he should be in. Somehow he doesn't fit, kind of stiff, but it was wonderful working with him; I enjoyed it very much. I don't know what to tell you about him. I think he has left the Los Angeles area, and I think he now lives in Northern California. I don't know if he works any more.

Man in audience: I fell in love with you back in the early fifties when you made a movie with Burt Lancaster, *South Sea Woman.*[183]

Virginia: That was fun. I liked Burt very much. He's an interesting man; he's also very intense, but he's not as dislikeable as Kirk Douglas. *[Laughter]* Burt Lancaster is likeable, very intelligent, he reads a lot, and he doesn't suffer fools well. I did two pictures with him and I enjoyed both of them very much. He had to exercise all the time. He'd go into the gym at the studio and work out all the time because he was a trapeze performer at one time.

In one picture, *The Flame and the Arrow,*[184] he did all those trapeze stunts himself. You saw his face [on screen as he was] doing that, so he had to keep in condition. I don't think he does that any more; after all, he's pretty old. We had a love scene in *The Flame and the Arrow*, and he was supposed to be angry because I was a noble woman, and he was mad at noble people and people of social classes. So he grabbed me, and he's supposed to kiss me and be mad at me at the same time. When he kissed me I swear I thought my mouth was broken, he was so violent. *[Laughter]* And I thought, oh, I lost my front teeth! *[Laughter]* That was some kiss, I want to tell you! I don't ever want to kiss him again! *[Laughter]* And my arms were black and blue.

David: Well, I think that brings up a subject that we've got to explore a little bit: If you didn't like doing love scenes with Burt Lancaster, who did you like doing the love scenes with?

Virginia: [Coyly] Gregory Peck! He was really good at love scenes. I think this dramatic coach he used to go to advised him on how to do a love scene. She used to specialize in that. A lot of men in movies get too rough for a woman. You know, women like sensitive, soft love making; they don't like rough stuff. And Gregory Peck was the best kisser.

David: You hear so often from actors and actresses that, oh, they don't like to do those love scenes, they just feel so uncomfortable doing them, and

that they're embarrassed, and all that sort of thing. But I don't seem to be hearing you say that; you sound as if they were enjoyable.

Virginia: They were embarrassing, but if it's handled correctly, you can enjoy it.

David: And with Gregory Peck it was easy to enjoy.

Virginia: Right!

Man in audience: What was it like working with William Wyler as a director?

Virginia: He was a magnificent director. He has gotten more Oscars than any other director. I must say he was easy to work with; he didn't have any problems with me. I enjoyed working with him. He was silent most of the time. You know, he worked with Bette Davis, and she said to him, "Willy, when I finish a scene you don't say it's good, you don't say it's bad. I mean, come on, what is it?" So from then on, after each scene, he'd say, "Wonderful, Bette! Wonderful, wonderful; oh, that was magnificent!" Finally she said, "Oh, go back to the other way." *[Laughter]*

Man in audience: What do you consider the film that you like the most that you've done?

Virginia: *She's Working Her Way through College*, musical, Ronald Reagan.

David: Gene Nelson was also in it. He's an actor, a dancer to begin with, that I always enjoyed so much on the screen. I know he went on to be a successful director, but I miss him as a dancer.

Virginia: I loved working with Gene because we got to dance together. You know, he was my dancing partner and I enjoyed it so much.

David: Was he as good a dancer as I thought he was as I watched him?

Virginia: He did some steps that I didn't like, and he made me learn how to do it his way. The steps were kind of backwards, if you know what

Virginia Mayo struts her stuff for a very disapproving Ronald Reagan in
She's Working Her Way through College.

I mean. He sort of went left instead of right and the dancing was
confusing for me. He had his own style that I couldn't follow at times.
Other than that, we got along great.

David: Was he doing his own choreography for the most part?

Virginia: For the most part. They let him do that.

David: I'm a little bit surprised to hear you say that *She's Working Her Way
through College* was your favorite film.

Virginia: I think it's just because of the dancing and [being] a musical. I liked the musicals the best.

David: Well, they certainly were enjoyable, and the studios are not making many musicals these days.

Virginia: No, they're not. It's very sad. I mean, when is Patrick Swayze going to make another musical? If he doesn't do it soon, he'll be too old! I'd love to see him dance some more.

David: He was marvelous in *Dirty Dancing*, of course. How would you rank him among dancers you've seen or worked with yourself in films?

Virginia: Just about the top. I would say he's really tops. Well, who dances in pictures any more, not many?

David: That's true, but would you rank him right up there with the great dancers in the past?

Virginia: Well, Fred Astaire was about the best, and then Gene Kelly and he [Swayze] would rate among that category.

David: That is high praise indeed.

Virginia: Yeah. Well, he's a ballet dancer, you know.

David: You never had the opportunity to work with Astaire or Kelly, did you?

Virginia: No.

David: That is a shame. I would have enjoyed that match-up.

Virginia: I would have enjoyed it, yeah.

Man in audience: Would you comment on working with Randolph Scott in *Westbound?*[185]

Virginia: I had hardly any scenes with him. I hardly knew the man. Well, I didn't like doing the picture in the first place. I was having some dental work and I told the studio I couldn't work for several weeks. And they said, "Oh, we'll wait." I didn't want them to wait. *[Laughter]* I wanted to recover in peace, and, anyway, the part was about this big [demonstrating the smallness with her hands]. It was a terrible part!

David: It was a very strange movie role for you. It was shown here at the film festival the other night, and it was as if—pardon me for saying this—the studio was angry with you and was giving you a role that wasn't appropriate for you.

Virginia: Well, they were! This man, the director Bud Boetticher, put his girlfriend [Karen Steele] in the lead. So she's playing the lead, and I'm playing a bit part!

David: And it was even suggested at the end that Randolph Scott was going to come back to her. I thought it was rather absurd, because that did not seem appropriate at all at the end of the movie.

Virginia: I haven't seen the picture recently so I don't [remember] what it's all about.

David: That was right near the end of your time at Warner Brothers, and that was also about the end of studio contract players too. Was the studio trying to find reason to cancel your contract?

Virginia: They used to do that to all of the people when they ended their contracts. They tried to put you [in a picture you didn't want to do] and have you say that you didn't want to do it. Then they'd put you [on suspension] so they wouldn't have to pay you any more. They liked to do that to you, sort of punish you.

Lady in audience: You mentioned Patrick Swayze among the newer group of actors today. Do you go to the movies much and, if so, who do you enjoy watching?

Virginia: I go to the movies as much as I can. I don't go to see *Gremlins,* uh! I wouldn't go see that! There are a lot of pictures I don't like, but I do go to the movies whenever I can. I like Mel Gibson; he's so darling. I like Goldie Hawn, but I didn't like the picture they did together very much, *Bird on the Wire.* But I still like them both.

David: Have you had a chance to see *Dick Tracy?*

Virginia: Yes.

David: What did you think of that?

Virginia: Well, it was too loud. The sound they put in the theaters is deafening and that interferes with my enjoyment. It was pretty good though; I enjoyed Madonna. I thought she was pretty and fascinating. I like the women in pictures; they don't have enough women [in pictures] for my satisfaction.

David: Glen Close, is she an actress you admire?

Virginia: Yes. That was a good picture, *Fatal Attraction;* that was a very interesting picture.

Man in audience: Could you comment on the amount of money some stars are making today—and some of them with very little talent, I think—as compared with the money you were making in films?

Virginia: I know; we got just peanuts. The stars today are making outrageous salaries. I mean, when you take someone like Bruce Willis who makes twelve million dollars. I wouldn't even walk across the street to see him. I don't think he has anything, but that's just my opinion. I don't understand it; how they get so much money.

David: Doris Day was at Warner Brothers for so many years when you were there. You worked with her in *West Point Story* and a little bit in *Starlift.*

Virginia: Well, Doris was so sparkly and full of laughter and fun that we used to call her Sparkle Plenty, and she was lots of fun. She was very vivacious, as we all know. She married her agent, Marty Melcher, and they proceeded to make pictures together at various studios, which made it great for her because all the stories were tailored to her. They made a lot of money, and then when he died, I don't know what happened to the money but it seems that it was all siphoned off somehow. And the judge couldn't figure out what happened to the money. And if the judge can't figure it out, we certainly never have gotten the truth out of that. I suspect mafia.

David: For several years you must have been pretty much in competition with Doris for the musical roles at Warner Brothers. Did you two get along all right at the studio even though you were in competition?

Virginia: We got along okay. Some of the roles she got I would like to have had. I was a little jealous of her.

David: Jack Warner, the head of Warner Brothers, we haven't discussed him today. Did you have many dealings with Jack Warner?

Virginia: Well, not really. I never tangled with him. Whenever I had any dealing with the studio officials, I always dealt with Steve Trilling, who was his assistant. I always felt it was easier to keep a balance if I didn't deal with Jack Warner. When you go to people's houses—Jack Warner always gave great parties—you can't argue about money the next day. So I never did that; I always dealt with Steve Trilling.

Jack Warner gave these fabulous parties at his house, a mansion still there in Beverly Hills, a huge estate with the gorgeous house. They were interesting parties because the elite of Hollywood would be there. At dinner—a sumptuous meal always—Jack Warner wanted people to get up and make a speech or make some joke. He was quite a joke teller. He'd say, "Okay, Michael O'Shea, get up and say something." They [the guests] always used to hate it so, all these people who were invited; they'd have to get up and say some funny joke. So, finally, we just stopped going to the parties.

David: You were a star working in pictures during what most of us think of the golden age of Hollywood, the forties and on into the fifties before television sort of took over. Who were your friends? Were they for the most part in or outside the business?

Virginia Mayo and I are nearing the end of our conversation at the
1990 Raleigh Western Film Fair.

Virginia: I didn't have too many friends in the business. Really I didn't
have time, not the way that I worked, constantly. You had to get your
rest. You only had Sundays off and on Sundays you'd just fall apart,
you'd be so tired. There wasn't a lot of time for friendships. I have my
friend from way back—school days—that I still am in touch with all
the time. Oh, I had some friends like Vera Ellen,[186] who has since
died, and Steve Cochran, who has since died. So I haven't many friends
in the business. I will see somebody like Rhonda Fleming,[187] who's
an old friend, but we don't socialize, [only] very, very seldom.

David: You've made a lot of films during your long career, and I hear that
you've recently completed a new one.

Virginia: Yes, I did about forty-five pictures. I did a picture in March of
this year called *Evil Spirits*,[188] which is a horror film, and it probably
will be horrible. *[Laughter]* But, anyway, it's the last thing that I did.

Man in audience: What did you think of Elvis Presley?

Virginia: I didn't like him at all. I didn't like his singing or his looks.
[Shrugs] I guess I'm one in a million—everybody else does.

David: One of the very nice things about talking with you today is that
you are so candid. It's delightful to have someone who speaks her
mind. *[Audience applause]*

Virginia: I'd better keep my mouth shut! *[Laughter]* Kirk Douglas will come [looking] for me!

Man in audience: What are your future plans?

Virginia: Just keep breathing. *[Laughter]* I think I have to go; I'm getting tired of talking.

David: Well, before we let you go, we want to thank you so much. This has been a wonderful time that we've spent with you.

Virginia: Thank you. *[Applause]*

The last evening of the western film festivals there is always a banquet where the guest stars are feted and given a plaque in commemoration of their appearance at the festival. The guests express their "thank you" for being asked to the festival; some will sing, if that is their thing, others, like Lash LaRue and Jimmy Rogers (the son of Will Rogers), may recite a poem or deliver another type of recitation or remembrance. Virginia expressed her thanks for being asked to the festival, said she appreciated the plaque, and then made mouths drop by exclaiming, "I don't know why you people come to look at these broken-down movies."

Virginia Mayo and I—along with some helpful prompting from our audience—covered many of the highlights of her career during our conversation—and that's about all one can hope to do in a little over an hour—but, of course, there was so much more that could have been asked and said. In her film career which ran for well over four decades there are other films and other costars that I wish we could have discussed: *The Silver Chalice*[189] with Paul Newman, *Along the Great Divide*[190] with Kirk Douglas, *Great Day in the Morning*[191] with Robert Stack, *King Richard and the Crusaders*[192] with Rex Harrison—after all, she made over fifty pictures during those decades.

And she cut a wide acting swath too during her long career as a leading lady: she held her own as a comic foil for such comedians as Bob Hope, Danny Kaye, and Milton Berle. She displayed her dramatic acting ability in such films as *The Best Years of Our Lives* and *White Heat*—has there ever been as tough a gun-moll/two-timing wife as her Verna Jarrett opposite Cagney's Cody Jarrett? She radiated blowtorch heat as a voluptuous, sexy siren in *South Sea Woman, Pearl of the South Pacific*,[193] and *The Flame and the Arrow*. And then there were the musicals mentioned in our conversation that she loved the most and that greatly added to her résumé for versatility as a performer—but you get the idea.

Virginia was sixty-nine at the time we met in Raleigh and by then her active career had pretty much wound down. The horror film she had just completed, *Evil Spirits*, was her last—and just as horrible as she suspected it would be. After a brief run in a few theaters, it rested on a shelf until finally being released on DVD in 2005.

Virginia returned to her long-time home in Thousand Oaks, California, where she pursued her avocation of painting, working in both watercolors and oils. She had a close bond with her daughter Mary Catherine and stated that the role of her life was playing "loving grandmother" to her three grandsons. Virginia never remarried after the death of her husband Michael O'Shea in 1973.

During the 1990s she decided to donate her extensive collection of show business memorabilia to the Thousand Oaks Library, which was not far from where she had lived since the fifties. In 1996 she received a star on the St Louis Walk of Fame. She was touched that her hometown would remember her early experience in the ballet corps of the St. Louis Municipal Opera and would honor her in this way. Of course, they remembered her more familiarly as a Hollywood and stage star. (Many years earlier she had received her star on the Hollywood Walk of Fame.)

Later in the decade she began work on her autobiography which was published in 2002 under the title *Virginia Mayo: The Best Years of My Life* as told to LC Van Savage and published by BeachHouse Books. I smiled as I read her book; she had lost none of her cynicism, and her candidness about fellow actors and show business in general was unchecked. It was a delightful read.

Early in the new century her health began to fail and eventually she reluctantly entered a nursing facility near her home. On January 17, 2005, Virginia Mayo, died of pneumonia and heart failure. She was eighty-four. Funeral services were private. The family suggested that memorial donations be made in her name to the St. Louis Municipal Opera.

Show business historian Jeanine Basinger wrote in the *Los Angeles Times* obituary that "Virginia Mayo was one of the truly great beauties of her era, and I think that people forget what a big star she really was. She played with all the big names of her era, in both comedies and dramas. Mayo appeared in films that guarantee her place in film history, including *White Heat* and *The Best Years of Our Lives*. But she also was a great foil for comedians, and that's a difficult role to play, and she did it well."

Roddy McDowall

January 23, 1978

"Plays happen to have the chance of disappearing sooner than movies because the emulsion stays around."

This was the "official" Roddy McDowall publicity photo at the time of
our conversation in 1978.

Roddy McDowall came to Fort Lauderdale to perform in English playwright Simon Gray's *Otherwise Engaged* just at the time I needed to talk to him about some well-known animals: Lassie, Flicka, and Thunderhead—not to mention some apes that Roddy had been associating with in more recent years. I was about mid-way on my book *The Great Show Business Animals* and how convenient it was that Roddy McDowall would be appearing at a nearby theater and might perhaps be amenable to a conversation.

Roddy's PR man assured me on the phone that the actor had a deep affection for the animals he had performed with so many years before—*and* the movies too. He felt certain that Mr. McDowall would want to talk to me about them. I made sure that Mr. PR Man also realized that I wanted to include some other career material for my radio program. "If Mr. McDowall is available for the one, I'm sure there would be no problem with the other," he responded pleasantly. "I'll get back to you very soon."

The man was as good as his word; I heard back from him within the hour: "Yes, Mr. McDowall would very much like to talk with you about Lassie and whatever else you have in mind. Could you meet with him after the Saturday evening performance?" "Yes," I shot back quickly. "How many tickets would you like Mr. McDowall to leave for you at the box office?" "One would be just fine, thank you." And we said our goodbyes. My goodness, I wish all meetings with show business personalities could be arranged that easily.

I decided to make a full day of it. Leaving my home in Sarasota about noon on Saturday, I arrived in Fort Lauderdale about three o'clock and made hotel arrangements for the night at a location near the theater, which left me some time to roam the shops in the area and get dinner. I was particularly drawn to the antique and collectible shops where sometimes one could pick up interesting show business memorabilia for a pittance—remember this was before eBay and the internet. In one shop I stumbled upon a few old, eight-by-ten movie photos and one, in particular, of Roddy McDowall that I dickered for—but more about that later when I'm talking with Roddy.

I find it astonishing that I have absolutely no remembrance of the show that I saw that evening—it is a complete blank in my mind. Thank goodness we mentioned the play by name in our later recorded conversation; otherwise I would have no knowledge of it. Anyway, I *do* remember that after the show Mr. PR Man escorted me to a lower-level kitchen area in the theater where "Mr. McDowall" was going to meet me presently. While we waited, we exchanged the type of awkward chit-chat that people use to fill up awkward periods of time.

But it was only a few minutes later that Roddy arrived, freshly showered, wafting some pleasant masculine scent before him, and wearing a jumpsuit that gave him an adventurous aura. PR Man introduced us and then excused himself as Roddy and I shook hands and got comfortable with each other by utilizing a bit more chit-chat—this time about how much I had enjoyed the show [whatever it was] and his appreciation of my comments.

Roddy then asked if I minded if we stood while talking; I assured him that I didn't and that the only other time I could remember doing a standup conversation was with Mel Tormé before a nightclub performance. We both chuckled at that. But no more chit-chat; it was time to get down to the serious business of canines, equines, primates, and whatever else evolved from our conversation.

David: You were a child actor in England, and I read somewhere that you moved to the United States around 1940.

Roddy: My father sent my mother and sister to the United States at the end of 1940 to live with her relatives in America. That was in October of 1940. I had made films, some twenty films, in England before coming to America.

David: The first really big motion picture that you made in America was *How Green Was My Valley*[194] directed by John Ford.

Roddy: Yes, I was an accident that I got *How Green Was My Valley*. I was here for two weeks and by fluke got the role. But the *first* film I made in the United States was *Man Hunt*,[195] a Fritz Lange[196] film also with Walter Pidgeon. Then *How Green Was My Valley* was made. I was contracted when in New York to do that—and taken to the West Coast.

David: How did they discover you in New York as a young actor and take you off to California.

Roddy: My mother, based on the fact that she had worked very hard to get me work in England, coming to America she heard that MGM was looking for a little boy for *The Yearling* and took me to MGM in New York and they said that they didn't think I was the right type at all, but over at Twentieth Century-Fox they were looking for a child for *How Green Was My Valley*, which was going to be made. So my mother took me there, and it was just such a fluke. It just happened to be the right moment, that's all.

David: By the way, it just popped into my head. I interviewed Bobby Morse[197] down in Miami Beach yesterday, and he said to be sure and say hello to Roddy.

Roddy: Oh, thank you. Yes, we did a film—*The Loved One*[198]—together.

David: Let's go to *My Friend Flicka*[199] and *Thunderhead, Son of Flicka*.[200] As you know, I am involved in writing a book on show business animals,[201] and I'm intrigued with your work in those two movies.

Roddy: Really! Why?

David: Well, because you were such an accomplished young actor at the time and in viewing those movies you seemed to be an accomplished horseman. Were you really?

Roddy: Oh, well, yes, I was. But I didn't become one until, actually, for *My Friend Flicka*. I was very young, twelve or thirteen, and I loved horses. During the progress of two or three films that involved horses, I was

Young Roddy is getting a little sympathetic advice from ranch hand James Bell about the injured Flicka in this scene from *My Friend Flicka*.

trained to ride English, bareback, Western, and to run a race. I was trained to run a race in *Thunderhead*. I always thought I was wrong for those films, actually, for the two films, because I was still tremendously English.

David: That was a question I wanted to ask you. How did you get rid of your English accent?

Roddy: Well, I didn't. In that film it is very prevalent. I'd only been here, I think, a year and a half. The reason the film worked, historically, is that it was the first major piece about an animal that had been made in about ten years. *My Friend Flicka* and *Lassie Come Home*[202] were made at the same time. In fact, they had to stop *Lassie Come Home* until I finished *My Friend Flicka*. I think that one big reason for their successes was the fact that they were the first for many years about animals.

David: They were very scenic and they were in Technicolor too.

Roddy: Actually, *Lassie Come Home* and, I think, *Thunderhead* were the first monopack films made, the first use of monopack Technicolor, which is the one-strip Technicolor.

David: I didn't realize that.

Roddy: Sequences of *Lassie Come Home* and then in *Thunderhead*. And the lights were excruciatingly hot to work under. The animals used to fall asleep. It was boiling under those lights.

David: Did you shoot *My Friend Flicka* and *Thunderhead, Son of Flicka* in Wyoming where the stories take place?

Roddy: No, in Kanab, Utah, Cedar City, and Bryce Canyon in Bryce National Park, all in that area of Utah. Part of *Thunderhead* was done at a county race track up in Oregon.

Roddy signed this photo as we talked. I had purchased it in a collectibles' shop the afternoon before our conversation in 1978. The scene is from *Thunderhead, Son of Flicka.*

David: I've got an old photo that I picked up today at a collectibles store here in Fort Lauderdale of you in the *Thunderhead* race. I was astounded when I found it because it was not a store that carried many things of that type, and they just happened to have it among a few other photographs. [Roddy cleverly autographed the photo for me.] *Lassie Come Home* was Elizabeth Taylor's first major motion picture—and you've been lifelong friends since then.

Roddy: Yes, we have.

David: And worked in several pictures together.

Roddy: We've made three films together. After *Lassie Come Home* we did one called *The White Cliffs of Dover*,[203] and then years later a film called *Cleopatra*.[204] Those are the three we have done together, but we've known each other, really, since 1942, since *Lassie Come Home*.

David: Does *Lassie Come Home* have a special place in your memory in any way?

Roddy: Yes, it's one of the three films I was emotionally attached to that I made as a child—the other two being *How Green Was My Valley* and *The White Cliffs of Dover*. I was very fond of making them. I was extremely happy making *Lassie Come Home*. I loved the dog; the dog was extraordinary, an absolutely extraordinary animal. It was a very happy movie to make and a very good movie.

David: It certainly was, and I have a very vivid image of sitting in the Rivoli Theatre in Elyria, Ohio, crying my eyes out, my mother and I.

Roddy: It's a lovely film even today.

David: Yes, and I just recently saw the *Lassie with Love* documentary that you partly hosted and that had excerpts from *Lassie Come Home,* and I'm afraid that I got misty eyed all over again. I'm a sucker for an animal story.

Roddy: The actors in it were so good—Dame May Whitty,[205] Nigel Bruce,[206] Edmund Gwenn.[207] It was just a beautifully made film.

David: Did you observe the handling of Lassie by Rudd Weatherwax?[208]

Roddy: His training of the dog must have been phenomenal because the dog was absolutely amazing, stunning, absolutely stunning! He was very good with his animals as far as I can remember and very good in relation to how the animals related to the people with whom they had to work. I only had the highest admiration actually, not only for Weatherwax, but for all the animal trainers that I worked with in lots of films—I mean down to the *Apes* movies where there were animals as well as humans as animals. They're very efficient and extremely, well, elegant about the way they do what they do.

David: I talked with Myrna Loy recently . . .

Roddy: Yes.

David: And she was reminiscing about *The Thin Man* series with Asta the dog, and she said that Asta was a trained dog and they never let any of the actors play with or pet Asta. How about with Lassie; were you allowed to play or romp with Lassie?

Roddy: Yes. In fact, Weatherwax let the dog stay overnight one night at my house before we worked together, which was an extraordinary and very sensible thing to do, and that dog was extremely adaptable. There were a lot of Lassies, of course; I'm talking about the original dog. The dog remembered also, remembered the people; it had a real connection [with me]. It's a little different for Myrna with Asta because it was sort of a different relationship. A dog and a child, when they work together, have to connect, otherwise it simply wouldn't work.

Just a boy and his dog. Lassie would accompany Roddy's character to school each morning and then return when school let out. The scene, of course, is from *Lassie Come Home.*

David: There's that beautiful scene near the end of the movie where you come out of the school house and Lassie, all bedraggled, is under the tree. . .

Roddy: They put ice cream on my face!

David: *[Laugh]* You anticipated my question about how they got the dog to lick your face so lovingly.

Roddy: They did! That's what they did.

David: Any incidents on the Lassie set that come to mind? You were just a little boy at that time.

Roddy: Well, I wasn't that little; I looked smaller than I was. Actually, in 1942 I was going on fourteen—I was born in 1928, so I was fourteen—and I had been working a long time. The film, just the memory of it, is that it was just such an incredibly happy movie to work on; it was just a very special atmosphere and I can't pin that down; it was intangibles. I will always remember it as a particularly happy experience—not glamorous or anything like that—I'm not talking about in a fantasy; it was just a lovely experience.

David: As Roddy McDowall, little boy, did you want to have a dog like Lassie that you could take home with you?

Roddy: No, because there was only one Lassie. In fact, I never wanted a collie after that dog because that dog was so phenomenal. I mean, if they had given me Lassie I'm sure I would have taken it, but the point is the dog was just very special. I don't think I ever felt that way about any of the other animals I worked with. The horses I worked with I liked, but there was never the same connection. I really adored Lassie.

David: One of the directors that I admire—and I'm certainly not alone in saying this—is Orson Welles, and you had the opportunity to work with Orson Welles in *Macbeth*[209] back in 1948. Tell me about it, if you would.

Roddy: It wasn't released for a long time after it was made, I mean three or four years, and the film is much purged.[210] All I really remember about it was that it was fascinating to work with Orson. I was only about eighteen then, eighteen or nineteen, and we did it, first of all, on the stage at the centennial at the University of Utah right before hand [before the filming], and I was very young. I was sort of beginning my adult work.

I was very frightened and extremely tenuous. I was fascinated by him—I still am—because he is so larger than life—no pun intended at all. He is just a very opulent figure, both in appetites and learning. It was a little peculiar in the filming of it because it was done like a musical—it was pre-recorded because they decided to make it in a very short period of time. So it was done working to playbacks.[211] So that . . . It just was an odd experience. [*Chuckle*]

David: And it was done at Republic Pictures, a B movie studio mostly known for Gene Autry and Roy Rogers Westerns. . .

Roddy: He's an original.

David: He certainly is. Do you have any incidents, anecdotes from the set that come to mind? I know you did it in about twenty-eight days.

Roddy: I think it was twenty-one days—maybe it was twenty-eight. Not really, not at the moment that I can conjure up. It was a unique experience all the way around.

David: And it was your first adult role, wasn't it?

Roddy: Well, let's see. At that time I had done *Holiday in Mexico*[212] where I suppose I was sixteen or seventeen years old, but it was the first heavy material that I'd done in my late teens and among the first things that I had done on the stage.

David: Was it your first Shakespeare?

Roddy: Ah, no, as a tiny child I had done some Shakespeare. But, yes, I would say really the first thing.

David: As a trained actor.

Roddy: No, I wasn't trained by then. I didn't really start to train until I grew up and went to New York. Outside of elocution classes when I was very small in England, I was never trained other than just by the experience of doing it, which I suppose is the best training one can have—unless it is misused.

David: You made a series of B movies for Monogram Pictures, and I think you were associate producer.

Roddy: Yes. There were six of them. The only one having any attempt at distinction was a film called *Kidnapped*,[213] the Robert Louis Stevenson one. But they were sort of slapped together, and it was in that cusp area where I was eighteen, nineteen, twenty years old, but the preconceived notion about me was that I was still a child actor, so the material that one was working with was not complicated in any sense.

David: But you managed to be associate producer as well as actor.

Roddy: Well, I very much wanted to be, but primarily what I learned in that situation was what not to do, so that was really what that experience was.

David: And suddenly in 1952, right after this Monogram experience, you left Hollywood and went to New York—and you didn't make another movie that I know of until 1960.

Roddy: Is *Subterraneans*[214] 1960?

David: Yes.

Roddy: Oh, yes, well, it would have been made in 1959. Yes, that's right, the reason being that I went to New York just because there really wasn't any place for me to expand or to attempt to work because I was a pre-conceived notion.

David: Were you having trouble getting out of adolescence as far as your roles were concerned.

Roddy: No, I don't know that I ever have gotten out of adolescence. [Laugh] But the point is that I was a child actor in people's minds, and that was that! And on the other side of the coin, I didn't really know how the hell to use whatever talent I did have. And I was fortunate I left when I did because it was the beginning of all the live television in New York, which I didn't really realize at the time. It is in that arena that I began to work a great deal and to learn and to go and study and, one thing working hand in hand with the other, I had an opportunity to at least find out how to be an actor, what it took to be one.

The reason I didn't make films during that period is that the films that were coming along that I could have done were not as interesting to do as the plays I was involved in at the time, and the films I wanted to make, I couldn't get. And that's why there is such a gap in film work.

David: It seems as if you did a number of shows in New York that were not what you would call commercial projects: *Misalliance*,[215] for example.

Roddy: *Misalliance* was a big hit. *Misalliance* was the first play I did in New York, and it was a big hit. It opened for a two-week run and ran a season. But then, which is always true in the theater and movies too—it's only, wow, a small percentage of the product that one is in that is successful. Plays happen to have the chance of disappearing sooner than movies because the emulsion stays around. In New York I think I did something like twenty plays, but I think only three or four of them were plays that ran.

David: *No Time for Sergeants*[216] is one that everyone remembers, along with *Camelot*[217] and *Compulsion*.[218] You received wonderful reviews for all three of those Broadway shows, so you must have been very pleased.

Roddy: Yes, but then there were a dozen other plays that opened and closed, and one didn't realize that that was going to happen. *[Laugh]*

David: *Planet of the Apes*.[219] Everybody saw *Planet of the Apes* and the sequels, and they were utterly fascinated with the performance you gave and with the makeup you wore. I know you've been asked this a million times, but can you comment on the makeup and the process?

Roddy: Yes, I can, and rather simply, actually. It's not a makeup; it's an appliance, incidentally, it's an appliance piece. It's much more complicated than being makeup, and it's the most phenomenal invention in that area that I've ever encountered. Brilliantly thought out, painful and difficult to deal with, but extremely challenging as an acting assignment to get through all that. It is something that I am very happy I was involved in.

David: Let's say the call was for 9:00 a.m. on the set. What time would you have to start putting the makeup on?

Roddy: Well, the makeup took three and a half hours to get fully ready—and a great deal of patience—both on the behalf of the person being made up and the makeup man doing it.

David: Okay, when you broke for lunch . . .

Roddy's involvement in the *Planet of the Apes* film and television franchise consumed about six years of his acting career.

Roddy: Oh, you didn't, didn't eat. I'd sleep because when you are in something like that for that many hours, it's always beginning to come off from the moment it was put on, so it's easier not to eat except through a straw, liquids, you know. And it was very tiring, *extremely* tiring.

David: There was a TV series[220] attempted.

Roddy: We did thirteen.

David: Why didn't it work? The movies were fantastically successful.

Roddy: There was nothing wrong with the TV series. It was just on opposite *Sanford and Son* and didn't break those ratings and so went off the air. I mean, that's the name of that game! Television is not a positive game; it's a killing game. It's not the quality of the show that is the important thing; it's what other show it is doing in! That's the important thing. There was nothing wrong with the *Apes* television series, and it should never have gone off.

David: No. I saw several episodes and I thought it was well done.

Roddy: It was well done, yeah.

David: Do you have a favorite stage, TV, movie role?

Roddy: I don't have a favorite because it's a very long working life—it's forty-five years—and there's a tremendous amount of product inside those years, a great many things for tiny reasons—I mean obscure things—that were very revealing and interesting to do at that time in my life.

This play that I'm doing now is fascinating for me to do at this time in my life. I'm grateful to be working with the people I'm working with. I'm not being a Pollyanna. It's a very difficult play and it's a very special experience as a performer for me. It's an intriguing exercise.

David: And we're talking about *Otherwise Engaged*.[221]

Roddy: Oh, yes, yes! And the generosity of the actors, it's a wonderful experience. But I don't have *a* favorite.

David: Do you have a favorite medium?

Roddy: No. What is good in whatever medium it is in becomes then a rare and particular experience. What's bad in whatever medium, yeach! They can all be rewarding and they can all be terrifying, each of them.

David: Thank you, Roddy McDowall, very much!

Roddy: Thank you.

Roddy was forty-nine years old when we talked in 1978. He would live for another twenty years and those years would be filled with work in all media. Looking at his filmography from 1978 on, there were twenty-some films in which he appeared or narrated or did voice work. Some of the most memorable include *Evil under the Sun*,[222] *Fright Night*,[223] *Fright Night II*[224], and his last film *A Bug's Life*.[225]

During these same years he appeared in episodes of some of television's most popular series, as varied as *The New Adventures of Wonder Woman, Fantasy Island, Hart to Hart, Hotel, Murder She Wrote, The New Lassie, Remember WENN*, and the list goes on. He was a game show regular for years on *Hollywood Squares*.

In between films and television work Roddy also returned to stage work repeatedly. In 1980 he performed the leading role of Elwood P. Dowd in the popular comedy *Harvey* in San Antonio for forty-four performances and New Orleans for forty-one performances. He starred in a national tour of *Dial M for Murder* for one hundred and fifty performances between September of 1995 and March of 1996. He returned to Broadway in November of 1997 and performed Scrooge in *A Christmas Carol*, which ran until January 4, 1998.

And then there were special events that he was involved with: He and Michael Feinstein hosted "Carnegie Hall Celebrates the Glorious MGM Musicals" on July 15, 16, 1997. He went to Gstaad, Switzerland, to host the Fourth Annual CineMusic Festival, "A Celebration of Julie Andrews" on March 13, 1998. He even provided cruise ship entertainment when he performed *Love Letters* with Mariette Hartley on June 1, 1998, aboard the *Queen Elizabeth II* from South Hampton to New York.

And then there was his photography career. He became known as an accomplished portrait photographer whose photos of Katharine Hepburn, Spencer Tracy, and Mia Farrow appeared in such magazines as *Life* and *Look*. He published several luxury photo books with the title *Double Exposure* with the sequels adding the suffix *Take Two, Take Three*, etc. The books featured portraits of famous individuals with short commentaries of each by other famous people. The beautifully produced volumes proved to be very popular.

Late in his life he served on executive boards of the Screen Actors Guild and the Academy of Motion Picture Arts and Sciences. A lifelong film collector, he worked with the National Film Preservation Board to see that film classics and even run-of-the-mill features be preserved. In August of 1998 he was elected president of the Academy Foundation.

Probably the nicest thing that can be said for Roddy McDowall is the fact that everyone who knew him loved him. He was one of the last links back to the "Golden Age of Hollywood," and he was much loved for his kindness and loyalty. Life-long friend Elizabeth Taylor referred to him as the one friend to whom she confided everything, and who was always understanding. He appears to have made few if any enemies during his lifetime and was beloved by the old timers as well as the newer faces in Hollywood.

Roddy, as most people of his era, was a smoker and began to have serious health problems by 1998 when he had surgery for prostate cancer. In the 1990s he began a long battle with lung cancer while still carrying out his professional activities. But lung cancer is a formidable enemy.

On October 3, 1998, Roddy McDowall died at his home in the Studio City area of Los Angeles. Dennis Osborne, a screenwriter friend who had cared for him during his last few months, said, "It was very peaceful. It was just as he wanted it. It was exactly the way he planned." Later it was announced that his remains were cremated by the Neptune Society.

A few days before his death the Academy of Motion Picture Arts and Sciences named its photo archive after him. Longtime friend Angela Lansbury, deeply moved by Roddy's death, said that he was "one of the most wonderful friends anybody could possibly have." Roddy McDowall was only seventy at the time of his death.

Spanky McFarland

June 24, 1977

"I am Spanky. That's the only role I ever played."

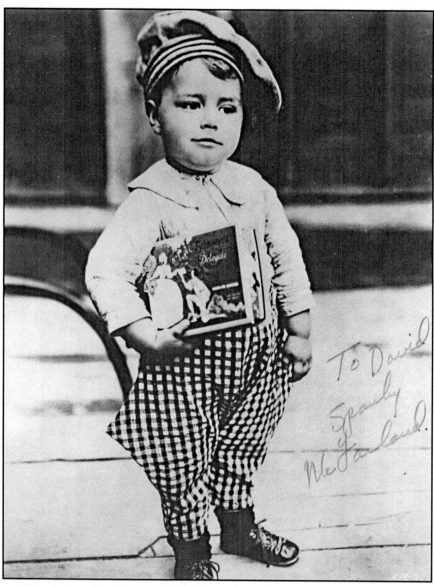

Take a look at this photo and you don't have to wonder why Spanky McFarland
was one of the most successful child stars in Hollywood.

I missed the silent *Our Gang* comedies of the 1920s by the happenstance of not being born yet. And then just about the time I was old enough to go to the movies in the mid-1940s, the *Our Gang* shorts stopped production. By the time the series was sold to television, I had grown up and didn't have much interest in the everyday activities of these little tykes, charming as they might be.

But at some point along the line I must have watched a few of the shorts on television because—like everyone—I knew the names of the major cast members, at least those of the late 1930s and early forties. There was "Alfalfa," Darla, "Buckwheat," "Porky" and "Spanky," among others. Late in the series Bobby Blake came onto the scene as "Mickey," but I never knew him as part of the "gang." I knew him only as "Little Beaver" in the Republic Pictures Red Ryder series of the middle forties.

So, anyway, time flies, the years pass, and I am at the Houstoncon film festival in the summer of 1977, and who should be one of the guest stars but George "Spanky" McFarland of *Our Gang* fame, undoubtedly the most famous of those child actors. I was at the con primarily to talk with several of the other guest stars, George Takei and Jock Mahoney in particular, but most especially I wanted to visit again with Roy Rogers, the King of the Cowboys, whom I had interviewed a few months before for my then forthcoming book *The Singing Cowboys* and who was scheduled to be in Houston for the con.

But Spanky McFarland would be an additional coup for my radio show, and I set about locating him for a conversation. Many child stars can go completely unnoticed as adults, their features changing considerably as they move into adulthood and middle age—which was about the place where Spanky would be. Not so with George McFarland; he was

George is seen here schmoozing with the fans in the dealers' room in Houston.

immediately identifiable as "Spanky" as I encountered him in the hotel hallway while on my way to my room; he was just a grownup version of the chubby, little, round-faced boy he had been.

"Yes," he said, he would be amenable to meeting with me, "tomorrow, but let's meet in my room rather than in the dining room or dealers' room; they're so crowded and we'll keep getting interrupted." "That's okay by me," I said, and we agreed to meet at one o'clock the next day, right after lunch.

During those twenty-four hours before we met again, I had a chance to observe George around the con, interacting with the fans. He seemed to be a man who was comfortable schmoozing with the public, signing autographs, but, at the same time, he seemed a bit distant while answering questions about the films and his co-players from forty years before. I guess what I'm getting at is that there wasn't a great deal of "warmth" about him, he didn't seem to make a definite "connection" with those around him—at least that was the way I saw him, and the next day I felt it in our conversation.

David: George "Spanky" McFarland, I think everyone is delighted that you've been able to attend Houstoncon this year as one of the guest stars. Let me begin by asking a pretty stock question. How did you happen to be cast in the *Our Gang* comedies when you were a little boy?

Spanky: Of course, it goes back a long way to 1931. I was residing in Dallas, Texas, with my family, and I had an aunt who lived in Fort Worth. I was doing some local advertising in Dallas for, of all things, the Dr. Pepper Company, which had just started then, and for a local clothing store, A. Harris & Company, which is now part of Sanger-Harris, which is the biggest department store in Dallas, Texas.[226] I had some local publicity and she [Spanky's aunt] sent copies in to Hal Roach,[227] and they sent for me to make a screen test. I got lucky and stayed for thirteen years.

David: How did you happen to be dubbed with the name "Spanky"?

Spanky: Well, there have been several stories about it, but actually my first director, Bob McGowan, gave me the name "Spanky." And I don't know why; nobody knows. Maybe because I just look spankable, I don't know.

David: *[Laugh]* There was a story about your mother supposedly saying that if you didn't behave, "spanky, spanky."

Spanky: No, no, that's not true.

David: So you were in the *Our Gang* series for thirteen years. When you left the series was it because you'd outgrown it?

Spanky: Primarily. The series had reached an end. Hal Roach had sold the gang to MGM in 1938, and MGM was discontinuing the series—this was in 1944—and they would not renegotiate a long-term contract. In fact, I worked up until the last five or six comedies that were made on a per-comedy basis, as far as a contract was concerned. Then I just didn't make any more.

David: Do you know off hand how many of these shorts you were in?

Spanky: About a hundred and fifty.[228]

David: You did some other films during the *Our Gang* series, didn't you?

Spanky: Well, the gang made a feature film entitled *General Spanky*;[229] this was in 1936, '37, somewhere in there. I made several films during my tenure with the gang,[230] but I only made one feature film after I left the gang, and that was *Woman in the Window*[231] with Eddie G. Robinson—and that was a very small part in that [film].

David: Who in the Our Gang cast were you particularly close to?

Spanky: None of 'em.

David: None of them? *[Laugh]* That seems a little odd given that you had worked with the kids in so many films.

Spanky is seen here with his regular gang from the late 1930s and early forties. Left to right: Spanky, Billy "Buckwheat" Thomas, Eugene "Porky" Lee, Carl "Alfalfa" Switzer, and Darla Hood.

Spanky: I am one of these people they call loners. I'm gregarious and I mix well because I *do* like people. I don't have to have people. I can spend the day right here in this room completely by myself and be very happy. I enjoy what I'm doing here at the con, you know, because it's good for the ego, and I meet a lot of nice people such as yourself. But I'm a loner.

I don't like to get real close to people, and I don't know why. It's not because I'm afraid of losing a friendship. It's just that I will be friendly with people, but if given my druthers, as we say in Texas, I can be just as happy by myself as in a crowd.

David: How did the *Our Gang* kids get along? Did they scrap and squabble?

Spanky: No, we were well monitored by the parents. The state of California furnished a person from the California State Welfare Department, which bears a little different connotation from the word "welfare" today. He was there or she was there to make certain the children were not abused or overworked, to make sure that they attended school three hours a day, whether they shot a picture or not.

The parents were very mother-henish about the kids. There was no horseplay allowed except in some isolated cases. About the only mischief maker was Alfalfa, and there really wasn't too much of that. A lot of the stories that Bobby Blake or Robert Blake tells about stuffing rolls of toilet paper down the commodes at MGM is a bunch of malarkey. I don't know where he got that idea; now, he may have done it, but I'll guarantee it if his daddy had known about it, he wouldn't have been able to sit down for a week. I know I wouldn't have because my father was very strict with me.

David: Working as you were on the *Our Gang* series and getting three hours of classes a day, do you feel that you were able to get a good education?

Spanky: I think so. In fact, I'm most appreciative of the basic elementary education that I received on the set. Mrs. Fern Carter was our teacher for, gosh, from when I started school until I started junior high school in North Hollywood. I think I was extremely well prepared to go to

Spanky is getting some homework help from his pal Pete the pup.

junior high school, having gone to the studio private school for whatever the required amount of time was, six years, I think.

David: Have you found it exasperating over the years to be typed as "Spanky"?

Spanky: No, because I *am* Spanky. That's the only role I ever played.

David: And as an adult have you found that confining, exasperating in any way?

Spanky: Not exasperating; that's the wrong term. I find it gets in the way sometimes with my private business. In my private business life people will find out that I am Spanky. When I go to make a business call, if they know [that I'm Spanky], that will get in the way of the real purpose for my being there.

Not that I mind talking about it, but Spanky doesn't make me any money anymore. George McFarland puts the bread on the table now. Although I don't mind reminiscing about my past, in my business venture it gets in the way sometimes. It takes valuable time away from me and my customer to talk about something that's not going to make either one of us any money.

David: By my question I didn't mean to suggest that there was anything wrong with being Spanky; Spanky is loved around the world.

Spanky: No, no, I understand and I don't deny it. Just like here at the Houstoncon, I'm having a ball, and I would not be here were I not Spanky. While I'm here, I'm "Spanky." There will be people coming to visit me that I know here in Houston that know me as "George." Even though they know I'm "Spanky," I'm still "George" to them because they're business associates of mine.

David: You have children, I know.

Spanky: Oh, yes. I have a son Vern, and he's going to college down at Galveston, just fifty miles from here at Moody College, down at the marine biology school. I have a daughter Betsy who is a junior in high school, and we live up in the Fort Worth area. My wife is named Doris, and we've been married twenty-one years, going on twenty-two.

David: Certainly as your children were growing up, they had to see the *Our Gang* series on television, called *The Little Rascals*[232] on TV, I guess. Did they ever look at that little boy on the series and then look at you and say, "Gee, was that really you, Dad?"

Spanky: No. I'm sure maybe the thought crossed their minds, but we've never really had that kind of a conversation about it. They've never asked me how it was to be in pictures. They grew up with it, you know, and even though I don't use the term "Spanky" anymore, it's hard to ignore it and hard to keep it down.

Of course, with all the memorabilia around my house from the comedies and the conversation that does exist around Spanky and the fact that they have grown up with me and that they've seen the comedies over the period of their lifetime, they ah, it's just kind of—I never really have asked what they thought about it.

They seem to handle it very well. If someone asks them if their father is Spanky McFarland, they say, "Yeah." But they don't go down the street saying, "Hey, guess what? My father is Spanky McFarland." I think that they are proud of the fact that I was Spanky, but I think the family and our relationship with "Spanky" is well in line. We keep them separated pretty well.

David: What's George McFarland doing these days?

Spanky: George McFarland is district manager for Magic Chef, Incorporated, out of Cleveland, Tennessee. For those of you who don't know who Magic Chef is, perish forbid, Magic Chef is one of the oldest cooking range manufacturers in the United States. Of course, now we're into microwave products and refrigerators, anything for the kitchen. I have a territory in Texas, including Fort Worth.

David: Do you ever get the old bug to go back and get in front of the camera again?

Spanky: Absolutely none. I can satisfy what ham ego I've got left in me by doing what you saw me do ten minutes ago.

David: Signing autographs, talking with the fans. . . .

Spanky: Signing autographs, being Spanky McFarland for a short period of time out of my life. It gives me kind of a hiatus from the business world. It lets me be Spanky, who I can't ignore; I will be Spanky until the day I die. But other than that, this nicely does it, and then come Monday morning it's back on my head.

David: Thank you George "Spanky" McFarland.

Spanky: Thank you.

And so George, I guess, was "back on his head" on Monday after our brief conversation. I got back to my main business at the con with Jocko Mahoney, George Takei, Roy Rogers, and others, but I spent some time thinking about George during the rest of my time in Houston.

He didn't seem like a very happy man, and I wondered how much it had to do with coming to the con and having all the fans remind him of his glory days as Spanky that faded so quickly when he was just com-

George was kept busy signing autographs for the fans at Houstoncon.

ing into his teen years—and now here it was so many years later. He had been quoted as saying, "I wouldn't take a million dollars for the experience . . . and I wouldn't take a penny to do it again. As a kid I had everything I wanted, we had a good life but when it was over . . . it was over."

Apparently he didn't want it to be totally over because back in the fifties after he came out of the Air Force, he created and hosted a daily kids TV show which ran from 1955 until 1960 called *Spanky's Clubhouse* on KOTV in Tulsa, Oklahoma. A couple of still photos I've seen from the program show George in a sort of grownup Spanky costume, wearing his trademark cap from the old days. He had a studio audience of kids and played games, told stories, and had comedy skits that served as wraparounds for re-runs of *The Little Rascal* film comedies.

Between 1960 and when I met up with him in Houston in 1977, George apparently had held several jobs prior to the Magic Chef position he had when we talked. Sometime not too long afterwards, though, he moved on to Philco-Ford Television where he rose to the position of sales executive and from which he eventually retired. Late in life he conceded that if he could have lived his life over, he would have skipped the *Our Gang* years, finished his schooling, gone to college, and maybe become the president of a corporation.

But still George couldn't resist when an occasional show business opportunity came along in later years. In the mid-1980s he appeared in a bizarre Texas-made science fiction/Western movie entitled *The Aurora Encounter*,[233] in which he played a governor. In 1993 the opportunity came along to make a guest appearance on the popular NBC sitcom *Cheers*, in which he appeared as himself in the episode entitled "Woody Gets an Election." Also during those later years he helped raise money for charity by playing in a number of pro-am celebrity golf tournaments.

But George was not to live to be an old man. On June 30, 1993, he was rushed to the Baylor Medical Center of Grapevine in Grapevine, Texas, with signs of apparent heart problems. He died less than an hour later at the emergency room. George was only sixty-four years old. The cause of death was later given as a heart attack. He was survived by his wife Doris and their children. It was reported later that his remains were cremated.

In January of 1994, six months after his death, George "Spanky" McFarland received his star on the Hollywood Walk of Fame. The only other *Our Gang* member to be so honored is Jackie Cooper.

Molly Picon

January 24, 1978

*"Wherever I can make people laugh,
that's the job I want to do."*

Molly signed the photo, looked at it, and said, "Did I spell that right?" I assured
her that I loved it that way, and we both had a laugh.

I must admit that I had only a limited knowledge of Molly Picon's work on stage and in the movies when I got a call asking if I would like to talk with her about her career for my radio program. Molly was in Sarasota appearing at the Golden Apple Dinner Theatre, hence the invitation to meet with her. Sure, I was always looking for interesting show business people for the program and, yes, I knew that she had had a distinguished career, especially on stage—only I didn't know much more than that about her. A time was set for our meeting, and that meant that it was time for a bit of research on my part.

I did remember back in the 1960s going to the Hanna Theater in Cleveland, Ohio, to see *Milk and Honey*, the Jerry Herman musical, and Molly Picon was there playing the Jewish lady who sang a song about her beloved "Hymie." I liked the show so much that I even bought the Broadway cast album. I must have seen the show prior to its Broadway opening in 1961 when it was still in tryout towns getting ready for Broadway, unless it was the touring show after it closed in 1963—it gets fuzzy after all these years. Anyway, I saw it and was impressed.

In my research I discovered that Molly was one of those rare performers who loved to tour with a show, and she had done her share of touring over the years, including at age fifteen touring as "Topsy" in *Uncle Tom's Cabin* in the Yiddish theater, performing in English, German or Yiddish, depending on her audience. She toured extensively with *Milk and Honey* after the long Broadway run and more recently she had toured in *Hello, Dolly*.

I learned that Molly's life-long partner and husband Jacob Kalish had died three years earlier in 1975. When I met with Molly, it was almost as if Jacob were still there, because his name came up repeatedly. She always called him "Yonkel," because as she tried to explain years later in her autobiography, "Yonkel is the Yiddish for Jacob and Yiddish is the

MOLLY PICON
IN
HELLO, DOLLY!

Jewish for Jewish—I hope that's clear." Well, clear or not, her love for him was deep and abiding, and I could not help but feel that he must be in the next room waiting for her to finish talking with me.

We were to have our meeting at the home of Robert Turoff, the producer and director of the Golden Apple. I pulled into his drive right on time for our two o'clock meeting armed with my tape recorder and the expectation of an interesting time because my research had revealed that this was one fascinating lady!

Molly greeted me warmly when I arrived at the side door, ushering me into the kitchen. I was immediately struck by what a tiny little thing she was, even with her silvery gray hair piled high atop her head. It was chilly in Sarasota that January day, so she was attired in dark blue slacks and wearing an attractive gray, cardigan sweater with the sleeves pushed up a few inches from her wrists. She belied her age by the way she bustled around getting two tall glasses and pouring us some freshly-brewed iced tea from the pitcher she took from the refrigerator. After the usual amenities we moved to the kitchen counter where we sat opposite each other on stools, sipped our tea, and chatted.

David: Molly, I understand that your career started in Philadelphia many, many years ago, about 1904, something like that, and you have been called for many years now the First Lady of the Yiddish Theater. I'm just a country boy from Ohio; I never got to go to the Yiddish theater. Tell me about it.

Molly: Well, evidently you never got to Cleveland, because the Yiddish theater in my day played all over the states. We were one of the many ethnic theaters in the country. There were French and Russian and Polish and Yugoslavian and even Chinese theater, run by a Jew, a man by the name of Moskovich, *and* the Yiddish theater. Our theater survived after all those other theaters disappeared. We still survived as we still survive in history, because we are a stubborn people.

It was a very live ethnic theater, and we catered to the immigrants because they were the ones who understood the language. So all through the big immigration we had a big audience. Now, after the holocaust and the loss of six million Jews and the cut down in immigration, we were left with the older people who still understood but didn't speak the language any more, because they too, they had been immigrants and they had learned to speak English. They only used the Yiddish when their children were around and they didn't want them to know what they were saying. So the children never learned the language.

Now with the loss of immigration and practically the loss of the language, the theater has finally given up. Last year was the first year in a hundred years that we had no Yiddish theater in New York, and it's a great loss to us. It was a wonderful, vital, vibrant, theater and somehow our actors had no background, they had no education, many of them couldn't even write or read, but they had great talent and they had energy and vitality and a great dedication. The only time they wouldn't go on was if they were dead; that was the only time they wouldn't go on, but otherwise, no matter how ill they were or what tragedies they had in their families, they went on to do the show. We don't have that any more in the American theater.

I regret greatly that I had to convert and come into the American theater because I had no more room to function in the Yiddish theater. Now there's another funny aspect to this. This generation of Jews, the younger people, are very curious about what they have lost. They lost all the ethnic humor, all the things grandma used to say that everybody laughed at, and they don't know what they are. So there are many schools and colleges that have classes in Yiddish now beside the Hebrew, which is the language of Israel. They hope eventually the language will be reborn.

Personally, I don't see how, because I have studied many languages and I find out that if I'm on a language I don't hear, I can never learn it. I can learn to read and understand, but I can't learn to hear the sound because I don't hear the sound.

We are a people who live by miracles. Many years ago we met Ben Gurion in Israel, and we spoke of the miracles of Israel and so forth, and he said, "In Israel if you don't believe in miracles, you are not a realist." So I take his guideline and hope this miracle might happen to the Yiddish language, so we can go back again and have a thriving Yiddish theater.

David: What was the Yiddish theater like compared to, let's say, Broadway theater as it has existed in the United States for the last fifty years.

Molly: Well, I think the Yiddish theater eventually started to imitate Broadway because of the lack of people who understood what we call "pure Yiddish." We had to Anglicize so that very often almost half of our plays were in English *and* in Yiddish. The first act would probably be about immigrants coming from Europe and speaking the language and the second act would be with the children who spoke in English to their parents, so you got the English/Yiddish which I called bastardizing because it was not a pure language anymore.

But we had great actors; we had wonderful actors, and many of them converted and went into the American theater. Paul Muni,[234] of course, is *the* example. I played with Paul when I met my husband [to be] in Boston, and he [Yonkel, Molly's future husband] wrote the first play for me. I was always a hundred pounds or under. And the stars of those days were big, heavy women. I couldn't play one of those ladies so Yonkel—now let me explain to you that Yonkel is the Yiddish for Jacob, and he always used to say that his gentile friends called him Yonkel and all of his Yiddish friends called him Jack, which is natural—Yonkel wrote this play about a little boy for me.

It was a kind of Peter Pan play and I was a thirteen year old boy. Paul Muni was in the cast there in Boston. He was two years older than I, but he played my grandfather, because even then he was doing character roles. At the time his name was Moony Weisenfreund and then he changed it to Paul Muni, and he became one of the great actors in the American theater.

Our theater imitated the Broadway theater. I did only musicals. We started out with chorus girls only sixty and over. When Yonkel took over, he finally got their granddaughters into the chorus and little by little we took on the Broadway color. But we didn't play Broadway shows. In the early Yiddish theater when I played in Philadelphia, we did everything: we did Shakespeare, I did *Uncle Tom's Cabin*; I did "Topsy" in Yiddish. Shall I sing you the song?

David: I'd love to have you do that.

Molly: Topsy says, "Shoo, fly, don't bother me. Shoo, Fly, don't bother me, Shoo fly don't bother me, for I belongs to the company B." And in Yiddish it was, [sings in Yiddish]. Now that only means, "Go away, fly, and don't bother me. If not, I will make cornmeal mush out of you." *[Laugh]* It's a very funny song. And the whole cast played with a Southern accent; I think it must have been funny. I don't remember because I was a child.

David: Had to be, had to be! Maurice Schwartz was a leading Yiddish actor, I believe.

Molly: Well, he and Ben Ami started the literary Yiddish theater, because before that it was lighter, you know. We played Goldfaden, who was our Gilbert and Sullivan. He wrote musical comedies mostly on Biblical characters, and then we played what they called *shund*, a junk

theater to them—just the everyday themes, and this was not litera-
ture. But we had great writers; we had Sholem Aleichem who eventually reached the world with a story that he wrote eighty or ninety
years ago, but it was so universal that now it is accepted all over the
world, *Fiddler on the Roof*. So Schwartz and Ami started the literary
theater and they did a beautiful job of it, wonderful performances,
and they also had a group of great actors; Muni was in that group,
too, and Bertha Kalish, who was a great actress and eventually came
to the American theater, and Schwartz, himself, who did some plays
on Broadway.

David: I have a very, very close friend here in Sarasota who played in
Merchant of Venice to Maurice Schwartz's Shylock, which was done, I
believe, on Broadway as part of a vaudeville show. It was a condensed
version as part of a vaudeville show years and years ago.

Molly: Yes. Well, when I played vaudeville when I started, they used to
do sketches, and Nazimova,[235] the great Russian actress, did a sketch
on one of the shows that I was in and Sarah Bernhardt[236] was in a
sketch. I wasn't with her, but Belle Baker[237] was with her. She was a
great vaudeville act. Belle Baker and Fanny Brice,[238] they were all in
vaudeville, and in the vaudeville of those days they used to have one
act that did a little sketch—we called them a "sketch" in those days.

David: Did Fanny Brice ever do any Yiddish theater?

Molly: No, but she did Yiddish characters and she was one of the funniest ladies in the business.

David: I'm afraid that I only knew Fanny Brice as . . . .

Molly: Baby Snooks.

David: And she was absolutely delightful as Baby Snooks on radio. I would
give anything if I could have known her as she was in the theater.

Molly: She was one of the great comediennes of our day, yes.

David: You and your late husband Jacob Kalich did a "Mr. and Mrs." radio program for some twenty years.

Molly: Well, we did five shows a week for Maxwell House Coffee and Jello. Yonkel actually was the first one to invent that "Jello, everybody" hello. Then Jack Benny used it. But every year we did a different format. One year was my story, you know. Then another year we dramatized stories that people sent in. And then we did all the [Yiddish] plays, little condensed versions of the plays.

I must tell you one funny story. We used to broadcast from the Carnegie Chambers, which is the little hall above Carnegie Hall. We sent out tickets to anybody that wanted them, and an old lady came in one evening and she showed the ticket to the usher and he pointed upstairs. She looked at him as if he was crazy. She wasn't going to walk upstairs, and she sat downstairs in the orchestra [of Carnegie Hall]. And Arthur Toscanini was conducting a Brahms symphony and it went on and on and on. Finally she called the usher over and said, "Such a long overture; when does Molly Picon come on?" *[Both laugh]* But it was a very good program and it lasted nineteen or twenty years, and then we kind of got weary of it.

David: And this was during the thirties and forties?

Molly: Yes.

David: And it wasn't anything like the Dorothy and Dick[239] radio program. You didn't do just a conversation—talking back and forth at the breakfast table—on your program.

Molly: No, no. I did a lot of songs, and I used to translate from the French and the German and the English into Yiddish and do the whole Yiddish repertoire of music. I would do three songs a show and then we would do our little skits between.

David: Now, let me make sure I have this correctly. Was this done in Yiddish or in English?

Molly: No, it was done in Yiddish.

David: It was all in Yiddish!

Molly: Yes, yes. We had a station, WEVD, that did just Yiddish programs, and we don't have that any more.

David: No, unfortunately. Let's move on, if we may, to *Come Blow Your Horn*,[240] a movie back about 1963 with Frank Sinatra. You played Frank Sinatra's mother in this wonderful Neil Simon comedy, and Lee J. Cobb played your husband. Frank Sinatra has been an idol for me all my years, so I've got to ask what it was like to play Frank Sinatra's mother and work on the set every day with him during the production of that movie.

Molly: When he comes on the set, he's just another actor; he's not Frank Sinatra. But he's one of the most professional professionals that I've ever worked with. He is the first one in, he knows his lines perfectly, he knows exactly what he wants to do, and he works quickly. And if you are professional as he is, he'll give you the sky, because he likes to get out. He has other interests besides making a picture.

I was there for ten weeks with him, and I had ten days in one spot of the film when I didn't have to work. He said to me and Yonkel, who was with me, "Have you ever been to Las Vegas?" We said no. And he said, "I'll send you." So he sent us in his plane, just Yonkel and me in this tremendous plane to Las Vegas to the Sands Hotel.

We went all over and saw every play and every actor and all over the tabs were picked up. We did not pay a penny. So, finally, when we had to go back, Yonkel said, "Look, Molly, we should gamble at least because this is his hotel. We should show him our appreciation." But we hadn't taken any money along, so I said, "Maybe he left some credit for us, as they do."

So I went over to the cashier and said, "Did Frank leave any credit for us?" She said, "Yes." I said, "How much? She said, "Twenty thousand dollars." Yonkel said, "Ho, Ho, he wants your salary back!" Well, we played and we lost two hundred dollars, and I have the feeling they'll never ask us back again to the Sands Hotel. *[Both laugh]*

David: *Milk and Honey*, Broadway musical, 1961. I believe it was your first Broadway musical, and it had a cast that included Robert Weede,[241] Mimi Benzell,[242] and I saw you in that show and just loved

In a change from Molly's usual casting, this time she was an *Italian* mother, married to Lee J. Cobb with sons Frank Sinatra and Tony Bill in Neil Simon's *Come Blow Your Horn.*

it, thought it was a wonderful, wonderful performance all around. You sang a couple of songs in that show.

Molly: Well, I sang "Hymn to Hymie," which was a show stopper, and "Chin Up, Ladies," which was another show stopper. With "Chin Up, Ladies" we had a rather funny experience in New Haven where we tried out [prior to going to Broadway]. They wrote it after we opened, feeling that I could handle another number, and so I needed another costume and other shoes.

They fixed up a costume for me but we didn't get the shoes, so I went to a shoe store and said, "Look, I need these shoes and you've got to rubberize them so I don't slip, and I need them for tonight." He said, "No, I can't do it." I said, "You've got to do it." He said, "If you give me two tickets." I said, "I'll give you two tickets." And so I got the shoes, and he came to see the show that night.

I stopped the show with "Chin Up, Ladies." After the show he came backstage and said, "See, you stopped the show with my shoes." *[Both laugh]* Really, it's such a reaction. People always see everything in their own image; anything that relates to them, that's the big event of the night. So his shoes were the hit of the show that night.

David: Right! As a theater director I discovered that the costumer, for instance, only noticed whether the costumes looked right on the performers during the production. She didn't care if they said their lines right or moved as they were supposed to, but if there was one tiny bit of costume out of place, that she noticed immediately.

Molly: Well, that's true of every phase of show business.

David: How did you happen to appear in three episodes of Car *54, Where Are You?* That seems totally alien to all the rest of your show business experience.

Molly: I don't know why they asked for me. They just engaged me, and we had a lovely, lovely relationship. The three that I did were very good.

David: Did you play the same role in each?

Molly: The same role, yes. It was about a lady in an apartment house that the government wanted to take down. She had a lease, and they couldn't get her out of it because her dog used to go away and come back three months later. She was waiting for that dog to get back, and she wouldn't get out of the apartment. They tried all kinds of things to get her out. It was very funny. The dog came back eventually, and they got her out.

I have been very flexible as a performer. From my childhood on I played in the Yiddish theater one night and then in the American theater the next night. In Philadelphia I did *Broadway Jones*, which is a George M. Cohan[243] comedy with Blanche Yurka,[244] who is a classical actress.

David: She appeared with John Barrymore in *Hamlet.*

Molly: Yes, *Hamlet*, and she did *Medea*. She did all [the classics], and she also did *Broadway Jones* in a repertory theater, every week they had another play. And I played in the German *Turngemeinde* because Yiddish and German are close enough so that I could sound German enough for them. I also did amateur nights in Philadelphia, where they had the hook and all of that business. And vaudeville, the kind of vaudeville that was—what did they call it then; they didn't call it vaudeville. It was a two-reel picture and one act. Nickelodeon is what they called it. You paid a nickel [to get in].

So I've done all these things all through my life, sort of jumped from one medium to another and it made me flexible. I can sing in a revolving door; I'm not boasting; I'm just telling you that my experience has given me the security to work in any medium. I've played Madison Square Garden; I've played in the Sarasota theater to two hundred and fifty or sixty people. That makes no difference to me. I don't see audiences; I don't see an arena, I just see what I'm doing and the actors I'm working with.

David: In the *Fiddler on the Roof*[45] movie, you played Yente the matchmaker. Vincent Canby, *The New York Times* critic, said, "The single most touching performance was that of Molly Picon—outrageously authentic."

Molly: A Yenta is a woman who is a busybody. She mixes into everybody's affairs. In the story she arranges the marriages. She gets the bride and groom together, and the whole little town is scared to death of her, the girls especially—"She'll get her an ugly old man, and once she gives her approval, that's it!"

We had a very funny experience with that. One of the critics—I'm not going to mention her name; the lady writes in a magazine—was very angry with me because I didn't play the part as it was portrayed in New York. In the play she was a bright, red-haired woman and she'd say, "Oh, have I got a bridegroom for you, this that and the other." Our director Norman Jewison[246] said to the woman who played opposite me, that played Golda, "I want to tape the two of you together so I get the quality of your voices." When the playback came we sounded very much alike.

He said, "Molly, I'm in trouble. If I'm focusing on you, they'll think you're talking when she's talking. If I focus on her, they'll think she's talking when you're talking. What can I do about it?" I said,

The butcher, Lazar Wolf (Paul Mann), and the Matchmaker, Yente (Molly Picon)
walk through the streets of their tiny Russian village to attend a wedding in
Fiddler on the Roof.

"Why can't she be another [type of] character?" He said, "Well, I always imagined that she'd be a little old lady with a cane." I said, "I know what you mean." I had played such a character in the Yiddish theater called the "Baba Yachna." "Yachna" is another form of Yente. I said, "You mean a lady who would say, [doing a character voice] 'Oy, Goldy, have I got a thing for you, you'll never see such a bargain in all your life.'" And I talked that way. He said, "That's what I want!"

So he was the one who gave me permission to do the part that way, but this lady [critic] said, "How did she dare do this? Why did Jewison let her get away with it?" It was his direction, you see. Anyway, it was a very good part for me, and I enjoyed doing it.

David: It must have been quite an experience filming that movie.

Molly: It was filmed in Yugoslavia. Actually, they tried to get Russia to allow the filming; they wouldn't accept it. Poland wouldn't accept it, and the next country was Yugoslavia, which has a countryside like

Russia and Poland. Finally they let it in because we were going to bring about eight million dollars with us. Tito was no fool!

We were billeted in Zagreb, which is a big city. We filmed in a little village which was about an hour's ride from where we were billeted. Every morning we were up at six o'clock all through the cold winter and taken in the car to Lechinik. Lechinik is just a country village and they had the little huts, little houses where all the people lived. The plumbing was all outdoors, the outdoor johns and the water and all.

But they did have television and television antennas. Of course, you couldn't have that as background for a Russian picture back in the... God knows when. *[Laugh]* So they had to take them off. And that was the only thing the peasants regretted, because their favorite television show was *Peyton Place*, which is rather odd for a little village called Lechinik. Well, anyhow, they had to take the television antennas down.

The roads were all mud roads. They had to macadamize them because they couldn't get the heavy equipment in that came from London and New York, the cameras and all the sets and things. Then they had to put mud on top of the macadam so that the audience wouldn't see it; that was another expense.

They also brought along what we call in our language "honey wagons"; actually, these are mechanized toilets, because they had no toilets there. They placed them in strategic places where we could see them, his and hers. So that was fine. But at night, when we had the wedding scene which was filmed at night, we couldn't find them.

They had engaged all the peasant people there to be extras, you know, just to stand around in the background. So I asked one of these little old ladies through an interpreter if she had a toilet. She said, "Yes." I said, "Where is it?" She pointed across the way, and I went across to her house, and there it was outdoors. It was a little outhouse. So I went in and closed the door and I felt a draft on my back. I looked around, and there was no back! *[Both laugh]* So I came back to her and I said, "Look, lady, there is no back there!" And she said to me, "Who knows you from the back, lady." *[Both laugh]*

Of course, the whole experience of filming with these people, they were so excited and everybody was being an actor and actress, and there was one scene in a synagogue where they were all praying—and, of course, it's a Jewish film. There was this little old Yugoslavian man who was supposed to be scared to death; he had nothing to say, but he had to shake up and down, up and down. So Yonkel, who was also in the film, said "It's all right. You're fine, you're fine." And this little old man *crossed* himself! *[Both laugh]* Little things like that happened, and the whole experience was really wonderful. We had a great time.

And another funny thing about the show: Now this was written by Sholem Aleichem, which means "peace be with you," and it's a pseudonym; it's not his name. He wrote it seventy or eighty years ago about his family in a little town in Russia. This story turns out to be such a universal story that it has been played in the theater in every country—in Turkey, in France, in England, and even in Japan. In every country they play it in their own image because the problems are universal, not Yiddish. It's the break of tradition and the family life that's broken up and the rebellion against the government. All these things are going on today as they went on eighty years ago.

The writer Jule Styne[247] went to see the opening of a production in Japan, because he was interested [in how it would be performed]—he thought it would be a kabuki play—and it was done, more or less, in kabuki style. The producer came out after the show and said to him, "I don't know how you can do this play in New York; it's a Japanese story!" *[Both laugh]* which just shows you the universality of the story itself.

David: *Fiddler on the Roof* is the only show that I ever stood through on Broadway. There were no tickets available; there was standing room only, so my wife and I stood throughout the entire show and loved every minute of it!

Molly: I want to show you how theater people don't know anything about theater. We were there opening night. We knew everybody: Zero [Mostel[248]] and [Boris] Aronson[249] who did the wonderful sets, and all the others. We were just uplifted; it was just *so* beautiful. We came out after the show and said, "For New York it's a great play; outside New York, nothing!" *[Both laugh]* Which it didn't turn out to be, as you see!

David: It turned out to be a great show in all ways. *For Pete's Sake* sounds like an exclamation, but it's also the title of a 1974 film that you did with Barbra Streisand. In the film you played a Brooklyn madam who congratulates Barbra at one point for coming to realize that "sex, after all, is a business, not a pleasure."[250] *[Both laugh]*

Molly: That's putting it nicely. Well, there was a little bit of controversy between me and Yonkel about accepting the part. I said, "Look, I don't want to be typed as just one kind of Yiddish mama. Let me do this; let me see if I can do this." And it turned out very nicely.

The only fault that I found with it was that they changed the end of the film because Barbra didn't have enough to do in the last scene, and she protects herself—which I don't blame her for. But in that [cut] scene I told why I became a madam. She had a son and that son was a genius, and she had to subsidize the boy; she had to pay for his college studies and to pay for the magazine he wanted to publish, and all that. This was the only way she could do it. So there was some reason for her being a madam.

When they took that out, they took out some of the sympathy the character might have had, but I had the comedy and that was enough. And I rather enjoyed it. Then they asked me to do another film—one of those airplane things—and I was to do a drunk in it, a lady drunk. I think Myrna Loy did it afterwards.[251] But Yonkel said, "No, Molly, I can't allow that. A madam and a drunk in one season; your whole image will be destroyed!" [*Both laugh*] So I didn't do the second one.

I did another airport-themed film: *Murder on Flight 502.*[252] That was rather good, too. It was made just for television. I was just a lady with a man who was not well [Walter Pidgeon]; I was going to take care of him. And in the conclusion I say, "I'll go with you." And he says to me, "Do you think it befitting that we take one room together; you know we're not married." I said, "So, they'll say I'm a swinger!" Then I said to the director, "You know, I don't think "befitting" is a word this man would use; I would say, "Do you think it "kosher" for us to. . . ." and he did; he used the word.

David: You are here in Sarasota at the Golden Apple Dinner Theater starring in *The Second Time Around*,[253] and I understand that you're leaving shortly to go down to Miami Beach to the Golden Apple at the Deauville.

Molly: I'm doing the same play [there] at the Golden Apple for six weeks, but I found out today from Robert Turoff, who is director and producer—one of the most legitimate directors in regional theater, let me tell you; he puts on beautiful performances—He just told me that he's bringing us back here for four more weeks after the Deauville because they are all sold out here and there is such a demand. He says the people are very militant about it: "What do you mean you have no tickets?" And so he's bringing us back.

David: Very good! Tell me a little bit about the play, if you will.

Molly: Well, the play is simply about a problem that many of our older citizens face in the country. It's a man of sixty-five and a lady of sixty-four who want to live together without marrying because she will have to lose her social security if they marry, and they can't get along on just what he has. This is the theme of the play.

So many people in the audience recognize their own lives and identify with us. In the play they also have her son and his wife and his daughter and her husband who have their own marital problems. He also has the grandson who is so shocked when he hears that the old people are going to live together that he says at the end, "Look, grandpa, shacking up is *our* thing. If you do it, what's left for us?" So you have the three generations and the problems that are very prevalent today.

David: Was this role written for you?

Molly: I think so. I think Henry Denker in writing the play thought of me. It's a charming part, and I enjoy doing it. And the people come backstage and they're very enthusiastic. One lady came backstage and she said, "You know, Molly, this play is homemade," which means that she understood every word! [Laugh] And they are so kind, and they're so thankful—as if I am doing them a personal favor.

David: Well, you are, you are.

Molly: I have written a book, and I'm going to call it The Sound of Laughter.[254] And I'm going to tell you why. If you want to wind up this interview with this, I'd be very pleased. Simon and Shuster were on the phone this morning and they gave me the leave for another four weeks to finish the play, and then we shall finish the book.

Yonkel and I, after the holocaust, we went to the displaced persons camps and we entertained all over Europe for six months, giving free

concerts wherever there were people left, wherever there were survivors. When I played in Warsaw in 1921, 2, and 3, there were one million Jews there. When I played there now, there were five thousand.

This is the story: In one of the performances in a bombed out little theater somewhere, a lady came with a child we thought was an infant but must have been two or three years old, but an emaciated little thing, and she started to cry, the baby. Yonkel went over to her and said, "Why did you bring a baby to a concert?" And she said, "My child has never heard the sound of laughter, and I don't want her to grow up without hearing people laugh."

And this has been my goal from then on: Wherever I can make people laugh, that's the job I want to do.

David: And you've succeed admirably.

Molly: Thank you.

David: Thank *you*, Molly Picon.

Molly was eighty years old at the time of our conversation, but you would never have known it. She could have played early sixties on stage, and, in fact, her career on stage, television, and the movies was a long way from being over. When she completed her run in *The Second Time Around*, she created and toured with a one-woman show entitled *Hello, Molly*, which she performed on and off for the next several years.

In 1979 she and her widowed sister, Helen Silverblatt, moved near Lincoln Center in New York and vowed that they would only speak Yiddish to each other for the rest of their lives. In the summer of 1980 she received the Creative Achievement Award of the Performing Arts Unit of B'nai B'rith, and her autobiography was published by Simon and Schuster. Around that same time she was filming *The Cannonball Run*[255] (of all things) with Burt Reynolds and Farrah Fawcett, playing an elderly Jewish lady named "Mrs. Goldfarb." Three years later she would film the sequel, *Cannonball Run II*,[256] playing the same role—again with Reynolds but now including her old pal Frank Sinatra.

And the lifetime achievement awards continued to come her way: In 1981 she was elected to the Broadway Hall of Fame. In 1985 the Congress of Jewish Culture awarded her a "Goldie," named after the "father" of the

Yiddish theater, Abraham Goldfaden. She accepted the award wearing a boy's tuxedo in homage to the many years in which she had dressed in little boy's clothes on stage.

During these same years she continued to make appearances on many television shows of the era. She played a character called "Mother Mishkin" on a *Vegas$* episode in 1978, joined *Trapper John, M.D.* for a 1980 episode entitled "If You Can't Stand the Heat," and was "Grandma Mona" on a couple of episodes of *The Facts of Life* in the early 1980s.

Certainly Molly's most touching television performance was a half-hour drama entitled *Grandma Didn't Wave Back* on NBC in November of 1982, dealing with old age, senility, and Alzheimer's disease. John J. O'Connor, writing in *The New York Times*, stated that there was "one big reason for watching the little film about an eleven-year-old girl and her reactions to the fact that her treasured grandmother is sliding into senility . . . . The extra and special ingredient is Molly Picon in the role of the grandmother." O'Connor went on to write, "There is nothing overwhelming here, but Miss Picon makes this short film something special."

And, sadly, the role in *Grandma Didn't Wave Back* turned out to be prophetic too. As early as 1979 Molly began to experience the effects of a mild case of Bell's palsy. By the late eighties it had evolved into Alzheimer's disease, and she was unable to perform any more. She had been called, "The girl who gets older every year and younger every day," but now the "older" took precedence over the "younger" and her great vitality was sapped by the dread disease. Molly died on April 5, 1992, at the age of ninety-two. She was buried in the Yiddish section of the Mount Hebron Cemetery.

Fifteen years after Molly's death the New York Public Library for the Performing Arts had an exhibition of more than two hundred items of theater memorabilia from Molly's collection. The exhibition was entitled *Molly Picon: Yiddish Star, American Star* and ran from June 26 through September 22, 2007.

During the years she performed her one-woman show she thanked her audience by saying, "How can I tell all the people who have laughed and cried with me through seventy-five years in the theater, all over the world, when I was up and when I was down, and especially now that I am on my own, how can I tell you how much your love for me has gladdened my heart through a wonderful life?"

How do we say, "Thank you" to you, Molly?

Vincent Price

March 9, 1978

"A man who limits his interests limits his life."

This composite photo of Vincent Price was taken in the lobby of the Hyatt House during the time of our conversation.

I knew I wasn't going to get much time alone with Vincent Price when our meeting was set up. He was in town with his one-man show about Oscar Wilde, *Diversions and Delights*, which was only playing a long weekend of performances at Sarasota's Van Wezel Performing Arts Hall. My PR contact at the theater cautioned me that following my brief conversation with Mr. Price there would be a rush of print, radio, and TV people descending on the Hyatt House, where he was residing, to also talk with him. "So try to keep it short!"

I was scrambling to get to the Hyatt even earlier than the scheduled 1:30 p.m. meeting time in the lobby. The snow birds—what Sarasotans call winter tourists—were still out in force on the highway this March day as I wound my way from my home to the Hyatt. I thought maybe if I got there a little early, I might get lucky and have Mr. Price come down from his suite a bit early. I got even luckier.

Vincent Price was already seated in the luxuriously-appointed lobby, dapperly dressed in a navy blue suit, jaunty white handkerchief in his breast pocket, his powder blue shirt with a variegated rust tie setting off the ensemble; he was alone in the huge lobby, smoking a cigarette and appearing care free.

If you didn't already know it, his appearance told you that here was a class act! He exuded a sense of sophistication, urbanity, and maybe more than a touch of world weariness, for he had seen it all in his long career—the successes and the flops that any performer experiences when he puts himself out there in the business of show for as long as Vincent Price had. But here he was by his very appearance silently exclaiming that all was right in his world.

I introduced myself; he greeted me warmly in the way that performers do who meet perfect strangers on a regular basis and proceed to tell them their life stories. If there was any wariness there, his manner belied it. He seemed genuinely pleased to meet yet another journalist in another city and to talk about his long career and the show in which he was currently appearing—but I hoped to throw him a surprise or two with the subject matter I had selected for our conversation.

David: I'd like to talk for a few minutes about several things that you did some years back. I trust that a happy, long-ago memory for you is the radio series you did called *The Saint.*[257]

Vincent: *The Saint*, oh, my Lord, yes! I certainly do remember it; it was four years of my life doing *The Saint.* I loved it; I thought it was an absolutely wonderful program.

David: It was during the late 1940s and early fifties when you were doing that program. It appears that they tailored the character a little to you; at least it seems so because you have interests in art and gourmet food. . . .

Vincent: Leslie Charteris,[258] you know, is a very famous gourmet cook, and so an awful lot of Leslie Charteris is in there too. Actually, Leslie always thought of himself as the Saint, and he really wanted to play it desperately on the radio, but they wouldn't let him. *[Laugh]* He was always such a pain in the neck that they kept him out of the studios. I finally met him a few years later after I had finished *The Saint.* An awful lot of what Leslie Charteris got into the books is actually part of my life too, as you've mentioned. I think that was one of the reasons I was cast as the Saint.

David: Yes. It seems like perfect type casting.

Vincent: Yes, it was absolutely perfect.

David: Going back to the time when radio was in its peak years, you worked just about every radio drama series there was. You've worked on stage and motion pictures, television, and radio. Did you find that you had to shift gears, let's say, in radio as compared to motion picture work?

Vincent: No, I found radio probably the greatest training ground for an actor that there is, and many actors in the business have come out of radio because in radio you had to do everything. You as the actor created the sets, the costumes, the atmosphere—and the audience had to do a lot of work too, which was very good for them.

I don't think television gives the audience much to do. Those [radio] shows, like one I did called "Three Skeleton Key,"[259] which was about a group of men trapped in a lighthouse with rats invading it, won every award that year.

David: Yes, I have that program on tape, and as a radio show, being a theater of the mind, required much of the audience—mentally visualizing the lighthouse, the rats gnawing to get inside, the fear of the trapped men.

Vincent: It was absolutely wonderful, and it still holds up today. And now there are hundreds of kids who collect old radio shows, all over the country. Are you one of them?

David: I'm not a kid, but I'm one of them.

Vincent: Those old programs are wonderful, they really are! I just got a copy of one that somebody sent me the other day, a tape that they took off of the record of Bette Davis and Herbert Marshall and myself in *The Letter*,[260] the Somerset Maugham thing. My God, it's *good!* It really holds up.

David: Was that done on *Lux* . . .

Vincent: Yes, *Lux Radio Theatre*.[261] Yeah.

David: That was such a great radio series.

Vincent: I did *Song of Bernadette*[262] on there, all kinds of shows.

David: You were under contract to Twentieth Century-Fox during most of the 1940s and made so many movies that show up on television now.

Based on a Maxwell Anderson story, *The Eve of St. Mark* dealt with the struggles of young soldiers going off to war. William Eythe and Vincent Price are pictured here.

Vincent: Oh, yes, and some really good ones.

David: Yes. *Laura*,[263] *Dragonwyck*[264] and *Leave Her to Heaven*.[265]

Vincent: *Keys of the Kingdom*.[266] Yes, they were wonderful movies, they really were.

David: Do you have any particular one of those movies that is an especially fond remembrance for you?

Vincent: Yes, I think there was one from that time that is not on television very much because it was about draftees in World War II, and it was called *The Eve of St. Mark*.[267] It was a marvelous picture and received great critical acclaim at the time. Unfortunately, it is a little dated because we've had several little contretemps since then. I think it was almost the best part I ever had in movies. It was a marvelous part.

David: Back about 1960 you began a series of pictures for producer/ director Roger Corman for American-International Pictures, and many of them were loosely based on Edgar Allen Poe stories, such as *The Raven*,[268] *House of Usher*,[269] and *Tales of Terror*.[270]

Vincent: *[Laughing] Loosely* based on Edgar Allan Poe, yes.

David: During most of the sixties you worked in this series of films. They were fun films, they were campy. Some of them, like *The Bat*,[271] were played straight, however.

Vincent: Yeah, some of them.

David: During the forties and fifties you established such a reputation as a distinguished actor at Twentieth Century-Fox and elsewhere. I just wondered how you felt working in campy horror films.

Vincent: I survived! I survived! *[Laughing]*

Vincent Price starred in the horror film *The Bat*.

David: Did you ever say, "What in the world am I doing in this?"

Vincent: No, I didn't. I loved them, and they have proven very popular.
. .

David: Yes! I don't mean to denigrate them.

Vincent: No, I know, and they still play all of the time on television. No, I think the thing that happened—I was trying to figure it out—was that Basil Rathbone and myself and Boris [Karloff] and all of us were brought out to Hollywood right after the beginnings of talking pictures because many of the silent picture stars couldn't talk or couldn't be recorded. We all had our heyday at that time, and then came along a different group of actors, like Marlon Brando, who you couldn't understand, and Jimmy Dean, and a few others like those.

I remember a very famous director saying at that time, "I would never knowingly hire an actor with a good voice." And I said, "Oh, don't give me that crap! You've never had an actor in any of your

Boris Karloff, Peter Lorre, and Vincent Price in a scene from the popular
1962 horror film entitled *Tales of Terror*.

pictures that didn't have a good voice." But it all changed though in the 1950s and became Robert De Niro and all that sort of thing. So actors like myself and Basil were relegated to the costume pictures and to the thrillers, the horror pictures—whatever you want to call them—and they did help us to survive a very bad time.

David: And they made a pile of money!

Vincent: Yes, they made a pile of money!

David: You have written a book: *I Know What I Like. . .*

Vincent: Yeah, *I Like What I Know.*[272] *[Laugh]*

David: Did I say it backwards? I tried so hard not to say it backwards. *[Laugh]*

Vincent: *[Laughing]* I know, but everybody does.

David: When you were just a little tyke, you displayed this interest in the artwork of famous artists. To what do you attribute this early interest?

Vincent: Well, I went to this progressive school which was something new, and art was sort of the concentration—art and drama and theater and expressing yourself. It didn't help you much to get into college; I had tutoring after that. In St Louis, where I'm from, we had a marvelous museum and the museum worked a great deal with this school I went to, and I think that was really my inspiration—working through the museum. I am probably the biggest museum-goer that ever lived. I go to every museum as much as I can possibly go.

David: I believe you've said that of all the forms of entertainment in which you've been involved, television is not really a favorite. Is that right?

Vincent: No, I think television is a wonderful entertainment medium. I wouldn't play it down for a minute, but for the actor working in it, it is very unsatisfactory. It's done too quickly. I mean, the really good shows take six days or eight days, and the movies for television only take a little more time. No, I think the fact that they are done so quickly means that they [the actors] aren't really prepared as well as maybe they could be.

Of course, there are some of them that achieve it. I think, for instance, among the comedy shows *The Jeffersons* and *The Mary Tyler Moore Show* are absolutely marvelous. Each week it is like a little play on a certain area of comedy. But for the most part I don't really think they come off as well as the theater or the movies.

And now I'm back in the theater again doing a play about Oscar Wilde, which I think is probably the best thing I've ever done in my life.

David: Yes, I wanted to ask you about *Diversions and Delights*.[273] I've been told that you are taking the show to New York after you leave Sarasota.

Vincent: Yes, I open in Baltimore for three weeks and then I go into New York. I've already played Boston and Washington and San Francisco and Chicago.

David: And the word that I've read in the papers is that it is just great!

Vincent: It has gotten marvelous critical acclaim; it's a wonderful play.

David: Tell me a little bit about it. I know it's a one-man show.

Vincent: It's a one-man show, but the thing that's good about it is that it's about a man who probably had the greatest sense of humor in the world and was one of the greatest conversationalists. So when you speak Oscar Wilde, you are speaking the English language as it should be.

David: It's quite a feat of makeup too. Isn't it?

Vincent: Not really. I wear a wig and . . .

David: I've seen a photo of you in the part, and it seemed as if it required quite a bit of makeup.

Vincent: No, actually, in a funny way, I look a little bit like Oscar Wilde, but instead of hiding things like a double chin, I let it all hang out. *[Laugh]* It just works! This takes place at the end of Wilde's life when he was wearing hand-me-down clothes but still [presented himself] with a kind of elegance.

It's very touching and a very funny play with some of the most brilliant comments on life and morality, humor, his tour of America, women and men, politicians, and authors—it's got a little bit of everything in it.

David: I am looking forward to seeing it this evening. Thank you very much, Vincent Price.

Vincent: Thank you. Loved it!

Vincent's performances of *Diversions and Delights* were sellout or close to sell out at Sarasota's Van Wezel Performing Arts Hall. After the following three weeks in Baltimore, he took the show to New York where to everyone's amazement the show was not successful. "That's show business," as they say. In the summer of 1979, he had the experience of performing his Oscar Wilde show at the Tabor Opera House in Leadville, Colorado, on the very same stage where Wilde had appeared some ninety-six years before during an American tour.

At the time of our conversation Vincent was sixty-seven years old and had pretty much left motion pictures—or they had pretty much left him. The hugely popular cycle of Gothic horror films had all but played out by the late1970s, but Vincent was to make several more bottom-of-the-barrel films of this type in the early 1980s, usually costarring with other actors of the genre—John Carradine, Christopher Lee, Peter Cushing, Donald Pleasance—or nobodies.

There were a few bright spots during these later years of his career. In 1982 he was asked by Michael Jackson to provide a "rap" voiceover for the title track of Michael's *Thriller* album. Vincent said of the experience, "I didn't think anything would happen with it. Then it came out and sold forty million copies! I didn't do it for the money, because I didn't have a percentage of it. It was just fun to do. You know, to be identified with the most popular record ever made is not just chopped liver! It has really done me a lot of good, because it has given me a new audience."

In the same year of 1982, Vincent agreed to narrate in rhyme a short animated film (approximately six minutes long) for a then-unknown, fledgling director named Tim Burton. The film was entitled *Vincent*[274] and concerned a young boy named Vincent Malloy who dreams of being just like Vincent Price and drifts off into macabre daydreams much to the annoyance of his mother. Vincent delighted in saying, "Tim Burton's *Vincent* was immortality—better than a star on Hollywood Boulevard."

The short film became a precursor for Vincent Price's last memorable screen appearance eight years later as "The Inventor" in the now-famous director's *Edward Scissorhands*.[275]

Between the two Burton films director Lindsay Anderson cast Vincent as an aging roué in his autumnal, bittersweet film, *The Whales of August*,[276] which became the final film appearance for Lillian Gish and the next-to-last film role for Bette Davis.

Vincent was married to his third wife, Australian actress Coral Browne, at the time of our conversation. He had met her while she was playing one of his victims in the 1973 film *Theatre of Blood*.[277] His first two marriages had ended in divorce. He had a son, Vincent Barrett Price, with his first wife, former actress Edith Barrett, whom he divorced in 1948 after ten years of marriage. In 1949 he married Mary Grant, a wealthy art connoisseur, who donated many art works and a considerable amount of money to East Los Angeles College to endow a Vincent and Mary Price Gallery at the college. They had a daughter, Victoria, who was born in 1962. That marriage lasted until 1973. Marriage to Coral Browne followed in 1974.

In the spring of 1979, Vincent and Coral Browne hosted a limited-run TV series on CBS entitled *Time Express*. The rather novel idea for the show, sometimes compared to *Fantasy Island*, found Vincent and Coral portraying the charming, sophisticated hosts on a mysterious train called the *Time Express* which took passengers back in time to a place where they could relive or attempt to alter an important event in their lives. There were only four sixty-minute episodes produced. In addition to making many guest appearances on television shows of the era, Vincent became the weekly host of the PBS series *Mystery* from 1981 through 1989.

Vincent was a true Renaissance man. His interests were varied and wide ranging. He was a patron of the arts, whether it was stage, film, radio, television, or the visual arts. He loved being an actor in all the performing media, but he also was a frequent lecturer on art; a gourmet

Vincent Price is seen here as "The Inventor" in Tim Burton's production of *Edward Scissorhands*.

chef who published a number of cookbooks; an outspoken, liberal Democrat politically; and a passionate gardener. He even had his own mail-order book club in the 1970s called "Vincent Price Books," which specialized in mystery, horror, and detective novels. He said, "A man who limits his interests limits his life."

He was devastated when his beloved wife Coral Browne died of breast cancer on May 29, 1991, just two days after his eightieth birthday. He himself was in failing health at that time. His long addiction to smoking—I remember that he was constantly smoking cigarettes during our conversation in 1978—had now brought on emphysema, and he was further weakened by Parkinson's disease. And then, finally, there was lung cancer. He said resignedly, "I hate being old and ill! Don't get old if you can avoid it."

Vincent Price died on October 25, 1993, and his body was cremated. Later his ashes were scattered by his family off the Pacific coast near Malibu.

Gordon Scott

July 9, 1993

"I like sex, although it's very difficult on a vine."

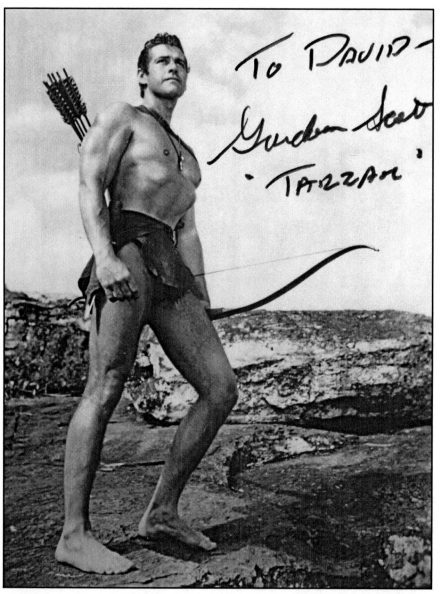

Gordon Scott was about midway in his Tarzan career when this photo was taken.

I have to tell you that I had a bone to pick with Gordon Scott before I even met him in Charlotte, North Carolina, at the 1993 Charlotte Western Film Fair. Here's what happened: Back a few years before that, I had acquired several really extraordinary black and white photos of Gordon from one of his Tarzan films, and by some fortunate occurrence I had been given Gordon's address in California. For the first and only time in my life, I decided to trouble a film star for a couple of autographs. I sent two of the photos to Gordon and asked if he might sign them. I enclosed a stamped, self-addressed envelope, of course, for him to return them. Days, weeks passed, and I didn't get my photos returned—and *never* got them.

Well, one shouldn't hold a grudge, I guess, and despite the fact that my photos were still missing, I was pleased to hear that Gordon was to be a guest star at the Film Fair. It had become my custom during the 1980s and nineties to attend the Western Film Fair in Charlotte to promote the books I had written in the western genre and to see old friends that I had gotten to know through the years. In addition, the good folks in charge usually asked me to host a guest star panel session, which was always enjoyable.

The guest star lineup for 1993 was typical of what one would expect at a western festival, although the pickings were getting slim because the best-loved of the western films were made in the thirties, forties, and fifties, and many of those performers, sadly, had gone to that great roundup in the sky. Anyway, the lineup did include a few heroes like Lash LaRue of B-westerns, Robert Horton of TV's *Wagon Train*, and Richard Simmons who starred in *Sergeant Preston of the Yukon* on TV. Cowboy sidekicks were represented by Richard "Chito" Martin from the Tim Holt westerns. Then there were a couple of guest villains whose names would only be known to dyed-in-the-wool western fans. The same could be said for the several heroines that were invited except for Mary Murphy, who was not really known for westerns but got her great break as Marlon Brando's leading lady in *The Wild One*. Gordon Scott was there because he had starred in a few of spaghetti westerns in Italy after he gave up swinging on the Tarzan vine.

It was on the second afternoon of the Film Fair that I hosted a guest star panel which consisted of Gordon Scott, Richard Martin, and Mary Murphy. For our purposes only the Gordon Scott portion is included. (In fact, I used Richard Martin's comments in my book *Tim Holt*, which came out a number of years ago, and Mary Murphy, a delightful lady, unfortunately had little to say about Marlon Brando except that he was "interesting" and "different"; therefore, I decided not to include her offerings.)

When Gordon arrived in the panel room he was dressed in a loose-fitting, white sweater-shirt with an aqua open-at-the-neck short-sleeve shirt under it. His dark brown hair, still worn Tarzan-full, was now engulfed with gray, and he wore a full gray moustache. His demeanor was jaunty, and he seemed to be in a fun mood as I introduced him to the Film Fair audience. I invited the audience to participate too by asking questions of Gordon as the opportunity arose. With that we began:

David: Gordon Scott, we hear stories about the young lady sitting on a stool in a Los Angeles drugstore and being discovered by Hollywood. Wasn't your discovery by Hollywood about as unlikely—something along the lines of you were working at a health spa flexing your muscles when you were discovered?

Gordon: No, I was at the Sahara Hotel in Las Vegas. I was working there at the time; I had the health club and taught swimming. I had four people working for me. An agent from Hollywood was up there on his honeymoon, and he came to me and said they were looking for a new Tarzan and he'd like to keep in contact with me and contact Sol Lesser who was producer [of the Tarzan films].

Two weeks later I got this agency contact with Walter Meyers, and he said that he had set up an appointment with Sol Lesser. I went down on a Wednesday and tested. They saw the film on Friday, and I

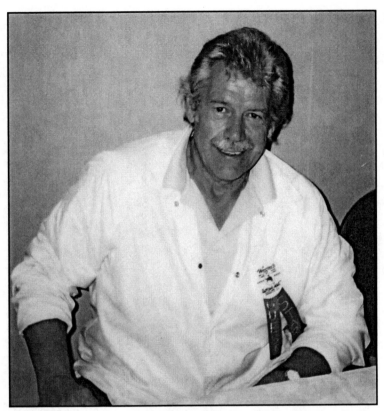

Gordon Scott is seen here at the time we met with the festival audience.

was signed Saturday. I didn't find out until later that there were twenty-five hundred people who tried out for the part. Now, I'm not sure of that; my God, that's a lot of people! But anybody who can sign a contract for seven years to run around the jungle in little leather knickers has a lot of guts. *[Audience laughter]*

I had great fun doing it; I worked with some great people: Sean Connery,[278] Anthony Quayle.[279] The trips to Africa were absolutely gorgeous. I had a lot of fun with the part; I made seven films [as Tarzan]. But I made fifty-two films *[sic]* in Europe; I was there for ten years. But I always enjoyed the Tarzans because where else can you, an intelligent man, *[Laugh]* run around in those little leather knickers—and I loved animals too, you see.

David: And you had had no experience prior to this. *Tarzan's Hidden Jungle*[280] was your first film.

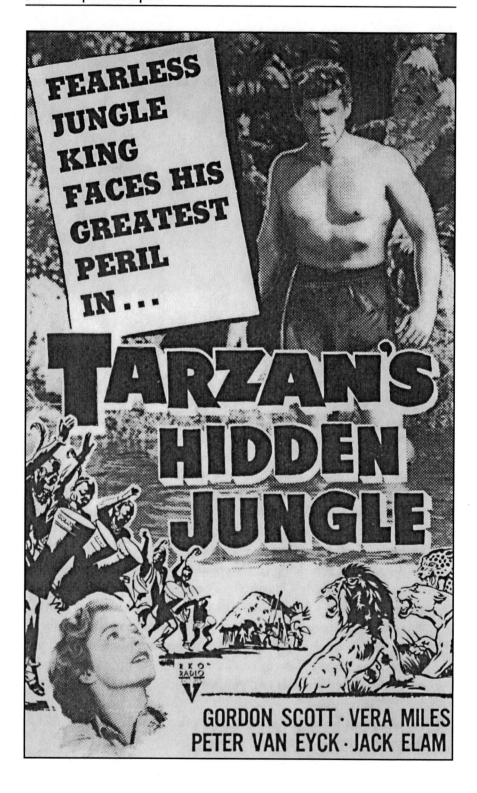

Gordon: That was my first one, and I wasn't really very good, but I got some great critique value in the Los Angeles papers. They said, "He has great potential," and they even mentioned in the article that "He could do other things other than Tarzans and westerns." And that was really a good compliment.

David: It's astounding that they would take a chance on an unknown.

Gordon: Well, I had a good background for the part; I had a gymnastics background, and I was a swimmer for the athletic club—as a matter of fact, I broke three of Weismuller's[281] records. I'm saying that not to brag about it but that we had different training methods than when John was training. He used to swim with his whole upper body out of the water, but his arms were so powerful that he'd really glide through it. Now, of course, you want to keep down and leave that mass out of the way.

Man in Audience: Would you comment on Vera Miles[282] who was in *Tarzan's Hidden Jungle?*

Gordon: Yes, I first met Vera in *Hidden Jungle.* We became very good friends; I actually fell in love with her on that film. We had a marvelous relationship, and we married. For nine years it was absolutely first class. Sometimes, you know, when you are in the business, you are away from each other for so long at a time that something happens, and the last eighteen months of our marriage it wasn't too pleasant. I'm being very personal about this because it really was the best time of my life. Now, if you want to get your hankies out . . . *[Laugh]* she's a marvelous girl and a fine actress. We have two fine children that love us both.

Man in audience: I understand you had a great fight scene with Jock Mahoney[283] in one of your Tarzan films where something unexpected happened. Could you tell us about it?

Gordon: We were in Africa and this fight sequence was at a place called Fourteen Falls, a beautiful area, water coming down, and a lot of noise. In the scene there were rocks in the water all around. We'd have a fight on one, and I'd knock Jock in the water [then he'd knock me in the water]. We kept doing this, knocking each other in the water. One time, as I was crawling up, he was supposed to grab onto my waist and pull me down. He grabbed onto my little knickers and pulled them right off. *[Audience laughter]* It was so loud that we couldn't hear the director calling, "Cut, cut, cut!" So we just kept on doing the fight. *[Audience laughter]* I don't think it was in the film, was it? *[Audience laughter]*

David: Since we're getting into very personal and intimate things, I have a question that I have to ask you that a number of people have men-

Anthony Quayle and Tarzan in the scene where the wire was used to secure Gordon.

tioned to me. In *Tarzan's Greatest Adventure*[284] you have a fantastic fight with Anthony Quayle high up on a rocky cliff. In the scene, if you look very, very carefully, you can see a wire coming from your loin cloth to off camera. . . .

Gordon: You bet your ass! *[Audience laughter]*

David: And a number of people have wondered how that was attached to you. [Handing Gordon a still photo from the film] This is from the scene with Anthony Quayle, but the wire was not attached for this still photo.

Gordon: There are damned few things you can tie it on to. *[Audience laughter]*

David: Well, that's what people were concerned about. *[Audience laughter]*

Gordon: [Gesturing to photo] See, the leather part of my outfit is right there, you see. And they put a strap in the back so that you couldn't see it visually—only if you had a fine eye—and then the wire was up here. That happened because we had rehearsed so much, and it was very hot and [there was] perspiration. The rocks became very slippery, very dangerous, and there was about a ninety-foot drop onto rocks below, so we wanted to make it look authentic, but we didn't want to lose old Tarzan.

David: [Handing Gordon another photo] In this shot you can see the hole in the loin cloth where they wrapped the wire around you apparently.

Gordon: [looking at photo] No, no, no, that's . . . . *[Gordon breaks up. Audience laughter]* Boy, you're a great straight man!

David: I'm just feeding you the lines! *[Audience laughter]*

Gordon: That is a great shot [referring to the first photo].

The loin cloth hole used for fastening the safety wire can be seen
in the "G" of the autograph.

David: That was a great scene too.

Man in audience: When Anthony Quayle had that wire around your
neck and you put your hands in to try to force it off. . . .

Gordon: [It was] an animal snare.

Man in audience: Did they give you anything to protect your hands
from that wire?

Gordon: No, I'm tough! *[Audience laughter]* You know, when I was in Africa, I really began to believe that I could do these things. And never put yourself in that position, because when you come back to reality— like New York or the lower east side—it's not good. I was in great shape, and you can fake those sorts of things. It wasn't that difficult.

David: On those last couple of films there seemed to be a whole attitude change regarding the character of Tarzan. He seemed far more serious.

Gordon: Well, the Edgar Rice Burroughs people wanted them to follow more closely the books by Burroughs. In the second seven years, if I had signed, they wanted to send Clayton [Tarzan's English name is John Clayton] to England to be educated and then come back again [to Africa] as they did in *Lord Greystoke*,[285] which I felt was a great film. So they wrote out Jane and Boy, the family unit, and tried to give him more interest in the action and introduced new female characters in the thing. And they [worked for] better story lines.

David: They put in even a hint of romance.

Gordon: Oh, yeah. I mean, I like sex, although it's very difficult on a vine. *[Audience laughter]* Let's get off this!

Woman in audience: I was wondering if Gordon has any animal stories about the Tarzan films.

Gordon: Yes, I do. One that was very dicey. I always had pretty good luck with animals, but this one time—after the filming was over— there were English newspapers that wanted an interview with me in Nairobi. We were all in this room. I was [sitting] on the floor. I had been working with a lion called Jackie, one with a big black mane. He came in the room with his owner, and I'm on the floor, and he came over and just flopped down [on the floor] because we just got along great together.

There were questions and answers, and I was just laying there scratching Jackie's stomach. A girl from *The Observer* had a flash camera and she flashed it, and he went nuts. I had a pair of slacks on, and as he got up, he had his "do" claw—they have a huge claw here [a few inches up the lion's leg] that they use to open up an animal's gut—and he took a swipe at the first thing near him, which was me. I was just leaping out of the way over a table, and he caught me in the lower calf. Finally the trainer got him calmed down and out of the room.

I walked around from [behind] the table, and this woman who had taken the shot looked down at my leg and fainted right on her back. I thought she had killed herself; she had hit very hard. I looked down and here was blood coming out of my leg. They took thirty-two stitches in my lower calf. That was about the worst that ever happened to me; I mean, I got bruised and scratched [many times].

David: There were some great publicity shots of you riding a giraffe. I never saw anyone else riding a giraffe.

Gordon: That was taken with a "wild" camera. We were on the northern frontier in Ethiopia in Kenya. We were driving along and saw this young giraffe eating at a tree. Mickey Carter, who was the cameraman, said, "I wonder if we can get that animal in the background and you just kind of walk across. It could be a great stock shot."

I said, "Sure, let's try it." I was in my [Tarzan] outfit. So I strapped on the knife and started walking out to this tree, about eighty yards, I guess. I was going to walk so that he could get a pan shot. I kept walking and getting closer, and he never moved; he just kept eating. And I wondered if I could get *really* close to him.

I got within twenty yards, and he turned around and looked at me. I thought, there he goes, but he didn't; he went right back to eating. And I got up to him—as close as you to me, David—so I grabbed his neck and did a kip up on him, and he took off. And we got this great shot.

The rhino was a different story! *[Audience laughter]* No joke! Thank God it wasn't a black; it was a white rhino. It was a male, and I jumped up on it, and it was so wide at the back that my legs were just really spread-eagled like this [demonstrating]. And the mate came up, and she took her horn and nudged my leg. And you could see the expression on my face that I wasn't concerned at all. *[Audience laughter]* They are big animals, big animals!

David: I can understand getting on the giraffe or the rhino, but getting *off* the giraffe would seem to be a problem.

Gordon: I did a back flip off it because it was heading off for lion country, and I looked like a two-hundred-and twenty-pound piece of roast beef. I didn't want to get too far away from the others.

Man in audience: Didn't you have a fight once with a large snake.

Gordon: We were shooting a film with a twenty-two-foot boa constrictor, and they brought the animal in a long box with heating elements in it to make it kind of dormant. The scene was that they put it on a branch, and it would crawl down to where "Jane" was sitting, and I rushed in and grabbed it by its neck and wrapped it around my body.

It was kind of dormant so you could work with the animal, but it [the first take] was a bad shot, so they said we'd have to do it again. The snake weighed about two hundred and twenty pounds and I couldn't quite get it [the scene] right—the way they wanted.

Gordon tussles with a twenty-two foot boa constrictor in this scene from *Tarzan's Fight for Life* (1958). That's Eve Brent looking on nervously.

So all this time the snake is waking up a little bit, and it got active. It was better for the scene because the tail would come up and waggle about, and it wrapped right around my crotch and my back—and began to squeeze. I was talking soprano by that time! So they [the crew] went in and unwrapped it from me, and we shot it once more and it was fine. We finally got the shot.

They're dangerous animals because their teeth when they open— the inside of their mouth is just dead white—are slanted at an angle. So once they grab you, you pull on it, and they just go in deeper. I had it by its neck, and it opened its mouth and, boy, it was frightening! But it was a good shot!

David: Sean Connery was in *Tarzan's Greatest Adventure* with you just before he became James Bond. Was there any indication that was about to happen?

Gordon: It was great for Sean but bad for our next film because we wanted him in the next Tarzan film. We were in Africa, and he was so good in the film. I liked him and I wanted to work with him. I don't think we had a scene together except the last one when I shot him with the arrow. So they asked Sean verbally, unfortunately, if he would like to do the next one as a different character. He said, "Yeah, but I have to go back to England and do this show for Cubby Broccoli and Harry Saltzman. That was *Dr. No*, and that was the first James Bond. We couldn't touch him after that.

Man in audience: In the action scenes did you have a double who handled the scenes for you?

Gordon: We had a stunt coordinator, but I was hard to double; they couldn't get up close with the camera, and I'd had all this experience with gymnastics and played all the sports, threw the javelin and even did all the track and field events. We would have people [stuntmen/ coordinator] lay out the type of fight we were going to do.

Somebody here mentioned Jock Mahoney and the fight scene we did. He was an incredible stunt man; that's how he really began [his career]. He was so easy to work with. I could take him in a fight scene and put him over my head, literally, and he weighed a hundred and ninety-five pounds. But those guys, they give a lift a little bit and help you; they give you all the help in the world. That's why in the

fight sequences in the films they use guys who are helping you all of the time, taking a punch or whatever, so they are making *you* look good. But I never really had to use one [a stunt double].

Man in audience: Scott, am I correct that *Tarzan and the Trappers*[286] was originally a black and white TV pilot?

Gordon: Yep.

Woman in audience: Can you tell us the circumstances around that and why it didn't go into a series?

Gordon: My contract stipulated that if I was going to do a television show that it would be a separate contract and for a lot more money than they were willing to offer.

Man in audience: Didn't you work with Steve Reeves[287] in an Italian film?

Gordon: I've known Steve since 1947 when we both got out of the service about the same time. We worked out together at Bert Goodrich's old gym in Hollywood. I was doing Tarzan from 1954 until 1961, and Steve had just gotten the part of Hercules in 1958 or '59. [Because of that] he was in Europe and I was traveling everywhere, so we didn't see too much of each other.

When I went to Rome, he was already an established actor there. Because we looked similar—we could be brothers—a director had the idea that we should do Romulus and Remus, the foundation of Rome, which we finally did. It was released here as *Duel of the Titans*.[288] When you're not working with English speaking actors, you have to be very careful with the cues. When I first went to Italy, I would read the script in Italian and then learn it phonetically.

David: Well, Gordon Scott, we want to thank you for being with us today at the Charlotte Film Fair.

Gordon: May I say something? I know most of you were not old enough to see my films when they were first released—young-looking audience and so forth—but you've treated me so kindly. Anyway, I have

Gordon strikes a muscular pose here in a scene from *Duel of the Titans*.

been very well received here, and I want to thank you guys; you're first class. *[Audience applause]*

David: Thank you, Gordon Scott.

Gordon was sixty-six when he appeared at the Western Film Fair in 1993. His film career had ended back in the late 1960s with an Italian Western entitled *The Tramplers*,[289] an Italian secret agent spy film called *Danger!! Death Ray*,[290] and, finally, a Spanish film, that to my knowledge, was never released in America, *Segretissimo*.[291] One account stated that he then returned to the United States "trailed by a reputation as a ladies' man that seldom paid his bills."[292]

The years passed after the Western Film Fair, and I was aware that Gordon became a regular at such events, although not back in Charlotte. His only activities during the 1980s and nineties seemed to be appearing at film festivals, traveling the autograph circuit, and selling Tarzan-type knives at these events. And then as we all moved into the Twenty-first Century, I heard nothing more about Gordon.

Gordon Scott died on April 30, 2007, and in the many obituaries that were published more details on his personal life were revealed. It seemed that Vera Miles was probably not his first wife, and there may have been three wives altogether and several children, but no account of wives and children seemed to be certain of accuracy.[293] He had a son, Michael, with Miles, but there was no mention of a second child as Gordon had claimed during the panel. No obituary that I could find indicated that he was anything but a lifeguard in Las Vegas when he was "discovered" by Hollywood—not, as he claimed, "running a health club" at the Sahara Hotel with "four people working for me."

According to a surviving brother, Rayfield Werschkul, Gordon was born with the name Gordon M. Werschkul in Portland, Maine, on August 3, 1926. He said, "We were a family of nine kids, and we all ended up going in different directions. I haven't seen Gordon, whom we called Pete, for eight or ten years. We just didn't keep in touch." Rayfield went on to say, "He was always a big spender and loved to party. If he had one weakness, it was women. They were always hitting on him."[294]

The most bizarre revelation was the fact that Gordon had spent the last five years of his life living in a row house owned by fans Roger and Betty Thomas of Baltimore's Brooklyn neighborhood in Maryland. Betty said, "My husband has been a fan of his since he was a child. He was his idol. When we were in Hollywood about eight years ago, we looked him up. They called each other several times, and then we invited him for a visit. He came and never left."[295]

Mr. Thomas, who is a retired factory worker, commented, "I haven't had much time to think about his death and let it sink in. He meant the world to me, and we had lots of good times together. I was blessed to have known him." Living at the Thomas house, Gordon was described as a "semi-recluse," who stayed in his room reading or watching television. Mr. Thomas went on, "I last saw him on Saturday and said, 'Gordon, we love you, and so does the dog and the bird.' He opened one eye for a moment and gave me a wink."[296]

Gordon died at John Hopkins Hospital after multiple heart surgeries earlier in the year which left him on life support that was eventually undermined by pneumonia. Estranged from his family, he was survived by a brother and two sisters, none of whom had seen him in years. Gordon Scott was eighty years old.

No, I never asked him about the photos.

George Takei

June 25, 1977

"'Takei' means 'warriors well,' so I suspect my ancestors ran the local pub for the Samurai way back when."

George Takei looks ready for action as Lieutenant Sulu of the
Starship *Enterprise* in *Star Trek*.

Most television series do not have much of an afterlife. They run their course and then slip into a nether world where they are pretty much forgotten or, rarely, acquire "cult" status whereby they achieve a sort of immortality and linger on the fringes of our memories unless moved briefly to center stage by the personal appearance or death of one of the actors in the series—the series itself hardly ever gets a rebirth, but it can happen.

The original *Star Trek* television series had gone off the air in 1969, and here it was 1977 and the show had acquired the cult status that few do and actor George Takei, "Sulu" on the series, was showing up at *Star Trek* and other nostalgia conventions to schmooze with the fans, sign autographs, mourn the demise of the series, and speculate on the viability and possibility of a regeneration of the show either in television or movie form.

Such was the situation at the 1977 Houstoncon nostalgia festival. It was not an exclusive camp for Trekkies, however, since there were star representatives for other genres present: Roy Rogers and Jock Mahoney for westerns and Spanky McFarland for the *Our Gang* group, for example, but the *Star Trek* fans were there in abundance, some dressed in costumes designating their favorite characters from the series.

Rumors were especially rife at that time that *Star Trek* might be revived on television or as movie, so I wanted to get the latest from Lieutenant Sulu of the Starship *Enterprise*. It would also be a great time to find out more about this Japanese-American actor who had become quite well known as a result of *Star Trek* and several films in which he had had small to medium-sized roles: Cary Grant's last film, *Walk, Don't Run,*[297] and John Wayne's *The Green Berets*[298] come to mind.

I called George at his suite in the convention hotel, and we arranged to meet late the next morning to talk about all things George Takei and

Above: Earlier in the day George signed autographs in the dealers' room at the Houstoncon festival.

Left: George Takei met with *Star Trek* fans at an afternoon seminar which was followed by a Q & A session.

Star Trek. Later on that day I had the chance to see George mingling with the fans and signing autographs. In addition, he had what might be called a seminar in one of the meeting rooms, which he followed with a Q & A with the fans. George exuded an enthusiasm and collegial demeanor that was not unlike the fans who came to see him.

Late the next morning a sportily clad and very gracious George Takei opened the door of his suite, bid me "Welcome," and asked if I would like coffee. I thanked him but declined. The suite provided for George was quite nice, with a living room on the main floor and what appeared to be a loft bedroom or sitting room atop a set of carpeted stairs.

We sat opposite each other, George on the sofa, me in an easy chair with a tape recorder on the empty coffee table between us. George, looking younger than his real age—he and I were close to the same age, in fact—seemed relaxed and supremely comfortable in his own skin as we made small talk for the first couple of minutes before we got down to business.

David: George, I have to ask you about your last name. I've heard it pronounced three different ways since I arrived here: "Tak-eye," "Tak-ee," and "Ta-kay." Straighten me out; which one is it?

George: Well, the last one is the correct pronunciation: "Ta-kay." It rhymes with Okay. I tell people "Tak-Eye" is another legitimate Japanese name, and I'm more than happy to accommodate if they want to call me that, but I think I should warn them that "Tak-eye" means "expensive." "Takei" means "warriors well," so I suspect my ancestors ran the local pub for the Samurai way back when.

David: Well, you're fortunate because you can say your name rhymes with "okay." In my case I have to say that my name rhymes with "brothel." *[Both laugh]* I know you've had extensive training as an actor; I know you had this long before you became known for *Star Trek*.

George: I guess my first training was in the backyard. I was an inveterate performer, and as a kid I used to put together backyard theatricals. Then, of course, in junior high school I was in the drama club, and in high school [the] drama class. My parents knew the direction I was headed and they didn't like it, so they tried to give me guidance into my second love which is architecture.

So I started off my college career up in Berkeley, the University of California at Berkeley, as an architecture student. After two years as an architecture student I decided that that was satisfying to me, but certainly I had a greater love and wanted to be honest with myself and true to myself. At least not have regrets later in life. I decided to be realistic, and I changed to theater arts.

So I transferred down to UCLA where I majored in theater arts and got my bachelor's degree and master's degree at UCLA. At the same time I was studying acting at the Desilu Workshop at Desilu Studios in Hollywood. I also squeezed in some post-graduate studies in England at the Shakespeare Institute at Stratford-on-Avon, and also a summer session in Japan at Sophia University where I studied contemporary and classical Japanese theater. So I cover the whole broad spectrum.

David: How did you happen to get into *Star Trek*,[299] this fantastically successful TV series?

George: It's really an extraordinary phenomenon in retrospect, but how I first stepped into it isn't that extraordinary. My agent called one morning with an interview. He said that it was a running part in a series and that was attractive. [It was to be] science fiction, which at that time I wasn't into, as they say. I had read some Ray Bradbury, but [I was] not really into it, but I thought it might be an interesting thing.

So I went to this interview with a man named Gene Roddenberry.[300] I didn't know who he was at the time. When I was interviewed I found him to be a fascinating person, but, frankly, my appraisal of the interview was that it wasn't successful because we didn't talk anything about my career. Gene wanted to cover the whole range of discussionaries except my career. We talked about current affairs, the theater, everything.

I walked out of that interview thinking it was very interesting, that he was an interesting man, but I probably didn't get the part. I discovered later that Gene really wasn't interested in discussing our acting careers; he just assumed that everyone that he was going to be interviewing were capable actors.

He wanted to find another dimension, that human factor beyond just being a professional actor, and I found that to be very interesting. I guess he found me interesting enough too because two days later my agent called and said I had the part. So it was a very un-dramatic way of stepping into *Star Trek*.

David: I remember that there was more than one pilot made for *Star Trek*. What brought that about?

George: There were two pilots made. One pilot was made with Jeffrey Hunter[301] as the captain. Then they decided to make a second pilot because the first one had interesting elements in it but didn't quite sell the show. I was in the second pilot where Bill Shatner came in as the captain. The only survivors from the first pilot were Leonard Nimoy and Majel Barrett.[302] Then in the second pilot Bill Shatner, me, and Jimmy Doohan came on. That pilot sold. Then when we started our first season with the first episode, DeForest [Kelly] came on and also Nichelle [Nichols] came on. In the second season Walter Koenig came on as Chekov, so that's the whole history of it.

David: Was it a happy set to work on? From all appearances it was tremendously so.

His eyes gazing into "space, the final frontier," Lt. Sulu sits at the helm of the Starship *Enterprise*. This shot is from the sixties television series.

George: For those who have seen the blooper reels, I think that's unquestionable evidence that we had fun while shooting *Star Trek*. I think also it was extraordinary in the combination of people that we had. We had people who were professional, and we were able to have that kind of fun and still get the film done and shot sometimes under schedule, usually on schedule, and very infrequently a little bit over schedule.

But that kind of fun doesn't happen on [just] any set because people get rather nervous because they have a schedule to meet, and if you have that kind of frivolity and you don't have people who are equipped to deal with it, then you usually run over schedule. I thought that kind of fun was essential in the quality that we got in the show because there is a lot of tension on a set when you *do* have to get things done on schedule. When you work under tension and there isn't that healthy release steam valve, then it shows in the performance and the quality of the work, I think, and so that was both therapeutic as well as a fun aspect of the show.

David: What was a normal schedule for shooting an episode; how many days did you have in which to do it?

George: We were on a six-day schedule, and that's not unusual for an hour show. Most half-hour shows are on a three-day schedule. We had five working days in a week, so it was a week plus a day to get an hour out. So we really had to move to get a show out in a week.

David: Who in the cast were you personally closest to? Was there any particular one?

George: Yes, I think so. First of all, on a professional basis, Leonard Nimoy[303] was an actor I had admired for quite some time before *Star Trek*. He wasn't the star that he became in *Star Trek*. I first saw him in a little theater play on Santa Monica Boulevard, a Jean Genet play, playing a rather introspective and somewhat sullen hostile prisoner, a convict. [It was] a very deep, profound, subtle performance, and I was really impressed by him. And then I saw him in a couple of TV things.

So when I discovered that I was going to be working with him on *Star Trek*, I was kind of intrigued to meet that man behind this actor I had been admiring. And I found him certainly to be that [a deep, profound performer]. I think that Spock is truly a Leonard Nimoy creation.

A lot of the things about Spock that are unique, Leonard brought to that character. He's a totally new creation. The writers really didn't have a hook on him; there were a lot of fuzzy areas, and it was Leonard's inventiveness as an actor that made him specific.

That Spock pinch is his creation, his contribution to the character. Also that Vulcan salute is Leonard's contribution. He's a very creative performer.

Beyond that I found while working in the series with him that we had a lot of common areas in terms of philosophy, thoughts on life, the political arena. As a matter of fact, we're both political animals, I think, and we found ourselves supporting the same candidates, involved in the same issues in the political arena, and so I have not only a great deal of respect for Leonard as an actor, but we found that we were working in concert in the non-acting arenas as well.

The *Star Trek* cast from left to right included James Doohan as "Scotty," DeForest Kelly as "Dr. McCoy," Walter Koenig as "Chekov," Marjel Barrett as "Nurse Chapel," William Shatner as "Captain Kirk," Nichelle Nichols as "Uhura," Leonard Nimoy as "Spock," and George Takei as "Sulu."

David: For many years prior to *Star Trek* I had been fascinated with some of the work of DeForest Kelly.[304] One movie in particular that he made in the late 1940s called *Fear in the Night*,[305] which you may or may not be familiar with, was a story of a man who under the powers of a hypnotist is made to commit a murder. As a consequence, I have been interested in his career and wonder if you could provide a thumbnail sketch of him.

George: I think the extraordinary thing about the cast of *Star Trek* was that Gene was able to select people and put us together where we all shared a common vibration, I suppose: with Leonard [being] a political activist, with DeForest [having] a very warm and human interest in other people. I found DeForest to be great set-side companion. He's a wonderful raconteur; he loves to shoot the breeze. Those long days on the set can get to be awfully wearing if you don't have a good raconteur around.

David: He seems to have dropped out of sight a little bit since *Star Trek*.

George: Well, I don't know. DeForest always says, "I'm lazy." *[Laugh]* So that could be part of it. But it's been true that De has been a little laid back in his acting career since *Star Trek*.

David: How do you account for the cult status that has grown around *Star Trek* and remains so strong after all these years? It's been almost ten years now since the program went out of production and yet it is still so tremendously popular.

George: I've had to sort of sit back and think on that question too. I really was overwhelmed when this phenomenon started happening, oh, I guess about two or three years after the cancellation of *Star Trek* when the syndication caught on. I think there are many elements that come into play here. I think that *Star Trek* is a good action/adventure series just on that surface level; it provides good entertainment. Beyond that I think *Star Trek* provided a great deal of substance as well, something that pricked the mind as well.

The late sixties were a very turbulent time for America, and I think that a lot of our shows made rather pertinent observations about the turmoil that was going on at that time. I think some of the other commentaries, be they political, sociological, human observations, that it made dealt with some of the verities of what people and civilization are all about.

Another aspect, I think, that made *Star Trek* unique was our technological speculations on the future. I think Gene exercised a great deal of care and integrity in that. We had consultation from the Rand Corporation so that even the seemingly farfetched speculations were somehow tied down into current scientific thought. That also gave another dimension to *Star Trek*, but, of course, we were cancelled.

We weren't obviously reaching our audience while we were on first run. I think that was because NBC really had no feel for a show as unusual, as unique, as distinctive as *Star Trek* was. They put us on the last season at ten o'clock on Friday night—the morgue hour.

David: Right, considered the worst hour on TV.

George: So I think the fourth factor that came in to contribute to this phenomenon was that in syndication we were finally placed in the programming schedule where we had access to our audience or the audience had access to us. They discovered us because we were on at a reasonable hour—seven o'clock, for example, when college students right after dinner might be relaxing for an hour before they started in on their homework, whatever. People who were out on Friday nights were around at the hours that we were on.

There's a new generation that discovered us: the kids. It was on at an hour that was accessible to them. I'm kind of overwhelmed and staggered and a little incredulous to be carrying on intelligent conversations with people who were born after the premiere of *Star Trek*. *[Laugh]*

David: Every so often the story comes out that there's going to be a *Star Trek* movie or that they are going to reactivate the TV series. What's the latest on that?

George: Well, the latest in this continuing saga of "The Perils of Pauline," I think, is just that: It's another episode in the continuing story. As you know, for about three years Paramount talked about the revival of *Star Trek* as a feature film. [They] periodically kept announcing start dates, which they kept pushing back. Finally they decided, no, that's not the direction they're going to go. And now the talk is of a television series return.

Gene is pursuing this very seriously with Paramount, and there seems to be some evidence of progress in that discussion. But at the same time there is enough evidence of reservation on their part too, so I'm not counting the chicks yet. I'm fairly well persuaded that Paramount eventually will agree to reviving *Star Trek* in some shape, form. When that's going to be is still a question mark.

The talk is, and I have my tongue well placed in my cheek when I say that the talk is, of a start in the fall with the premiere in the spring of a television series. But that's a very familiar echo of other statements from Paramount.[306]

David: It seems to me that the most logical thing might be a ninety-minute TV movie to test the waters again and then go into a series if the ratings are good.

George: Well, I don't think the waters need to be tested. It's been well splashed around already, and no gingerly dip of the toe is necessary, I think. The success of these [*Star Trek*] conventions well attests to the fact that there is an audience out there, and an audience that will pay money. That's the thing that Paramount keeps coming up with: *Star Trek* was available free on television before, and they have serious doubts as to whether an audience would pay money at the box office to see an extension of a show they saw for free.

I'm convinced that they are wrong in their fears there because conventions are being held all over the country—as a matter of fact, abroad as well in England and Germany and Japan—all being quite successful. So I'm convinced that there is a box office, tariff-paying audience out there, and yet somehow we can't seem to communicate that to the executive dumb heads at Paramount.

David: You know what might tip the scale is *Star Wars*. The success of that science fiction film may bring on a flood of science fiction films, and, of course, *Star Trek* would be one of the best in the field.

George: Yeah, in fact Paramount is always so consistent, their timing is so perfectly terrible. I think it was about two weeks before the premiere of *Star Wars* that Paramount announced that the feature film of *Star Trek* will *not* be—that they were canceling those plans.

Although I think *Star Wars* is quite different from *Star Trek*. *Star Wars* is fantasy escape. In fact, to me it was nostalgia. A lot of those episodes to me were echoes of films that I saw when I was a kid, the Saturday matinee [films like] *Flash Gordon* or there were reverberations of Errol Flynn's daring-dos or some of the World War Two war movies—the aerial dogfights. So it was really, to me, a harkening back to another time rather than a projecting forward to a futuristic time.

I have some regrets. I know that Lucas didn't intend for there to be any substance to *Star Wars*. It was supposed to be escape entertainment, but there were so many opportunities for a little bit of intelligence, a little bit of awareness of that situation. I think *Star Wars* could have become a classic but missed out on becoming that because of the unused opportunities for a little meaning, a little substance, a little significance . . . .

David: Which were all the qualities of *Star Trek*.

George: That's where *Star Trek* differed very definitively from *Star Wars*.

David: Do you have any fears of being typed as Lieutenant Sulu?

George: No, it hasn't been a problem for me at all. Since *Star Trek* I've played everything but a space-oriented person. As a matter of fact, I was up for an Emmy this year for *Baa, Baa Black Sheep*[307] in which I played a Japanese major who masterminds a plot to kidnap General McArthur and thus end World War Two. The best I did was kidnap Robert Conrad, and maybe that's why the Japanese didn't win. *[Both laugh]*

David: What are your interests other than acting, performing? You mentioned architecture.

George: As I said, I'm somewhat of a political animal too. Currently I'm serving on the board of directors of the Southern California Rapid Transit District as a representative of the city of Los Angeles. So that combines my political interests as well as my architecture and urban planning interests.

David: Let me toss you a philosophical question. What's your hoped for goal or accomplishment in life, either as an actor or as a person, however that question hits you?

George: I think it's really a blessing in this society now for one to not really be one thing. I think it's all up to that individual to use opportunities that our society and our time afford. I love acting; it's my life, but I also am a member of this community called, well, I'm a citizen of Los Angeles and I love my city and I'm deeply involved in civic activities. I'm also a member of this country and all that it stands for, all the ideals and opportunities. I think we have to participate and try to correct some of the failings of this country.

As a Japanese-American I know that democracy can fail. During the Second World War all of us Japanese-Americans were incarcerated purely because of our ancestry—no trial, no anything. This was a time when hysteria ran rampant, and people made judgments based on hysteria, lack of information, and pure adrenalin.

Democracy is a very fragile form of government, only as good as those of us who participate in it. That's why I think it [participation] is important. Yet democracy also has ideals that can be tremendously powerful, potent, and that too is given that power only by us who participate in it. It has ideals that need to be supported, and so I think it is important that the "idealers" participate and underline and give support to the strengths of democracy.

That's why I'm a participant in the political arena. I'm also a Democrat, I'll confess. My publicity agent tells me to never talk about politics, but that's me too, and I feel that I've got to be honest when I discuss this. So we have the opportunity to try to contribute to making this world a little bit better—by the world I mean in every sense a citizen of this country, but I'm also a citizen of this global society.

And we do live in a global civilization now. What happens on the other side of the planet affects us. We have a political leader in the Middle East who makes a decision on petroleum fuel and, all of a sudden, in our neighborhoods we have to line up around the gas station. Decisions made on another part of this planet have direct organic impact on our lives.

David: When George Takei has a day off, what does he like to do?

George: Well, you know, I consider every day a day off or a day on. I was saying that we don't wear labels. I'm an actor, certainly. I love that, but I also am a political activist, you might say. I'm an artist. I'm an urban planner, an architect. In the same way, every day provides a new kind of work, a new kind of challenge.

You know, you're affording me an opportunity to communicate with a lot of people and share some of my ideas and, hopefully, I can stimulate them. Arrogantly I say, perhaps inspire them, but at the same time, I'm at a convention with the opportunity for other people to make that kind of impact on me. They may share with me some of their ideas which may move me to do certain things.

So I think it's terrible when you have a day off. We should not have days off; we should always have days on. I think that's the way we should approach every day.

David: Thank you, George Takei.

George: Thank you, David.

I came away from our conversation with a warm feeling and deep respect for the man. He was obviously intelligent, sincere, and demonstrated an interest in the state of the world that went beyond the "for the press," self-serving comments that you hear frequently from actors who feel the need to demonstrate their connection and compassion for worthwhile causes and civic responsibilities—today we might say, to show how "green" their feelings are.

George only touched on his many civic and political activities as we talked. I discovered later how active he was in the Democratic Party and that he had served as an alternate delegate from California to the Democratic National Convention in 1972. This involvement in politics caused him to run for the Los Angeles City Council seat vacated when Tom Bradley became mayor in 1973. George finished second in a field of over a dozen candidates. Mayor Bradley later appointed George to the Board of Directors of the Southern California Rapid Transit District, which was instrumental in initiating and planning the Los Angeles subway system.

Only a few months after we talked, Paramount Pictures announced that *Star Trek: The Motion Picture* would go into production and that the entire cast of regulars from the TV series would again be aboard the *Enterprise*. Ultimately, over the next twelve years, George and the other original TV regulars would star in six big-budget *Star Trek* films: *Star Trek: The Motion Picture* (1979), *Star Trek II: The Wrath of Khan* (1982), *Star Trek III: The Search for Spock* (1984), *Star Trek IV: The Voyage Home* (1986), *Star Trek V: The Final Frontier* (1989), and *Star Trek VI: The Undiscovered Country* (1992).

In 1979 I was director of the federally-funded Sarasota Visual and Performing Arts Center, a magnet school in Sarasota, Florida. We had some special funding to bring in professional artists and performers to work with our students and to, hopefully, inspire involvement and excellence in the arts.[308] I contacted George to see if he would be available to spend a week with our students and to talk with them about the life of a working actor on stage, in television, and film.

George was intrigued with the prospect of working with the students and agreed to come to the program just a few weeks before *Star Trek: The Motion Picture* opened across the country. Needless to say, he was a big hit with the students. His ability to connect with them was fascinating to observe; there was an almost instant rapport.

While George was in town for the Visual and Performing Arts program, I invited him to have dinner with my wife Nancy and me. As I was driving him to our home, he asked if we might stop at a local bookstore to see if they were carrying his new science fiction novel. This was the first I had heard about his on-the-side writing career. We stopped at the bookstore and, yes, they had his recently published novel, *Mirror Friend, Mirror Foe*,[309] in stock. I bought a copy and asked George to sign it. Many years later in 1994 George would publish his autobiography entitled *To the Stars*,[310] which was very favorably reviewed.

The years passed and only infrequently would I hear about George's activities unless a new *Star Trek* movie was being released. I was aware that he and his *Star Trek* colleagues continued to make many appearances

George takes up the sword in NBC's *Heroes*.

at *Star Trek* conventions, which continued in popularity. He made several guest star appearances in the 1990s and early years of the new century on such TV shows as *3rd Rock from the Sun* and *Malcolm in the Middle* and made an appearance as himself on a *Will & Grace* episode. In a particularly funny *Scrubs* episode he portrayed a minister who "looked like Sulu." On stage he played the challenging role of the psychiatrist in an East West Players production of *Equus*. The East West Players is considered the foremost Asian American theater in the United States, and George serves as the chairman of the Council of Governors of the theater.

In late 2005 George was recruited by *The Howard Stern Show* to serve as the "official announcer" for the Sirius radio show. Stern claimed that he wanted him for the show because George's bass/baritone voice and perfect enunciation were very distinctive. George agreed to be "live" in the studio occasionally and to do pre-recordings as needed on the show. It was reported that he felt that his appearances on the Stern show revitalized his career and resulted in the audience seeing George in an all new light—indeed a more fun-loving, raucous light that only added to his popularity.

In January of 2007 George was cast in an eight-episode story arc on the popular NBC television series entitled *Heroes*, in which he played the father of series regular Masi Oka. George's character, Kaito Nakamura, rarely spoke a word of English in the episodes, and the dialogue exchanges with fellow Asian actor Masi Oka were almost entirely in Japanese. George's character was killed off during the second season, but he came back one final time in the third year premiere episode as a pre-recorded video message for his son made prior to his death.

Back in October of 2005 George had acknowledged publicly that he was gay and that he had been in a longtime relationship—eighteen years or so—with his partner Brad Altman. This revelation only came as a surprise to the public at large because George had never really kept his sexual orientation a secret, and to his many *Star Trek* fans it had long been an open secret.

When the California Supreme Court ruled positively on gay marriage in 2008, George and Brad were among the first to file for a marriage license in West Hollywood and were officially married on Sunday, September 14, 2008. His *Star Trek* comrades Walter Koenig and Nichelle Nichols served as best man and best lady for the ceremony which also included Hollywood executives, local and national government officials, and the couple's relatives.

As Spock would say, "May they live long and prosper."

Victor Sen Yung

February 6, 1978

*"He who takes whatever gods send with
smile has learned life's hardest lesson."*
— Charlie Chan

Victor Sen Yung appears here in his Hop Sing costume from the popular
television series, *Bonanza*.

I've tried to piece together just why I was in Miami, Florida, on that February morning in 1978 when I discovered that Victor Sen Yung was in the city. The thing is that I rarely had cause to visit this most southern major city we have in the state, but there I was eating breakfast in a hotel coffee shop and reading the *Miami Herald*.

In my browsing through the paper, I came upon a good-sized advertisement for the personal appearance of Victor Sen Yung, Hop Sing of the popular Western TV series *Bonanza*, as it went on to say. The ad indicated that he would be at the local Richards Department Store in the house-ware's department at 11:00, 2:00, and 4:00 p.m. that day demonstrating wok cooking. The ad urged ladies *and* gentlemen to attend and learn how to improve their skills with this novel pan, the wok. In addition he would be autographing copies of his book, *Victor Sen Yung's Great Wok Cookbook.*

I couldn't resist the enticement of the ad. Here was the Chinese cook that had worked in the employ of Ben Cartwright on the Ponderosa way out there in Nevada and had prepared the meals for Ben and his three sons, Adam, Hoss, and Little Joe. How many times had I seen him chase pie-stealing Hoss out of the kitchen, waving dangerously a huge meat cleaver? How many times had I vicariously sat with Ben and the boys at the Ponderosa dinner table, chowing down on one of Hop Sing's culinary creations as the beaming cook looked on expectantly for the praise that was sure to come?

But there were more happy memories for me that went all the way back to my childhood when my folks would give me a quarter for the Saturday matinee at the Lincoln Theater in Elyria, Ohio. I would purchase a ticket, popcorn, and a Coke and go into the "air cooled" theater and see this same Victor Sen Yung in a role I appreciated even more than Hop Sing: number two son, Jimmy Chan, of that great Chinese detective who lived in Honolulu and solved difficult cases all over the world, Charlie Chan. There was no question about it; I was going to visit the houseware's department of that store today.

The cashier at the coffee shop was able to give me directions to Richards (no apostrophe), and soon I was pulling into the parking garage near the store. I rode the escalator to the second floor where I discovered about thirty-five folding chairs set up near the middle of the floor, most of them occupied by ladies—no gentlemen. In front was a table with a hot plate on which the demonstration was about to take place; it was 11:00 I felt a little awkward, the only "gentleman" among all of these ladies, but there are times when a man has to be brave.

In a few moments a man came to the table in front of us—I figured he had to be the manager of the store—and introduced Victor Sen Yung, who entered vigorously from a side door dressed in what I would call a Chinese tunic, slacks, a white chef's apron, and Hop Sing's skullcap. He looked and acted—in the genial-but-humble Chinese manner—just the way you would expect, greeting us and beginning his wok demonstration in his Chinese accent that we all, I'm sure, remembered from his *Bonanza* years.

It took little time for Victor to win the hearts and minds of the group of ladies in front of him and the one gentleman. The demonstration was fast paced and efficient, and then there was time available for specific questions from the ladies regarding such wok matters as food preparation, gauging the time and temperature needed for preparing the meal in the best possible manner, etc. Victor handled the questions with the skill of a master chef. I was very impressed.

After about thirty minutes the demonstration and questions came to an end. We all applauded enthusiastically, Victor graciously bowed in the Chinese manner, a cashier magically appeared to take the money of those who wished to purchase a wok, and Victor adjourned to a table at the side where a number of ladies gathered to purchase an autographed copy of his book. And then it was over.

As Victor was rising from his autograph table, I walked over and introduced myself, told him of my radio program in Sarasota, and asked if I might talk with him about his film and TV career. (I was taken aback for a moment as he spoke to me in standard American English with no

Chinese accent—but, of course, there had been no accent when he played Jimmy Chan in all those films.) He seemed pleased and maybe flattered when I mentioned how much I enjoyed his Chan films from so many years before. It appeared that *Bonanza* had swallowed up remembrance of that earlier career as number two son for many people.

Victor indicated that he needed to talk with the store manager and get some lunch before his two o'clock demonstration, but if I could come back at one he would enjoy "talking about the old days," as he put it. I left, grabbed some lunch, and was back on the second floor with my tape recorder at one o'clock. Victor was waiting for me.

David: Many film fans remember you played number two son, Jimmy Chan, in quite a number of the Charlie Chan films, and they know you as Hop Sing on *Bonanza*. But let me go back and ask you a few questions about your early days of acting. You were very young at the time of the Chan films; did you have any acting experience before that?

Victor: No, I didn't do any acting until I got into the Charlie Chan series except for one thing: in 1936 I worked as an extra in *The Good Earth* with Paul Muni and Louise Rainer. I was one of the farmers on the farm that helped fight the fires and kill the pests that came. But I got into the Chan series just by accident.

After I graduated from college—I went to the University of Southern California—things were tough. I had a job selling flame proofing and moth proofing, so I made an appointment to go out to the studio to talk to them about that. I didn't know they were looking for a boy to do the part of the son in the Charlie Chan series. While I was there, they saw me and asked me to do a screen test, and that's how I got the part and got started.

David: Just that easy.

Victor: Just that easy, yes.

David: Keye Luke was the number one son before you. Do you know why he left the series?

Victor: Well, there were two reports. One of them was that he was going to be featured [in a film entitled] *The Son of Chan Carries On*[311] and that his agent held out for too much money, and they decided to go with another Charlie Chan and another son. The other story—and the one that I think is probably more likely—is that he was negotiating for a part in the Doctor Kildare series with Lionel Barrymore. He got into that series shortly after I got in the Charlie Chan series, and he worked at MGM for quite a few years as Dr. Lee in the Doctor Kildare series.[312]

David: *Charlie Chan in Honolulu.*[313]

Victor: That was the first one with Eddie Collins, Robert Barrat . . . .

David: And that was the first film with Sidney Toler playing Chan.

Victor: I started with Sidney Toler in the Charlie Chan series. Then when I came out of the service, I went back into the series and worked with him. He passed away [in 1947] and then they signed Roland Winters to do the part of Charlie Chan and I did six pictures with Roland Winters. Then they discontinued the series.

David: I noticed that you weren't in the Chan pictures during World War Two, and I wondered if that was because you were in the service.

Victor: Yes, I was in the service. I went in as a private and wound up in the first motion picture unit in Culver City, helping them make training films for the Army Air Force, but I was very dissatisfied and I kept requesting a transfer so I could get to China. Finally I ended up in New York in the *Winged Victory*[314] show. Oh, that was a great cast: Eddie O'Brien, Lee J. Cobb, just a great group of talent.

I was still unhappy, so while I was in New York I applied for OCS [Officer's Candidate School], and I was accepted by the board at Mitchell Field. Just when we went out to California to do the show [Winged Victory], I got my orders to go to OCS, so I wound up at Kelly Field, and then later went on up to Harvard Graduate School of Business Administration, and I wound up as a staff control officer down at Memphis, Tennessee.

In this scene from *The Trap* (1947), Sidney Toler as Chan is on the case with number two son Jimmy and Mantan Moreland as Birmingham, Charlie Chan's chauffeur.

David: Back to the Chan series. None of the actors who played Charlie Chan were Asian.

Victor: I think there was a main reason for that. In those days the star system was still very much a practice in the studios, and if they could build up anybody in the way of a name, they could use them in other parts and to do other shows. Also, I think they tried to maintain the appearance that Warner Oland first established as Charlie Chan, sort of stocky, with the mustache and the hat, you know. I had no objection to that.

Toler was very helpful to me. Because it was about the first chance I had to do anything in the way of a speaking part in a motion picture, he guided me and taught me a lot. When I started under contract to Fox, I went to a dramatic school and started to learn as much as I could about the business. Toler taught me a lot about comedy and about timing, especially. He was a great comedian.

David: It's hard to think of him as a comedian. On screen we see him as Charlie Chan, the famous Honolulu detective, and he's very serious, wary, and brimming over with Chinese aphorisms. Some of those, however, were very funny. ["Silence is golden, except in police station." "Confucius say, 'Hasty decision is like ancient egg—look good from outside.'"]

Victor: He was full of the devil, very jovial, great sense of humor. After we started the series, he bought a golf driving range right across the street from the studio. We used to have a lot of fun out there just hitting golf balls and chatting, you know.

David: Sidney Toler, our Charlie Chan, hitting golf balls!

Victor: Right! *[Laugh]* The reason for it [the driving range] was not so much the golf range itself. It was because it was near the studio, and it also had a little sandwich stand and a patio. It was kind of a gathering place for all the young actors. This was what he enjoyed, mingling with the younger people.

Mantan Moreland and Victor provided comedy relief when the series moved to Monogram Pictures in 1944.

David: The series was produced by Twentieth Century-Fox for a number of years and then it went to Monogram Pictures.

Victor: Yeah, that was during the war, while I was in the service. You see, during the time I was in the series, we worked three years and then the war broke out in Europe and then broke out in Asia. During that time Twentieth Century-Fox lost their foreign market, so as a result they discontinued the series because they couldn't recoup the cost of production by just American exhibition alone.[315]

David: So Monogram, a smaller studio, took over the series and added the character played by Mantan Moreland.

Victor: Birmingham Brown, the chauffeur.

David: Everybody remembers Birmingham, the Black chauffeur in the Chan films. He was just tremendously popular; I believe he died only a few years back.[316] What kind of a man was he on the set?

Victor: *[Chuckle]* Mantan was just like what you saw on the screen. He was a great dancer, a hoofer, and tap dancer. He was always kidding around, always had a fast quip.[317] A lot of people mistook him for Rochester, you know, Eddie Anderson [from the *Jack Benny Program*]. He laughed it off most of the time, but a lot of times he insisted that, after all, he did have an identity of his own.

David: He certainly did. How long did it generally take to produce one of the Charlie Chan films?

Victor: Well, when we were shooting at Twentieth Century-Fox, it took between twenty-five and thirty-eight days, depending on the production schedule. At Monogram it was almost like television, seven days, six days. They were quick, fast.

David: I know. Roland Winters has made the comment that they really ground those out fast, those last ones at Monogram. There was a gap of some years from the time the Charlie Chan series ended until we next became very aware of you on the *Bonanza* television series. Did you keep busy during those years?

Victor: Oh, yes. I concentrated on character work. There were a lot of shows that I did, features: *The Left Hand of God,*[318] *Blood Alley,*[319] *The Hunters.*[320] There were many roles where nobody recognized me. Like the part that I did on *Bonanza,* Hop Sing; it's difficult for a person to recognize me because [reverting to the pidgin-English Chinese he used as Hop Sing] I speak so differently and with the hat on [breaking off the dialect] I look like somebody else.

David: *Bonanza*[321] came along in 1959 and was the top show on television for quite a few years. How did you happen to get cast in *Bonanza?*

Victor: It was an interview. It was funny the way it happened because I walked in there speaking the way I am now [standard American English, no dialect]. I talked with a Mr. Stanley who was a producer on the show. He reached back on his desk and got a script and tossed it across the desk to me and said, "We have here in this show the part of a Chinese cook." And I went right into character [in pidgin-English Chinese], "Oh, you want Chinese cook? I can cook anything you like." That was it! That's how I got it.

David: Were you with the series right from the beginning?

Victor: Yes, my interview was for the pilot. Then after the pilot was made, it was picked up by RCA, the company that made the first color television sets.[322]

David: For NBC television and sponsored by Chevrolet.

Victor: I'm sure they already had the sponsorship set up. What they were trying to do was work out the problems of color television because *Bonanza* was the first color television series on the air.[323]

David: There were four stars on *Bonanza* for many years. Let me run their names by you for a comment. Lorne Greene, Ben Cartwright.

Victor: Major-domo, head of the house. He was that way off camera too, always. He's austere, speaks well with good enunciation, very serious, not much in the way of a fast sense of humor.[324]

Ben Cartwright (Lorne Greene) of *Bonanza* is seen here with his three sons: Hoss (Dan Blocker), Little Joe (Michael Landon), and Adam (Pernell Roberts). The *Bonanza* series ran for fourteen years on the NBC network.

David: Dan Blocker, Hoss.

Victor: Now Dan Blocker was different. He always liked to talk out of the corner of his mouth and was to me like a big teddy bear—a very lovable fellow with a very soft and tender heart, great fun to be with, a real buddy.[325]

David: Michael Landon, Little Joe.

Victor: At the beginning I thought that he was aloof because he didn't socialize much. He'd say hello and that would be about it. But I think he's a genius; his mind is going all the time, and he doesn't have time to waste on things that are insignificant. It proved itself in the fact that he is now producer, writer, director, and star of *Little House on the Prairie*. He's done well.[326]

David: Pernell Roberts, Adam.

Victor: Pernell is a very fine man, a good actor, a very sensitive man. He had a tendency at times to keep to himself, but he was very friendly. We became good friends and used to have dinner together and chatted a lot.

David: Why did he leave *Bonanza* before the series was over?

Victor: The understanding I had was that he wanted to go to Connecticut or some state on the Eastern Seaboard and set up a Shakespearian theater. He's a great Shakespearian actor. It didn't pan out because it's very difficult to set up that sort of thing. The ultra cultural Shakespearian theater is not that commercial. When he went back to Hollywood after that, he did a few things, and then he toured on the road with Ingrid Bergman for about two and a half, three years on stage. Now he's back in Hollywood working, very active.[327]

David: The *Bonanza* series seemed to run forever.

Victor: In terms of production we were in production for fourteen years. We've been in reruns now for many years.

David: You had the role of Hop Sing, the cook, and we all saw you it seems like every week. But I'm sure there were some weeks you weren't on the show. What was your schedule like?

Victor: It was very loose. I didn't really appear in that many shows. I would say that I've been in about twenty-five per cent of the shows. There was always some reference among the boys about Hop Sing cooking the dinner or just the fact that when they're shooting in the kitchen or the dining room table, it's more or less understood that I'm in the back or upstairs or doing something—that I'm around the place—so that people think that I worked in every show, but I didn't.

In the meantime what I did were a lot of other freelancing jobs, working in different pictures, and doing public relations work. It was at that time that I actually got started into doing public relations work for food companies. I started with a company called Genuwine, and then I was with Chun King for four years promoting their products all over the country.

Then when I had a little time on my hands after they cancelled the *Bonanza* series, I wrote this cook book, *The Great Wok Cook Book*, and from that I got into the development of a wok, and that's what I'm doing now. I'm here in the Richards stores. It has been very, very rewarding in many respects, and it is just beginning. I've only been at it now on the road tour and selling like this for about a year and a half.

David: You do a great job of it. I watched the program this morning and it was most fascinating. During your talk you mentioned the *Kung Fu*[328] series. Did you appear in many episodes of that series?

Victor: Yes, I did about eighteen of those shows over a period of about three years, but every show I worked in I played a different character. It was a lot of fun. The last one I did I played the part of a hermit that was up in the mountains and came down and saved the town. I was supposed to be about eighty-five years old with long scraggly hair. It was a two-part episode.

It was fun, and working with David Carradine was sort of . . . an experience, I would say. He had his own private life and all, but he was a great guy. I didn't know him as a child, but I remember his father quite well, John Carradine. He was under contract to Twentieth Century-Fox when I was there, when he was in *The Grapes of Wrath*. I used to see him on occasion and we would chat a bit.

I was just starting in then, working in the Charlie Chan series, and I'd look at these guys [under contract then at Twentieth Century-Fox]: John Carradine, Tyrone Power, and Don Ameche. I'd look at them with awe and thinking if I could only do what they are doing, and do it well. I just learned so much by watching them and finally going to USC and taking the courses in cinematography and motion picture production and film editing—just to learn the business, learn the trade. It's just like anything else; as you get along, you continue to learn, which makes life interesting.

David: Very nice talking with you, Victor Sen Yung.

Victor: Thank you, Dave. I really enjoyed it.

I left the Miami department store after our conversation, got my car out of the parking garage, and headed back to Sarasota. As I drove the long hours towards home, my mind lingered on Victor and the whole scene that I had visited that day. There was about Victor that day an aura of wistfulness and loneliness when he wasn't involved in his wok demonstration. There were moments as he recalled for me working in the Charlie Chan films and the later *Bonanza* series that he was exuberant and upbeat, but that faded into a distant stare as he finished. I could sense his discomfiture in this current role that life had found for him. The ladies enjoyed his "performance" as he spoke in his pidgin-English Chinese and extolled the wonders of the wok and his cookbook—and many of them had made a purchase. He succeeded admirably in this newest role, but. . . .

It appeared that for most of the ladies his Hop Sing years were at best only a dim memory and that Jimmy Chan was totally lost in the mist of memory. And, of course, why should that not be so? It had been years since Victor worked regularly in films and TV, and the audience had moved on. Only show business junkies remembered or cared to go back and check the résumé.

I wished afterwards that I had thought to ask him about the scary situation he had experienced six years previously. On July 5, 1972, he was traveling on a Pacific Southwest Airlines plane on a flight from Sacramento, California, to San Francisco when a hijacking attempt took place. The hijackers wanted the plane to be flown to Russia. When the FBI stormed the plane, Victor was accidentally shot in the back by an FBI bullet. He and one other passenger, who was also injured, survived, but the two hijackers and one other passenger died. I should have remembered the incident and asked him about it.

I had no way of knowing during our meeting that Victor was not doing well financially. But when you look back on the roles that he played over the years, it soon becomes evident that most of them were in low-budget pictures or were bit parts that would hardly pay more than union minimum. And he had reminded me in our conversation that during the *Bonanza* years, he wasn't in *that* many episodes and that the Hop Sing role was smaller than most people remembered. We tend to think that the actors we see on the screens must be rich *because* they are on the big and little screens. As Gershwin told us, "It ain't necessarily so."

Victor Sen Yung returned to Los Angeles when his short tour of department stores concluded and soon started work on a second cookbook. His first book had been a moderate success and, since he was recognized as an accomplished chef who specialized in Cantonese-style cooking, a second book seemed to be a good idea.

But the second book was not to be finished. He had been working in his apartment making clay ware and curing it in his kitchen oven when fate took a hand. Victor Sen Yung was found dead on January 9, 1980, from carbon monoxide poisoning due to a gas leak in the stove. At first authorities described the death as under "mysterious circumstances" but later determined that it was accidental.

Victor Sen Yung was survived by one child (from his marriage that had ended in divorce) and two grandchildren. Pernell Roberts, his friend from the *Bonanza* years, gave the eulogy at the funeral. He was buried in Greenlawn Memorial Park at Colma, California. It was reported that Victor Sen Yung was virtually penniless at his death.

Author David Rothel

About the Author

David Rothel is the author of twelve books, mostly in the western film history/biography genre (*Who Was That Masked Man: The Story of the Lone Ranger, The Singing Cowboys, An Ambush of Ghosts, Those Great Cowboy Sidekicks, Richard Boone: A Knight without Armor in a Savage Land,* etc.). He created and hosted a daily radio program in Sarasota, Florida, entitled *Nostalgia Newsbreak* which featured conversations with famous show business personalities. Mr. Rothel has been the Director of the federally-funded Sarasota Visual and Performing Arts Center and, in more recent years, Executive/Artistic Director of the Black Bear Dinner Theatre in North Georgia. He has been a contributor to NPR's *All Things Considered,* the BBC's *Omnibus,* and was twice interviewed by Leonard Maltin on *Entertainment Tonight.* He and his wife Nancy reside in Dahlonega, Georgia.

Notes

Milton Berle

1. *Milton Berle, an Autobiography* was written by Milton Berle and Haskel Frankel and published by Dell in 1975.

2. Some reports set the annual fee at $200,000 and stated that it was renegotiated in 1966 to $120,000 per year (or $60,000 if the actual fee was $100,000) to permit Milton to work on other networks. The $100,000 per year contract seems to be the more commonly accepted figure.

3. *Sun Valley Serenade*, Twentieth Century-Fox, (1941) Starred Sonja Henie, John Payne, Glenn Miller, Milton Berle, Lynn Bari, Joan Davis, Dorothy Dandridge.

4. *Whispering Ghosts*, Twentieth Century-Fox, (1942) starred Milton Berle, Brenda Joyce, John Shelton, John Carradine, Willie Best, Grady Sutton, Renie Riano.

5. *Over My Dead Body*, Twentieth Century-Fox, (1942) starred Milton Berle, Mary Beth Hughes, Reginald Denny, Frank Orth, Leon Belasco.

6. *It's a Mad, Mad, Mad, Mad World*, United Artists, (1963) starred Spencer Tracy, Milton Berle, Sid Caesar, Buddy Hackett, Ethel Merman, Mickey Rooney, Phil Silvers, and an all-star supporting cast.

7. *The Perils of Pauline*, Eclectic Film Co., (1914) starred Pearl White, Crane Wilbur, Paul Panzer, Francis Carlyle, Clifford Bruce, Milton Berle (uncredited), Sidney Blackmer (uncredited).

8. In his autobiography Milton goes on to say that he was "scared shitless, even when he (the director) went on to tell me that Pauline would save my life. Which is exactly what happened, except that at the crucial moment they threw a bundle of rags instead of me from the train."

9. *Hey, Abbott!*, VidAmerica, (1978) Milton Berle (narrator/host), Guest commentators: Steve Allen, Joe Besser, Phil Silvers.

10. Milton appeared as guest villain "Louie the Lilac" in several episodes of the *Batman* television series in the 1960s.

11. *Rebecca of Sunnybrook Farm,* Artcraft, (1917) starred Mary Pickford, Eugene O'Brien, Helen Jerome Eddy, Charles Ogle, Margorie Daw, Zasu Pitts.

12. United Artists was founded in 1919 by Mary Pickford, Charlie Chaplin, Douglas Fairbanks, and D. W. Griffith.

13. *Texaco Star Theater,* later *The Buick-Berle show,* even later *The Milton Berle Show,* ran from June of 1948 until 1956 on NBC, Tuesday nights from 8-9 p.m. A pioneering comedy/variety show on TV, it was credited with sparking the sales of television sets from 500,000 its first year to over 30 million sets by the time of the show's demise in 1956, thus creating the title "Mr. Television" for Milton.

14. Ben Bernie (May 30, 1891—October 23, 1943) is less remembered today than some of his contemporaries mentioned here. Bernie was a jazz violinist and radio personality who was introduced on his shows as "The Old Maestro." He was popular on radio from the late 1920s until his death in 1943. To boost his radio ratings in the late 1930s, Bernie and Walter Winchell, also popular on radio, staged a fake rivalry which transferred into two films *Wake up and Live* (1937) and *Love and Hisses* (1937) in which they played themselves.

15. Milt Josefsberg (June 29, 1911—December 14, 1987) was a top comedy writer for Jack Benny on radio and television, and later wrote for such TV shows as *All in the Family* and *The Lucy Show.*

16. Ted Healy (October 1, 1896—December 21, 1937) was a popular vaudeville performer, comedian, and actor in his own right who is remembered today primarily as the man who created the Three Stooges act. Ted Healy and His Stooges appeared in a string of Broadway shows (*A Night in Spain, A Night in Venice*) and the film *Soup to Nuts* (1930) before the Three Stooges went on their own.

17. Remember, Jimmy Carter was President at the time of my conversation with Milton, and President Carter had a trouble-prone brother, Billy Carter.

18. There was never a book by that title published by Milton, but it may have been re-titled *Milton Berle's Private Joke File: Over 10,000 of His Best Gags, Anecdotes, and One-liners.* It was published by Three Rivers Press in 1989 and was 672 pages in length.

19. *Two Heads Are Better than None* was based on the Children's show *Kenan & Kel,* a sitcom about two teenagers which ran on Nickelodeon from 1996 until 2000.

Lloyd Bridges

20. *The Great Wallendas,* Daniel Wilson Productions/NBC, (1978) starred Lloyd Bridges, Britt Ekland, Tiana Elg, Cathy Rigby, William Sadler, Isa Thomas, John Van Dreelen, Ben Fuhrman, Bruce Ornstein. The film tells the story of 'The Flying Wallendas," a family of circus acrobats (headed by father Karl) famous for their seven-person, high-wire pyramid act that ended in tragedy in Detroit on January 30, 1962, when Karl's son-in-law and nephew died and his son was crippled. It goes on to tell of their triumphant comeback in Fort Worth in 1963.

21. *The Lone Wolf Takes a Chance*, Columbia, (1941) starred Warren William, June Storey, Henry Wilcoxon, Eric Blore, Thurston Hall, Don Beddoe, Evalyn Knapp, Lloyd Bridges.

22. Green Mansions was a summer resort in the Adirondacks—Chesterton, New York, to be exact—that back in the 1930s was the summer home of the Group Theatre.

23. Harry Cohn (July 23, 1891—February 27, 1958) was the often-tyrannical president and production director of Columbia Pictures in Hollywood.

24. The Group Theatre was founded in New York by Harold Clurman, Cheryl Crawford, and Lee Strasberg in 1931 and stressed a forceful, naturalistic style of acting derived from the teachings of Constantin Stanislavski. The Actors Studio evolved out of the Group Theatre in later years.

25. Tommy Cook (July 5, 1930) was a child actor who first played Red Ryder's Indian friend Little Beaver in the 1940 film serial *The Adventures of Red Ryder* and then went on to play the role on radio. Tommy's film/radio career waned as he reach adulthood, but he became one of the leading junior tennis players in Southern California and eventually parlayed that into the role of emcee/producer/director of celebrity gala/charity events.

26. Reed Hadley (June 25, 1911—December 11, 1974) was a movie, radio, and television actor who frequently did voice-overs for documentaries. He played Red Ryder on radio, Zorro in the film serial *Zorro's Fighting Legion*, and starred in *Racket Squad* and *Public Defender* on TV in the 1950s.

27. *A Walk in the Sun*, Louis Milestone Productions, (1945) starred Dana Andrews, Richard Conte, George Tyne, John Ireland, Lloyd Bridges, Sterling Holloway, Norman Lloyd, Huntz Hall.

28. *Canyon Passage*, Universal, (1946) starred Dana Andrews, Brian Donlevy, Susan Hayward, Ward Bond, Hoagy Carmichael, Fay Holden, Lloyd Bridges, Andy Devine.

29. *Home of the Brave*, United Artists, (1949) starred Douglas Dick, Jeff Corey, Lloyd Bridges, Frank Lovejoy, James Edwards, Steve Brodie.

30. *Rocket Ship X-M*, Lippert Pictures, (1950) starred Lloyd Bridges, Osa Massen, John Emery, Noah Beery, Jr., Morris Ankrum.

31. *Little Big Horn*, Lippert Pictures (1951) starred Lloyd Bridges, John Ireland, Marie Windsor, Reed Hadley, Jim Davis, Hugh O'Brian, King Donovan, Sheb Wooley, Rodd Redwing.

32. *High Noon*, United Artists, (1952) starred Gary Cooper, Thomas Mitchell, Lloyd Bridges, Katy Jurado, Grace Kelly, Otto Kruger, Lon Chaney, Jr., Harry Morgan.

33. *The Rainmaker*, Paramount, (1956) starred Burt Lancaster, Katharine Hepburn, Wendell Corey, Lloyd Bridges, Earl Holliman, Wallace Ford.

34. *The Goddess*, Columbia, (1958) starred Kim Stanley, Lloyd Bridges, Steven Hill, Betty Lou Holland, Joan Copeland, Gerald Hiken, Patty Duke.

35. *Sea Hunt* was a syndicated television series that was produced between 1957 and 1961 and consisted of one hundred and fifty-six thirty-minute episodes. The series was produced by Ivan Tors, who also produced such other television shows such as *Flipper, Gentle Ben,* and *Daktari* in the 1960s.

36. Lloyd wasn't working too much at that time because of allegations that he had been involved with the Communist Party. Lloyd's involvement with the Actors Lab, which was considered by some to be a radical theater with ties to the Communist Party, led to his name being on the show business blacklist at the height of McCarthyism in the 1950s. He was later given clearance by the FBI.

37. *The Lloyd Bridges Show* ran from September 11, 1962 until August 27, 1963 on CBS. It was produced by Aaron Spelling (April 22, 1923—June 23, 2006), legendary film and television producer famous for producing such TV series as *Charlie's Angels, Beverly Hills 90210, Dynasty, The Mod Squad,* and many others.

38. *The Loner* ran from September 18, 1965, until April 30, 1966, on CBS. The series was created by Rod Serling (December 25, 1924—June 28, 1975), most famous for *The Twilight Zone,* and was a western that took place just after the Civil War. Serling also wrote a number of the twenty-six episodes in the series.

39. Richard Kiley (March 31, 1922—March 5, 1999) was a Tony, Emmy, and Golden Globe winner who originally starred in *Man of La Mancha* (1965) on Broadway. He also starred in such other Broadway musicals as *Kismet* (1953) and *No Strings* (1962).

40. José Ferrer (January 8, 1909—January 26, 1992) was a three-time Tony award winner for acting and directing, and an Academy Award winner for *Cyrano de Bergerac* (1950). He was also known for his two marriages to Rosemary Clooney which produced five children.

41. *Tucker: The Man and His Dream,* Paramount, (1988) starred Jeff Bridges, Joan Allen, Martin Landau, Frederic Forrest, Dean Stockwell, Mako, Lloyd Bridges (uncredited), Elias Koteas, Christian Slater.

42. *Harts of the West,* Kushner-Locke company/CBS, (September 25, 1993—June 18, 1994) starred Beau Bridges, with regulars Saginaw Grant, Meghann Haldeman, O-Lan Jones, Harley Jane Kozak, Sean Murray, Stephen Root, Talisa Soto, Nathan Watt, and Lloyd Bridges for seven episodes.

43. *Airplane,* Paramount, (1980) starred Robert Hays, Julie Hagerty, Leslie Nielsen, Robert Stack, Lloyd Bridges, Peter Graves, and guest stars.

44. *Airplane II: The Sequel,* Paramount, (1982) starred Robert Hays, Julie Hagerty, Lloyd Bridges, Chad Everett, Peter Graves, Chuck Connors, William Shatner, Raymond Burr, and many other guest stars.

45. *Hot Shots!,* Twentieth Century-Fox, (1991) starred Charlie Sheen, Cary Elwes, Lloyd Bridges, John Cryer, Valeria Golino, Kevin Dunn, Kristy Swanson, Efrem Zimbalist, Jr.

46. *Hot Shots! Part Deux,* Paramount, (1993) starred Charlie Sheen, Lloyd Bridges, Valeria Golino, Richard Crenna, Brenda Bakke, Miguel Ferrer, Rowan Atkinson.

47. *Jane Austin's Mafia,* Touchstone Pictures, (1998) starred Jay Mohr, Billy Burke, Christina Applegate, Lloyd Bridges, Pamela Gridley, Olympia Dukakis.

Hans Conreid

48. *The First Nighter Program*, as it was formally called, created the aura of a Broadway opening on the weekly programs. The scripts tended to be light, romantic comedies for the most part. Starting in December of 1930, the show ran with few breaks until 1952. Don Ameche became the first star of the program but left in the late 1930s for Hollywood. Barbara Luddy was the female star of the program for most of its years on the air.

49. These radio programs were broadcast from the studios of WXYZ in Detroit, Michigan, starting in the early 1930s and running through the mid 1950s.

50. The program was called *Streamlined Shakespeare* and was broadcast on NBC Blue during the summer of 1937. John Dunning in his book *Tune in Yesterday* states that "Barrymore offered the Bard in an unusual format—a narrative sketch, punctuated by dramatized scenes, and streamlined to 45 minutes each."

51. Mel Blanc (May 30, 1908-July 10, 1989) *The Mel Blanc Show* aired on CBS starting in 1946. In the show Mel ran a fix-shop and got embroiled in typical sitcom exploits. In the running scripts Mel was a member of "The Loyal Order of Benevolent Zebras" of which Hans, as "Mr. Cushing," was the Lodge president. The "Ugga-Bo" routine was the password for the Lodge and became a popular catch phrase on the show. Other radio favorites such as Alan Reed and Bea Benaderet showed up frequently on the half-hour weekly show.

52. *Life with Luigi* starring J. Carrol Naish (January 21, 1897-January 24, 1973) was a hugely popular radio situation comedy about Italian immigrants which ran on CBS from the fall of 1948 until 1953.

53. *My Friend Irma* starring Marie Wilson (August 19, 1916-November 23, 1972) was first heard on radio in early 1947 and concerned the adventures of a lovable "dumb blonde," "Irma," and her roommate "Jane," who narrated the programs and was the sane, practical person on the show. Each script had Irma interacting with the same group of people: "Mrs. O'Reilly her landlady, "Al" her boyfriend, "Mr. Clyde" her boss, and "Professor Kropotkin" who lived in the attic. The show ran on CBS until 1954 and spawned two film versions.

54. Gale Gordon (February 20, 1906-June 30, 1995) was a top character actor on radio and later television, best known, perhaps, as principal "Osgood Conklin" on the radio and TV versions of *Our Miss Brooks* and "Mr. Mooney" on Lucille Ball's second TV show, *The Lucy Show*.

55. *The Jack Paar Show* was a 1947 summer replacement for *The Jack Benny Program*. It was a sitcom much in the manner of the Benny program.

56. This was during Paar's tenure as host of the *Tonight Show*, 1957-1962.

57. Jack Paar's daughter Randy appeared occasionally on her father's television show over the years. Jack Paar (May 1, 1918-January 27, 2004) underwent triple-bypass heart surgery in 1998 and then suffered a stroke the year before he died, 2004.

58. *Make Room for Daddy* starring Danny Thomas (January 6, 1912-February 6, 1991) premiered in September of 1953 and was a sitcom about the life of "Danny

Williams," a nightclub comedian who struggles to maintain his work, a wife, and children. The show changed its name after three seasons and became *The Danny Thomas Show*. When it returned after a hiatus of several years, the show was re-titled *Danny Thomas in Make Room for Granddaddy* and ran until September of 1971.

59.   *The Tony Randall Show* ran from September of 1976 until March of 1978 on ABC and then CBS television. Randall played a Court of Common Pleas judge in the series and Hans, coming on the second season, played Tony's father, a liberal-minded character named Wyatt Franklin, who felt that his son was something of a stuffed shirt—like father like son, I guess.

60.   *Summer Stock*, MGM, (1950) starred Judy Garland, Gene Kelly, Eddie Bracken, Margorie Main, Gloria DeHaven, Phil Silvers, Hans Conried.

61.   *Peter Pan*, Walt Disney, (1953) starred voices of Bobby Driscoll, Kathryn Beaumont, Hans Conried, Bill Thompson, Heather Angel, Candy Candido, Tom Conway.

62.   *Three for Bedroom C*, Warner Bros., (1952) starred Gloria Swanson, Fred Clark, James Warren, Steve Brodie, Hans Conried.

63.   *The Monster That Challenged the World*, United Artists, (1957) starred Tim Holt, Audrey Dalton, Hans Conried, Casey Adams, Gordon Jones, Jody McCrea.

64.   *The Five Thousand Fingers of Dr. T*, Columbia Pictures, (1953) starred Peter Lind Hayes, Mary Healy, Tommy Rettig, Hans Conried.

65.   Dr. Suess was the pen name of Theodor Suess Geisel (March 2, 1904-September 24, 1991), known for such children's writings as *The Cat in the Hat, Horton Hears a Who!, How the Grinch Stole Christmas!*, and dozens more. Many of his stories, of course, have been made into films.

66.   Stanley Kramer (September 29, 1913-February 19, 2001), one of Hollywood's most successful producers and directors, is known for such films as *High Noon, On the Beach, Inherit the Wind, Guess Who's Coming to Dinner*, and *The Caine Mutiny*.

67.   *The Rocky and Bullwinkle Show* is the collective title for two popular animated TV series: *Rocky and His Friends* on ABC (1959-1961) and *The Bullwinkle Show* NBC (1961-1964). The latter show reverted to ABC briefly in 1964 and then was cancelled. The show(s) have been in reruns and syndication since then.

68.   *The Cat from Outer Space*, Walt Disney Productions, (1978) starred Ken Berry, Sandy Duncan, Harry Morgan, Roddy McDowall, McLean Stevenson, Jesse White, Alan Young, Hans Conried.

69.   *Oh, God! Book II*, Warner Bros., (1980) starred George Burns, Suzanne Pleshette, David Birney, Wilfrid Hyde-White, Howard Duff, Hans Conried.

70.   *Drak Pack* was an animated television series that aired on CBS Saturday mornings between September 6, 1980 and September 12, 1982.

71.   *The Second Time Around* AKA *Something Old, Something New*, a comedy about generational differences, was written by Henry Denker.

Dennis Day

72. Since Bobby Breen may have slipped off your show business radar, let me do a recap of his career. Bobby Breen was a Canadian-born boy soprano back in the 1930s, performing both in radio and films. Eddie Cantor has been given credit for "discovering" Bobby and featuring him on his hugely popular weekly radio show of the thirties. Breen added film work to his schedule in 1936 with *Let's Sing Again*. Altogether he made nine films, concluding with *Johnny Doughboy* in 1942. His performing career continued well into the 1960s, performing in nightclubs, on stage, and in a local TV show in New York City. Sometime in the 1970s he opened his booking agency in Sarasota, Florida, and began bringing in show business personalities to perform in the Florida condominium and retirement home circuit.

73. Larry Clinton was a prominent bandleader during the late 1930s until the start of World War Two and had a radio program for part of that period.

74. An air check is a demonstration recording, often intended to be used for later audition purposes.

75. Raymond Paige and Ray Block were orchestra conductors for CBS at the time. With the coming of television, Ray Block gained prominence as the musical conductor for the Ed Sullivan and Jackie Gleason shows.

76. Kenny Baker was Jack Benny's "boy singer" on his popular radio program during the 1930s. He was a tenor with a voice much like Dennis Day's.

77. Verna Felton became famous on radio for playing the grandmother of Red Skelton's character of "Junior the Mean Widdle Kid" on Skelton's radio series and for playing Dennis Day's mother on *The Jack Benny Program*. She was also widely known for providing the voices for many animated characters, most notably for the Fairy Godmother in Disney's Cinderella (1950).

78. Jerry Colonna, of course, was Bob Hope's longtime comic stooge on Hope's radio and later television shows.

79. Titus Moody was a crusty New England Yankee-type character who was a regular on the Allen's Alley segment of *The Fred Allen Show* on radio. The role was played by actor Parker Fennelly.

80. *A Day in the Life of Dennis Day* came to NBC radio as a weekly series on October 3, 1946, sponsored by Colgate-Palmolive. Dennis usually sang two songs during each episode of this situation-comedy-with- music. The show ran until 1951.

81. *Melody Time*, Walt Disney, released by RKO, (1948) starred Roy Rogers, Luana Patten, Bobby Driscoll, Ethel Smith, Bob Nolan, Sons of the Pioneers, and the voices of Buddy Clark, The Andrews Sisters, Fred Waring and his Pennsylvanians, Frances Langford, Dennis Day, with Freddy Martin and his Orchestra.

82. Cliff Arquette (December 28, 1905—September 23, 1974) was most famous for his role as comic country rustic "Charley Weaver." Arquette was a regular on Dennis's show and any number of other shows from the 1950s until his death. Most prominently he was a frequent guest on Jack Paar's *Tonight Show* and later

variety show and a panelist on *Hollywood Squares*.

83. *Buck Benny Rides Again*, Paramount, (1940) starred Jack Benny, Ellen Drew, Andy Devine, Phil Harris, Virginia Dale, Dennis Day, Eddie "Rochester" Anderson.

84. *Sleepy Lagoon*, Republic Pictures, (1943) starred Judy Canova, Dennis Day, Ruth Donnelly, Joe Sawyer, Ernest Truex, Douglas Fowley.

85. *Music in Manhattan*, RKO, (1944) starred Anne Shirley, Dennis Day, Phillip Terry, Raymond Walburn, Jane Darwell.

86. *I'll Get By*, Twentieth Century-Fox, (1950) starred June Haver, William Lundigan, Gloria DeHaven, Dennis Day, Thelma Ritter.

87. *Golden Girl*, Twentieth Century-Fox (1951) starred Mitzi Gaynor, Dale Robertson, Dennis Day, Una Merkel.

88. *The Girl Next Door*, Twentieth Century-Fox (1953) starred Dan Dailey, June Haver, Dennis Day, Cara Williams, Natalie Schafer.

89. Based on Dickens' *A Christmas Carol*, Rankin/Bass Productions produced *The Stingiest Man in Town* which starred Walter Matthau as Ebenezer Scrooge with Tom Bosley, Theodore Bikel, Robert Morse, and Dennis Day. There had been a live 1976 TV presentation of the same title starring Basil Rathbone in the Scrooge role.

Phyllis Diller

90. The three movies with Bob Hope were Boy, *Did I get a Wrong Number!* (1966), *Eight on the Lam* (1967), and *The Private Navy of Sgt. O'Farrell* (1968). The three films came late in Hope's movie career and were unsuccessful at the box office.

91. *Splendor in the Grass*, Warner Bros., (1961) starred Natalie Wood, Warren Beatty, Pat Hingle, and Phyllis Diller (way down in the cast listing). Elia Kazan directed from a script by William Inge.

92. Mary Louise Cecilia "Texas" Guinan (January 12, 1884—November 5, 1933) was a saloon keeper, actress, and entrepreneur famous for the catch phrase, "Hello, Suckers." Other actresses who played Texas Guinan or a character based on her included Betty Hutton, Mae West, Gladys George, and even Whoopi Goldberg who played a bartender named "Guinan" on *Star Trek: The Next Generation*.

93. Totie Fields (May 7, 1930—August 2, 1978) was a short, heavy-set, standup comedienne in the Phyllis Diller mold who frequently made fun of her weight, health problems, and looks. By the mid 1970s her health problems had became acute. Her left leg was amputated above the knee because of a blood clot. While recovering from the amputation, she had two heart attacks, and then breast cancer was discovered. She continued to make appearances throughout this time. Totie Fields died of a pulmonary embolism at her Las Vegas home shortly before she was to appear at the Sahara Hotel.

94. Joan Rivers (June 8, 1933) over the years—perhaps more than any other woman—continued to carry the standup comedienne banner that Phyllis Diller founded. In more recent years she has also acquired several other titles: actress, businesswoman, talk show host, and show business celebrity.

95. Elayne Boosler (August 18, 1952) was still a fledgling when Phyllis and I talked in 1978, but she became the first female comedienne to get her own comedy special on cable when Showtime aired her "Party of One" special in 1986. She has since had six more specials and is widely credited with opening doors to women in comedy.

96. Those two series were *The Pruitts of Southampton*, a sitcom that ran on ABC from September 6, 1966, through September 1, 1967, and *The Beautiful Phyllis Diller show*, a comedy-variety series that was on NBC from September 15, 1968, until December 22, 1968.

97. The show was a sitcom entitled *C.P.O. Sharkey* in which Rickles was cast as Chief Petty Officer Sharkey of the U.S. Navy. The show lasted from December 1, 1976, until July of 1978.

98. *The Adding Machine*, Universal Pictures, (1969) starred Milo O'Shea, Phyllis Diller, Billie Whitelaw, Sydney Chaplin.

99. Jerome Epstein (January 17, 1922—November 16, 1991) wrote the screenplay and directed *The Adding Machine*. As Phyllis mentions, he was with Charles Chaplin for many years. He was Chaplin's assistant on *Limelight* (1952), associate producer (uncredited) for *A King in New York* (1957), and was producer on Chaplin's last film, *A Countess from Hong Kong* (1967).

100. As of the year 2000, Phyllis had appeared for charity as a piano soloist with one hundred symphony orchestras across the United States, including performances in Dallas, Denver, Annapolis, Houston, Baltimore, Pittsburgh, Detroit, and Sarasota.

Tony Dow & Jerry Mathers

101. *Bury Me Dead*, Eagle-Lion (previously PRC), (1947) starred Cathy O'Donnell, June Lockhart, Hugh Beaumont, Mark Daniels.

102. *The Trouble with Harry*, Paramount, (1955) starred John Forsythe, Shirley MacLaine, Edmund Gwenn, Mildred Natwick, Mildred Dunnock, Jerry Mathers, Royal Dano.

103. Connelly and Moser along with Dick Conway were the creators of the show which originally ran from April 23, 1957, until June 20, 1963, for a total of 234 episodes.

104. Hugh Beaumont (February 16, 1909—May 14, 1982) continued his career for a few years after *Leave It to Beaver* ended, appearing as a guest actor on such shows as *The Virginian*, *Wagon Train*, and *Medical Center*. By 1970 he pretty much retired from acting and became a Christmas tree farmer in Minnesota, his

wife's home state. In 1972 he had the stroke that Tony referred to and never completely recovered from it. He died of a heart attack on May 14, 1982, while visiting his son Hunter, a psychology professor in Munich, Germany.

105. Paul Petersen (September 23, 1945) and Mickey Dolenz (March 8, 1945), of course, were popular child performers: Petersen's most prominent role was as son "Jeff" in the popular *Donna Reed Show* (1958-1966). Dolenz was the drummer and lead singer on *The Monkees* TV series (1966-1968) and much earlier, under the name Micky Braddock, was the title character in the TV series *Circus Boy* (1956-1958).

106. *Never Too Young* was a short-lived attempt by ABC-TV to create a teenage daytime soap opera. Tony, in a far cry from his all-American good son "Wally Cleaver" role, played "Chet," a race-car loving, reckless troublemaker. Others in the cast included Tommy Rettig in a post-*Lassie* role, John Lupton post-*Broken Arrow*, and Dack Rambo pre-*The Guns of Will Sonnett*. The series ran from September 27, 1965, until June 24, 1966.

Tom Ewell

107. *Adam's Rib*, MGM, (1949) starred Spencer Tracy, Katharine Hepburn, Judy Holliday, Tom Ewell, David Wayne, Jean Hagen, and Hope Emerson.

108. *Up Front*, Universal International Pictures, (1951) starred David Wayne (Joe), Tom Ewell (Willie), Jeffrey Lynn, and Richard Egan. *Back at the Front*, Universal International Pictures, (1952) starred Tom Ewell (Willie), Harvey Lembeck (Joe), Mari Blanchard, Richard Long, and Gregg Palmer.

109. *They Shall Not Die* by John Wexler opened on Broadway on February 21, 1934, and ran for 62 performances. In addition to Claude Rains, Ruth Gordon, and Tom Ewell, the cast included Dean Jagger, Thurston Hall, and Erskine Sanford.

110. *Ethan Frome* by Owen Davis and Donald Davis from a previous dramatization by Lowell Barrington of the novel by Edith Wharton opened on Broadway January 21, 1936, and ran for 120 performances. The cast included Ruth Gordon, Raymond Massey, Pauline Lord, Oliver Barbour, and Tom Ewell.

111. *John Loves Mary* by Norman Krasna opened on Broadway on February 4, 1947, and ran for 423 performances. Included in the cast were Tom Ewell, Nina Foch, Lyle Bettger, William Prince, and Max Showalter

112. *The Seven Year Itch* by George Axelrod opened on Broadway on November 20, 1952, and ran for 1141 performances. Included in the cast were Tom Ewell, Vanessa Brown, Marilyn Clark, Joan Donovan, Robert Emhardt, and Neva Patterson.

113. *The Tunnel of Love* by Joseph Fields and Peter DeVries, based on the novel by Peter DeVries, opened on Broadway February 13, 1957, and ran for 417 performances. Included in the cast were Tom Ewell, Sylvia Daneel, Elisabeth Fraser, Darren McGavin, Nancy Olson, and Elizabeth Wilson.

114. George S. Kaufman (November 16, 1889—June 2, 1961) was a playwright, theater director, producer, and humorist, among other things. He was known as "The Great Collaborator" because he frequently co-wrote with other playwrights. Some of his shows include *The Royal Family*, *Dinner at Eight*, and *Stage Door* with John P. Marquand. With Moss Hart his writings included *You Can't Take It with You* and *The Man Who Came to Dinner*. Kaufman directed such shows as *Of Mice and Men*, *The Front Page*, and *Guys and Dolls*. He was also an esteemed member of the celebrated Algonquin Round Table, a circle of witty writers and show business people.

115. In case you forgot, Huntington Hartford was an A&P heir.

116. Vanessa Brown (March 24, 1928—May 21, 1999) had an IQ of 165 which led to her being selected as a young panelist on the radio series entitled *Quiz Kids*. Her work there caused Hollywood to take an interest, and she first appeared on film in the David O. Selznick production of *Youth Runs Wild* (1944). Other films include *The Ghost and Mrs. Muir* (1947), *The Heiress* (1949), and *Tarzan and the Slave Girl* (1950). She worked a lot in television in the fifties (*Robert Montgomery Presents*, *The Philco Television Playhouse*). Vanessa originated the role of "The Girl" in the Broadway production of *The Seven Year Itch*. She continued to work in television in later years. Vanessa Brown died of breast cancer in 1999 at the age of seventy one.

117. Tom is referring, of course, to Robert Blake, the star of the television series *Baretta*. *Baretta* was a police drama about a streetwise, tough cop (Tony Baretta) who used unorthodox methods (disguises and such to infiltrate the bad guys, etc.) that ran on ABC television from January 17, 1975, until June 1, 1978. Tom played Billy Truman, a retired cop who was the manager and house detective at the hotel where Baretta lived. Tony had a pet cockatoo named Fred that Billy watched over when Tony was on the job.

118. *The Great Show Business Animals* by David Rothel was published in 1980 by A. S. Barnes & Company, Inc.

119. Hal Erickson, *All Movie Guide*.

Walter B. Gibson

120. Harry Houdini (March 24, 1874—October 31, 1926) was, of course, the famous magician and escape artist. A master of self-promotion, he was widely regarded as the greatest in his field. Late in life he turned his energies toward debunking psychics and mediums, a phenomenon of the times. His study of "magic" over the years had given him the knowledge to ferret out frauds that had been able to fool scientists and academics.

121. Howard Thurston (July 20, 1869—April 13, 1936) was another famous magician of the era. He called himself "The King of Cards" for his famous "rising card" trick. He had a huge touring vaudeville/magic show for many years. It took eight train cars to transport his props and magical devices as he traveled across the country. Thurston died of a stroke in his hometown of Columbus, Ohio.

122. *The Shadow* first went on the air in August of 1930 with Jack LaCurto as the Shadow/narrator. From 1930 through to the fall of 1937 the program continued in this manner with LaCurto followed by Frank Readick, George Earle, and Robert Hardy Andrews in the narrator's role.

123. Frank Gruber (February 2, 1904-December 9, 1969) was one of the great pulp writers, writing more than three hundred stories for over forty pulp magazines during the early years of his career. Later he turned to movies, writing screenplays for such films as *Northern Pursuit* (1942), two Sherlock Holmes films: *Terror by Night* (1946) and *Dressed to Kill* (1946), as well as films based on his own novels: *The Big Land* (1957), *Backlash* (1956). He later wrote for television series such as *Tales of Wells Fargo* (1957-1962), *The Texan* (1958-1960), and *Shotgun Slade* ((1959-1961).

124. Orson Welles (May 6, 1915-October 10, 1985) played the role of the Shadow from September 26, 1937, until late into 1938. It was at the beginning of his tenure of *The Shadow* that the character became an integral part of the story and not just a narrator.

125. John Houseman (September 22, 1902-October 31, 1988), along with Orson Wells, founded the Mercury Theatre, which produced several plays in New York in the late 1930s and early forties and is best remembered for the 1938 radio production of H. G. Wells' *The War of the Worlds*. He later went on his own and had a long career as a producer, director, and actor in films and television.

126. The "they" refers to other Mercury Theatre actors who frequently acted on *The Shadow*, most notably Agnes Morehead as Margo Lane.

127. Bill Johnstone (February 7, 1908-November 1, 1996) took over the role of the Shadow after Welles left in 1938 and played the role until 1943.

128. Bret Morrison (May 5, 1912-September 25, 1978) played the Shadow longer than any other actor, spending ten years in the role in two separate runs. He was the final actor to play the role when the radio series ended in 1954.

129. Harry Blackstone (September 27, 1885-November 16, 1965) was a famous magician and illusionist. "The Great Blackstone," as he was billed, gained much additional fame during World War Two when he toured the troupe camps as a USO entertainer.

130. Joseph Dunninger (April 28, 1892-March 9, 1975) was known as "The Amazing Dunninger" and was primarily a "mentalist," although he did do some magic. As a mentalist he was able to work his trade on radio starting in 1943 with *Dunninger the Mentalist* and continued his act when television came along in the late 1940s. Dunninger had his own show on network television as late as 1956.

131. *Houdini*, Paramount Pictures, (1953) starred Tony Curtis, Janet Leigh, Torin Thatcher, Ian Wolfe, Sig Ruman.

Myrna Loy

132. *The Desert Song*, Warner Bros., (1929) starred John Boles, Carlotta King, Myrna Loy, Louise Fazenda, Johnny Arthur, Edward Martindel, Jack Pratt.

133. *The Mask of Fu Manchu*, MGM, (1932) starred Boris Karloff, Lewis Stone, Karen Morley, Charles Starrett, Myrna Loy, Jean Hersholt, Lawrence Grant, David Torrence.

134. The Thin Man series consisted of six films that were produced by MGM. The films were *The Thin Man* (1934), *After the Thin Man* (1936), *Another Thin Man* (1939), *Shadow of the Thin Man* (1941), *The Thin Man Goes Home* (1944), and *Song of the Thin Man* (1947). W. S. Van Dyke directed the first four in the series. Richard Thorpe directed the fifth and Edward Buzzell the last. Many then little-known actors came out of the supporting casts to successful careers: James Stewart, Sam Levene, Cesar Romero, Penny Singleton, Barry Nelson and Donna Reed, just to mention a few.

135. W. S. "Woody" Van Dyke (March 21, 1889—February 5, 1943) started directing during silent films and by the advent of the sound era he was one of MGM's most capable directors. Known as "One Take Woody" because of the speed with which he completed his films, he received Academy Award nominations for *The Thin Man* (1934) and *San Francisco* (1936). His other outstanding films include *Trader Horn* (1931) *Tarzan the Ape Man* (1932), and *Rose Marie* (1936). His last film *was Journey for Margaret* (1942), by which time he had terminal cancer. He said goodbye to his wife, children, and boss Louis B. Mayer of MGM and committed suicide.

136. Dashiell Hammett, of course, was the author of hardboiled detective novels such as *The Maltese Falcon, The Thin Man*, and the *Glass Key*.

137. William Powell (July 29, 1892—March 5, 1984) was a three-time Oscar-nominated actor (*The Thin Man* in 1934, *My Man Godfrey* in 1936, and *Life with Father* in 1947). His other notable films included *The Great Ziegfeld* (1936), *Ziegfeld Follies* (1946), and *Mister Roberts* (1955) He died at age ninety one, thirty years after his retirement.

138. Actually James Cagney (July 17, 1899—March 30, 1986) came out of retirement after my conversation with Myrna Loy. He starred in the 1981 Miloš Forman film *Ragtime* and made a TV movie in 1983 for CBS entitled *Terrible Joe Moran*, and then re-retired.

139. William Powell was diagnosed with colon cancer during the mid thirties.

140. Actually Powell had played detective Philo Vance three previous times before *The Kennel Murder Case*, going back to 1929: *The Canary Murder Case* (1929), *The Greene Murder Case* (1929), and *The Benson Murder Case* (1930). The Philo Vance films were based on the popular novels of S. S Van Dine.

141. Actually, Nick, Jr. was in two films: *Another Thin Man* (1936) played by William A. Poulson in apparently his only film role and *Shadow of the Thin Man* (1941) where he was played by Dickie Hall who appeared in a number of films between 1941 and '45 and then disappeared from films.

142. *The Best Years of Our Lives*, Samuel Goldwyn, (1946) starred Myrna Loy, Fredric March, Dana Andrews, Teresa Wright, Virginia Mayo, Cathy O'Donnell, Hoagy Carmichael, Harold Russell.

143. *Mr. Blandings Builds His Dream House*, RKO Radio, (1946) starred Cary Grant, Myrna Loy, Melvyn Douglas, Reginald Denny, Louise Beavers, Harry Shannon, Lex Barker, Emory Parnell.

144. *The End*, United Artists, (1978) starred Burt Reynolds, Dom DeLuise, Sally Field, Strother Martin, David Steinberg, Joanne Woodward, Norman Fell, Myrna Loy, Kristy McNichol, Pat O'Brien, Robby Benson, Carl Reiner. The film had not yet been released when I talked with Myrna Loy.

145. Burt Reynolds directed *The End.*

146. *Cheaper by the Dozen*, Twentieth Century-Fox, (1950) starred Clifton Webb, Myrna Loy, Jeanne Crain, Betty Lynn. The sequel, *Belles on Their Toes*, was released in 1952 with pretty much the same cast except Clifton Webb, whose character had died in the interim.

Jock Mahoney

147. The *Range Rider* (1951-1953) was a syndicated television series produced by Gene Autry's Flying A Productions. There were seventy-nine half-hour episodes in the series which starred Jock Mahoney (billed as Jack for the series) and Dick Jones, a former child actor.

148. *Slim Carter*, Universal International, (1957) starred Jock Mahoney, Julie Adams, Tim Hovey, William Hopper, Ben Johnson, Margaret Field (Jock's wife), Bill Williams, Barbara Hale.

149. *Yancy Derringer* was an action/adventure series set in New Orleans right after the Civil War. Yancy was an ex-Confederate soldier/gambler/adventurer/lady's man who sometimes worked as a special agent in the city to prevent crimes and capture criminals. His constant companion was an Indian name Pahoo, played by actor X Brands.

150. *Tightrope* (1959-1960) starred Mike Connors and was a popular police drama which had a one-season, thirty-seven-episode run on CBS and then was dropped.

151. *Tarzan the Magnificent*, Paramount, (1960) starred Gordon Scott, Jock Mahoney, Betta St. John, John Carradine, Lionel Jeffries.

152. *Tarzan Goes to India*, MGM, (1962) starred Jock Mahoney, Jai, Leo Gordon, Mark Dana, Feroz Khan.

153. *Tarzan's Three Challenges*, MGM, (1963) starred Jock Mahoney, Woody Strode, Tsu Kobayashi, Ricky Der.

154. Jock reportedly had the stroke while filming an episode of the television series *Kung Fu* with David Carradine.

155. Jock had married Margaret Field in the 1950s and thus became the stepfather for her daughter Sally Field.

156. *Tarzan, the Ape Man*, MGM, (1981) starred Bo Derek, Richard Harris, John Phillip Law, Miles O'Keeffe, Wilfrid Hyde-White.

Virginia Mayo

157. Other guest stars announced for the 1990 Western Film Fair were Billy Benedict, MacDonald Carey, Frank Coghlan, Jr., Ben Cooper, Oliver Drake, Lash LaRue, Jimmy Rogers, and Virginia Vale.

158. Ken had been my film festival buddy and photographer for about as long as I had been attending these festivals. He had also accompanied me on my research trips

during the writing of several of my books, keeping a photographic record of where we went and who we met and talked to.

159. *Jack London*, United Artists, (1943) starred Michael O'Shea, Susan Hayward, Osa Massen, Harry Davenport, Frank Craven, Virginia Mayo.

160. *Up in Arms*, RKO, (1944) starred Danny Kaye, Dana Andrews, Constance Dowling, Dinah Shore, Louis Calhern.

161. *The Princess and the Pirate*, RKO, (1944) starred Bob Hope, Virginia Mayo, Walter Slezak, Walter Brennan, Victor McLaglen.

162. *The Best Years of Our Lives*, RKO, (1946) starred Myrna Loy, Fredric March, Dana Andrews, Teresa Wright, Virginia Mayo.

163. *The Secret Life of Walter Mitty*, RKO, (1947) starred Danny Kaye, Virginia Mayo, Boris Karloff.

164. *Wonder Man*, RKO, (1945) starred Danny Kaye, Virginia Mayo, Vera-Ellen, Donald Woods.

165. *The Kid from Brooklyn*, RKO, (1946) starred Danny Kaye, Virginia Mayo, Vera-Ellen, Steve Cochran, Eve Arden.

166. *White Heat*, Warner Bros., (1949) starred James Cagney, Virginia Mayo, Edmond O'Brien, Steve Cochran.

167. *Starlift*, Warner Bros., (1951) starred Janice Rule, Dick Wesson, and cameos by most Warner contract players: James Cagney, Virginia Mayo, Doris Day, Gordon MacRae, etc.

168. *West Point Story*, Warner Bros., (1950) starred James Cagney, Virginia Mayo, Doris Day, Gordon MacRae, Gene Nelson.

169. The number was "B'N'LYN (That's Where I Make Me Home In)." Jimmy was dressed in a flashy zoot suit and Virginia was in a slinky, sexy, show-girl-type gown.

170. *The Iron Mistress*, Warner Bros., (1952) starred Alan Ladd, Virginia Mayo, Joseph Calleia, Phyllis Kirk.

171. *The Carpetbaggers*, Paramount, (1964) starred George Peppard, Carroll Baker, Alan Ladd, Robert Cummings.

172. On January 29, 1964, Alan Ladd died in Palm Springs, California, of an overdose of alcohol and sedatives at the age of 50, a likely suicide.

173. *The Girl from Jones Beach*, Warner Bros., (1949) starred Ronald Reagan, Virginia Mayo, Eddie Bracken, Dona Drake, Henry Travers.

174. *Colorado Territory*, Warner Bros., (1949) starred Joel McCrea, Virginia Mayo, Dorothy Malone, Henry Hull.

175. *Always Leave Them Laughing*, Warner Bros. (1949) starred Milton Berle, Virginia Mayo, Ruth Roman, Bert Lahr, and Alan Hale.

176. *She's Working Her Way through College*, Warner Bros., (1952) starred Virginia Mayo, Ronald Reagan, Gene Nelson, Don DeFore, Phyllis Thaxter, Patrice Wymore, Roland Winters.

177. Jessica Tandy, of course, won the Oscar for *Driving Miss Daisy* (1989).

178. Michael O'Shea was a film and stage actor with an over-abundance of Irish charm who was active on stage and in films primarily from the 1940s to the sixties. He and Virginia were married in 1947 and had one daughter, Mary Catherine, who was born in 1953. He first gained prominence on stage in *The Eve of St. Mark* and then later reprised his stage role in the film version in 1944. His first film was *Lady of Burlesque* (1943) with Barbara Stanwyck. Subsequent films included musicals (*Something for the Boys*, 1944), Westerns (*Last of the Redmen*, 1947), and film noir (*Violence*, 1947, *Underworld Story*, 1950). He was a guest star on many TV shows and had his own series, *It's a Great Life*, from 1954-1956. Late in his career he toured with his wife Virginia in such shows as *George Washington Slept Here, Tunnel of Love* and the musical *Fiorello!* It has been reported that he was a "plainclothes operative for the CIA after retiring from show business." (I wish I'd known to ask Virginia about that during our conversation.) Michael O'Shea died of a heard attack on December 4, 1973, in Dallas, Texas.

179. *Captain Horatio Hornblower*, Warner Bros., (1951) starred Gregory Peck, Virginia Mayo, Robert Beatty.

180. Steve Cochran was a Goldwyn and later Warner contract player during the forties and early fifties, specializing in gangster and other assorted tough-guy roles. He appeared in several of Virginia Mayo's films.

181. Cochran died at age forty-eight on June 15, 1965, under curious circumstances. With a well-known reputation for womanizing, Cochran was on his yacht off the coast of Guatemala with three women when he died of acute lung infection. Since the women did not know how to operate the boat, it drifted for ten days before coming ashore in Port Champerico, Guatemala. As one might expect, the circumstances caused rumors of foul play, but nothing was turned up from a police investigation.

182. *Fort Dobbs*, Warner Bros., (1958) starred Clint Walker, Virginia Mayo, Brian Keith, Richard Eyer.

183. *South Sea Woman*, Warner Bros., (1953) starred Burt Lancaster, Virginia Mayo, Chuck Conners, Arthur Shields.

184. *The Flame and the Arrow*, Warner Bros., (1950) starred Burt Lancaster, Virginia Mayo, Robert Douglas, Aline McMahon, Nick Cravat.

185. *Westbound*, Warner Bros., (1959) starred Randolph Scott, Virginia Mayo, Karen Steele, Michael Pate, Andrew Duggan.

186. Vera-Ellen, of course, was a popular film dancer who worked in a couple of the Danny Kaye pictures with Virginia Mayo (*Wonder Man, The Kid from Brooklyn*) and then went on to MGM where she danced with Gene Kelly in *Words and Music* (1948) and *On the Town* (1949); and Fred Astaire in *Three Little Words* (1950) and *The Belle of New York* (1952). Her last major film was *White Christmas*, Paramount, (1954) with Bing Crosby and, once again, Danny Kaye.

187. The film actress Rhonda Fleming, for those few who might not know or remember, was a contemporary of Virginia Mayo who was especially known for her

beauty and flaming red hair. During her active years, mainly in the 1940s and fifties, she was often called the "Queen of Technicolor" because of her beautiful complexion and the fact that her red hair photographed so well in Technicolor. As of this writing Rhonda Fleming is eighty-six years old and married to her sixth husband.

188. *Evil Spirits*, Grand Am, (1990) starred Karen Black, Arte Johnson, Virginia Mayo, Michael Berryman, Martine Beswick, Bert Remsen, Anthony Eisley.

189. *The Silver Chalice*, Warner Bros., (1954) starred Virginia Mayo, Paul Newman, Pier Angeli, Jack Palance, Walter Hampton.

190. *Along the Great Divide*, Warner Bros., (1951) starred Kirk Douglas, Virginia Mayo, John Agar, Walter Brennan.

191. *Great Day in the Morning*, Warner Bros., (1956) starred Virginia Mayo, Robert Stack, Ruth Roman, Alex Nicol, Raymond Burr.

192. *King Richard and the Crusaders*, Warner Bros., (1954) starred Rex Harrison, Virginia Mayo, George Sanders, Laurence Harvey.

193. *Pearl of the South Pacific*, Warner Bros., (1955) starred Virginia Mayo, Dennis Morgan, David Farrar, Murvyn Vye.

Roddy McDowall

194. *How Green Was My Valley*, Twentieth Century-Fox, (1941) starred Walter Pidgeon, Maureen O'Hara, Anna Lee, Donald Crisp, Roddy McDowall, John Loder, Barry Fitzgerald, Patric Knowles, Arthur Shields.

195. *Man Hunt*, Twentieth Century-Fox, (1941) starred Walter Pidgeon, Joan Bennett, George Sanders, John Carradine, Roddy McDowall.

196. Fritz Lange (December 5, 1890—August 2, 1976) was an Austrian/German/American film director and screenwriter famous for utilizing German expressionism in many of his films, such as *M* and *Metropolis*. He was also an exponent of *film noir*, directing *The Big Heat* (1953) and *While the City Sleeps* (1956), among others.

197. Robert Morse (May 18, 1931) is best known for starring on Broadway and in the filmed version *of How to Succeed in Business without Really Trying.* Look for Bobby in volume two of *Opened Time Capsules.*

198. *The Loved One*, MGM, (1965) starred Robert Morse, Jonathan Winters, Anjanette Comer, Dana Andrews, Milton Berle, James Coburn, John Gielgud, Tab Hunter, Margaret Leighton, Liberace, Roddy McDowall, Robert Morley, Lionel Stander.

199. *My Friend Flicka*, Twentieth Century-Fox, (1943) starred Roddy McDowall, Preston Foster, Rita Johnson, James Bell, Patti Hale, Jeff Corey.

200. *Thunderhead, Son of Flicka*, Twentieth Century-Fox, (1945) starred Roddy McDowall, Preston Foster, Rita Johnson, James Bell, Patti Hale, Carleton Young, Ralph Sanford.

201. *The Great Show Business Animals* was published in 1980 by A. S. Barnes & Company, Inc.

202. *Lassie Come Home*, Twentieth Century-Fox, (1943) Roddy McDowall, Donald Crisp, Dame May Whitty, Edmund Gwenn, Nigel Bruce, Elsa Lanchester, Elizabeth Taylor, Alan Napier, Arthur Shields.

203. *The White Cliffs of Dover*, MGM, (1944) starred Irene Dunne, Alan Marshal, Roddy McDowall, Frank Morgan, Van Johnson, C. Aubrey Smith, Gladys Cooper, Peter Lawford, Dame May Whitty, Elizabeth Taylor, Norma Varden.

204. *Cleopatra*, Twentieth Century-Fox, (1963) starred Elizabeth Taylor, Richard Burton, Rex Harrison, Hume Cronyn, Martin Landau, Roddy McDowall.

205. Dame May Whitty (June 19, 1865—May 29, 1948) was an English actress who was Oscar-nominated for Best Supporting Actress for *Night Must Fall* (1937). She is best remembered for the lady who turns up missing in Alfred Hitchcock's *The Lady Vanishes* (1938).

206. Nigel Bruce (February 4, 1895—October 8, 1953) was an English character actor of stage, films, and radio who is most famous for his role of Dr. Watson in the Sherlock Holmes films and radio series.

207. Edmund Gwenn (September 26, 1875—September 6, 1959) was an Academy Award-winning English stage and film actor best known for his role as Kris Kringle in *Miracle on 34th Street* (1947) for which he won the Oscar for Best Supporting Actor. He was nominated again for Best Supporting Actor for *Mr. 880* (1950) but did not win.

208. Rudd Weatherwax (September 23, 1907—February 25, 1985) was an animal trainer who owned and trained Lassie for films, television, and even radio.

209. *Macbeth*, Republic Pictures, (1948) starred Orson Welles, Jeanette Nolan, Dan O'Herlihy, Roddy McDowall, Edgar Barrier, Alan Napier, Erskine Sanford, John Dierkes, Peggy Webber, Christopher Welles, Keene Curtis.

210. The film was not originally released until 1950, when a much edited version was released to mostly negative reviews. In 1980 the original uncut version with the original Scottish-tinged soundtrack was restored by the UCLA Film Archives and the Folger Shakespeare Library.

211. In other words, the actors lip-synced the entire film to their pre-recording of the script.

212. *Holiday in Mexico*, MGM (1946) starred Walter Pidgeon, José Iturbi, Roddy McDowall, Ilona Massey, Xavier Cugat, Jane Powell, Hugo Haas, Amparo Iturbi.

213. *Kidnapped*, Monogram Pictures, (1948) starred Roddy McDowall, Sue England, Dan O'Herlihy, Roland Winters, Jeff Corey, Erskine Sanford.

214. *The Subterraneans*, MGM, (1960) starred Leslie Caron, George Peppard, Janice Rule, Roddy McDowall, Anne Seymour, Jim Hutton, Scott Marlowe, Arte Johnson, Ruth Storey, Carmen McRae, André Previn.

215. *Misalliance* by George Bernard Shaw was written in 1909-1910. Roddy performed the play in New York in 1953.

216. *No Time for Sergeants*, the Ira Levine comedy, based on a novel by Mack Hyman, opened on Broadway on October 20, 1955, and ran for seven hundred and ninety-six performances. The show starred Andy Griffith, Myron McCormick, Roddy McDowall, and Don Knotts in his Broadway debut.

217. *Camelot*, with book and lyrics by Alan Jay Lerner and music by Frederic Loewe, opened on Broadway on December 3, 1960, and ran for eight hundred and seventy-three performances. The stars were Julie Andrews, Richard Burton, Roddy McDowall, and Robert Goulet in his Broadway debut.

218. *Compulsion* by Meyer Levin opened on Broadway on October 24, 1957, and ran for one hundred and forty performances. The show, based upon the famous Leopold and Loeb murder trial, starred Roddy McDowall, Dean Stockwell, Frank Conroy, Howard Da Silva, Ben Astar, Ina Balin, Michael Constantine.

219. *Planet of the Apes*, Twentieth Century-Fox, (1968) starred Charlton Heston, Roddy McDowall, Kim Hunter, Maurice Evans, James Whitmore, James Daly, Wright King.

220. The *Planet of the Apes* TV series was produced by Twentieth Century-Fox Television and ran on CBS from September 13, 1974, until December 20, 1974, consisting of fourteen one-hour episodes. The regulars on the series were Roddy McDowall, Ron Harper, James Naughton, and Mark Lenard.

221. *Otherwise Engaged* by English playwright Simon Gray has been described as a "bleakly comic play." After a run in London in 1975, the show traveled to Broadway, opening in February of 1977 with Tom Courtenay and Carolyn Lagerfelt in the cast. Roddy performed the show at the Parker Playhouse in Fort Lauderdale from January 9 through February 4, 1978.

222. *Evil Under the Sun*, Universal Pictures, (1982) starred Peter Ustinov, James Mason, Maggie Smith, Nicholas Clay, Jane Birkin, Colin Blakely, Sylvia Miles, Dennis Quilley, Roddy McDowall, Diana Rigg.

223. *Fright Night*, Columbia Pictures, (1985) starred Chris Sarandon, William Ragsdale, Amanda Bearse, Roddy McDowall, Stephen Geoffreys.

224. *Fright Night II*, TriStar Pictures, (1988) starred Roddy McDowall, William Ragsdale, Julie Carmen, Jon Gries, Russell Clark, Brian Thompson.

225. *A Bug's Life*, Pixar/Walt Disney Pictures, (1998) starred Dave Foley, Kevin Spacey, Julia Louis-Dreyfus, Hayden Panettiere, Phyllis Diller, David Hyde Pierce, Roddy McDowall as voice of Mr. Soil.

Spanky McFarland

226. The Sanger-Harris stores are now part of Macy's.

227. Hal Roach (January 14, 1892—November 2, 1992), over an extremely long career, was a movie and television producer who is especially remembered for the films of comics Harold Lloyd, Harry Langdon, and Laurel & Hardy. He also produced the *Our Gang* comedies.

228. George appears to be a bit on the high side with a hundred and fifty. Most sources give him credit for ninety-five *Our Gang* shorts and about seventeen other shorts or features, give or take a few.

229. *General Spanky*, Hal Roach Studios, (1936) starred George "Spanky" McFarland, Phillips Holmes, Ralph Morgan, Irving Pichel, Rosina Lawrence, Billie "Buckwheat" Thomas, Carl "Alfalfa" Switzer, Hobart Bosworth, Louise Beavers, Willie Best.

230. Most notable of those films are the Wheeler and Woolsey comedy *Kentucky Kernels* (1934) in which he played himself and The *Trail of the Lonesome Pine* (1936) with Sylvia Sidney, Fred MacMurray, and Henry Fonda. *Johnny Doughboy* (1942) with Jane Withers, Bobby Breen, and Carl "Alfalfa" Switzer was made just as Spanky concluded his Our Gang shorts.

231. *Woman in the Window*, RKO, (1945) starred Edward G. Robinson, Joan Bennett, Raymond Massey, Dan Duryea, Robert Blake (uncredited), George "Spanky" McFarland (uncredited).

232. When the *Our Gang* series was sold to television in the mid-1950s, the eighty Hal Roach-produced shorts with sound were syndicated under the title *The Little Rascals* because MGM retained the rights to the *Our Gang* trademark.

233. *The Aurora Encounter*, New World Pictures, (1986) starred Jack Elam, Peter Brown, Carol Bagdasarian, Dottie West, Will Mitchell, Charles B. Pierce, Mickey Hays, George "Spanky" McFarland.

Molly Picon

234. Paul Muni (September 22, 1895—August 25, 1967) was a highly respected actor of stage and films who won a Tony for *Inherit the Wind* (1956) on Broadway and was nominated five times for Academy Awards and won once for *The Story of Louis Pasteur* (1936).

235. Nazimova (May 22, 1879—July 13, 1945) was a Russian actress who was a pupil in Stanislavsky's acting company in Russia and studied his "method style" of acting. Later she became famous in America as a theater and film actress. Her flamboyant private life led to Hollywood gossip regarding her well-known bisexual lifestyle.

236. Sarah Bernhardt (October 22, 1844—March 26, 1923) became famous as a stage actress in Europe in the 1870s and soon crossed the ocean to America where she became even more famous as a serious dramatic actress. She became known as "The Devine Sarah."

237. Belle Baker (December 25, 1893—April 29, 1957) became famous as a vaudeville singer and later appeared on Broadway, in nightclubs, and on radio and television.

238. Fanny Brice (October 29, 1891—May 29, 1951) was a popular comedienne, singer, stage and film actress who is fondly remembered by radio fans for creating and starring in the popular program, *The Baby Snooks Show*, where she played a bratty little girl named Snooks. Fanny Brice's life was recounted in the Broadway musical *Funny Girl*.

239. The syndicated New York columnist (*The Voice of Broadway*) Dorothy Kilgallen and her husband Dick Kollmar did a long-running daily radio program entitled *Breakfast with Dorothy and Dick* which ran from 1945 until 1963.

240. *Come Blow Your Horn*, Paramount, (1963) starred Frank Sinatra, Lee J. Cobb, Molly Picon, Barbara Rush, Jill St. John, Dan Blocker, Phyllis McGuire, Tony Bill.

241. Robert Weede (February 22, 1903—July 9, 1972) was a highly regarded operatic baritone who debuted with the Metropolitan Opera in 1937 as Tonio in *Pagliacci* and went on to play major roles in such operas as *Aïda*, *Tosca*, and *Rigoletto*. He moved to Broadway in 1956 in Frank Loesser's hit show *The Most Happy Fellow* and followed that with *Milk and Honey* (1961-1963).

242. Mimi Benzell (May 6, 1924—December 23, 1970) was a soprano who performed with the Metropolitan Opera (*The Magic Flute*, *La Bohéme*, *Carmen*) before moving on to Broadway, television, and nightclubs. *Milk and Honey* was her only Broadway show.

243. George M. Cohan (July 3, 1878—November 5, 1942) was an American singer, dancer, actor, playwright, producer, director known as "The Man who owned Broadway" because of his varied abilities. Three of the four performers in the famous Cohan family were in the cast of *Broadway Jones* when it was on Broadway in 1912: George, his mother and father, but not his sister Josie.

244. Blanche Yurka ((June 18, 1887—June 6, 1974) was an American theater and film actress noted especially for her performance as Queen Gertrude in John Barrymore's 1922 Broadway production of *Hamlet* and for the role of Madame Defarge in *A Tale of Two Cities*, an MGM film of 1935.

245. *Fiddler on the Roof*, United Artists, (1971) starred Topol, Norma Crane, Leonard Frey, Molly Picon, Paul Mann, Rosemary Harris, Michele Marsh. The film won three Academy Awards and was nominated for an additional five, including Best Picture and Best Director.

246. Norman Jewison (July 21, 1926) is, of course, regarded as one of our outstanding Hollywood directors with such films as *In the Heat of the Night* (1967), *The Thomas Crown Affair* (1968), *Fiddler on the Roof* (1971) and *Jesus Christ Superstar* (1973) to his credit.

247. Jule Styne (December 31, 1905—September 26, 1994) was a famous Broadway songwriter of such shows as *Gentleman Prefer Blondes*, *Peter Pan*, *Bells Are Ringing*, *Gypsy*, and *Funny Girl*, as well as many songs for films, especially for Frank Sinatra.

248. Zero Mostel (February 28, 1915—September 8, 1977) was a famous actor of stage and movies who was best known for the role of Tevye in *Fiddler on the Roof*. Other famous roles included Pseudolus in *A Funny Thing Happened on the Way to the Forum*, and Max Bialystock in the fist movie version of *The Producers* (1968).

249. Boris Aronson (October 15, 1898—November 16, 1980) was an acclaimed scenic designer for Broadway and the Yiddish theater. Shows that he designed include *Fiddler on the Roof*, *Cabaret*, *Company*, *Follies*, *Zorba*, and *A Little Night Music*.

250. *For Pete's Sake*, Columbia Pictures, (1974) starred Barbra Streisand, Michael Sarrazin, Estelle Parsons, Molly Picon, William Redford, Heywood Hale Broun.

251. Myrna Loy, in fact, did play the role offered to Molly in the film *Airport 1975* (1974).

252. *Murder on Flight 502*, Spelling-Goldberg Productions/ABC, (1975) starred Ralph Bellamy, Polly Bergen, Theodore Bikel, Sonny Bono, Dane Clark, Lorraine Day, Fernando Lamas, George Maharis, Farrah Fawcett, Hugh O'Brian, Molly Picon, Walter Pidgeon, Robert Stack, Brooke Adams, Danny Bonaduce.

253. *The Second Time Around* by Henry Denker (see my conversation with him) was entitled *Something Old, Something New* when it opened on Broadway with Molly and Hans Conried in January of 1977 and was a failure. The show, however, was a hit in regional and dinner theaters across the country, before and after its Broadway flop.

254. The book was published two years after my conversation with Molly and was ultimately entitled simply *Molly! An Autobiography* by Molly Picon with Jean Grillo.

255. *The Cannonball Run*, Twentieth Century-Fox, (1981) starred Burt Reynolds; Roger Moore; Farrah Fawcett; Dom LeLuise; Dean Martin; Sammy Davis, Jr.; Jack Elam; Peter Fonda; Molly Picon; and many more "guest appearances."

256. *Cannonball Run II*, Warner Bros. (1984) starred Burt Reynolds; Dom DeLuise; Dean Martin; Sammy Davis, Jr.; Jamie Farr; Telly Savalas; Shirley MacLaine; Don Knotts; Frank Sinatra; Molly Picon; and many more "guest appearances."

Vincent Price

257. *The Saint* first joined the airwaves on NBC January 6, 1945, with Edgar Barrier playing the title role and sponsored by Bromo Seltzer. Later, in June of 1945, a new *Saint* ran during summer hiatus with Brian Aherne playing Simon Templar. Vincent Price was the star of the best-remembered radio version of *The Saint*. He started in the role during the summer of 1947 on CBS and then returned two years later in July of 1949 on Mutual, sponsored by the Ford Motor Company. The show moved to NBC in 1950 on a sustaining basis and Price ended his run on *The Saint* in May of 1951.

258. Leslie Charteris, the author of *The Saint* novels, novellas, and short stories, was born in Singapore on May 12, 1907, to a Chinese father and an English mother. The character of Simon Templar, the Saint, first appeared in Charteris's third novel, *Meet the Tiger*. He died on April 15, 1993, at his home in Windsor, Berkshire, England.

259. "Three Skeleton Key" was a memorable radio drama that was first broadcast on the CBS radio program *Escape* on November 15, 1949. Vincent Price was not in the original broadcast. Because of hundreds of requests, the story was rebroadcast four months later, this time with Price starring, and the program was stunning! (This, of course, was during the time when Price was regularly starring in *The Saint* weekly radio series.) Price portrayed Jean, the new lighthouse keeper who spots the rat infested ship that ultimately crashes onto Three Skeleton Key,

loosing the rats to then invade the lighthouse where Jean and his two compatriots are barricaded. A feeling of intense suspense and terror pervades the entire broadcast. Price reprised his role in another broadcast of the story on October 19, 1958, now on the weekly radio series, *Suspense*.

260. *The Lux Radio Theatre* production of *The Letter* was based upon the Warner Bros. film of 1940, directed by William Wyler and starring Bette Davis and Herbert Marshall. Vincent Price was not in the film.

261. *The Lux Radio Theatre* was first broadcast on NBC on October 14, 1934, dramatizing movies and sometimes Broadway plays (in the early days). In 1935 it moved to CBS and in 1936 Cecil B. DeMille became the host of the program and remained for many years, leaving at the start of the 1945 season. The show closed its long run on radio on June 7, 1955.

262. *The Lux Radio Theatre* production was based upon *The Song of Bernadette*, a 1943 Twentieth Century-Fox film which starred Jennifer Jones, William Eythe, Charles Bickford, Vincent Price, Lee J. Cobb, Anne Revere.

263. *Laura*, Twentieth Century-Fox, (1944) starred Gene Tierney, Dana Andrews, Clifton Webb, Vincent Price, Judith Anderson.

264. *Dragonwyck*, Twentieth Century-Fox, (1946) starred Gene Tierney, Walter Huston, Glenn Langan, Anne Revere, Spring Byington, Henry (Harry) Morgan, Jessica Tandy.

265. *Leave Her to Heaven*, Twentieth Century-Fox, (1945) starred Gene Tierney, Cornel Wilde, Jeanne Crain, Vincent Price, Ray Collins, Darryl Hickman, Gene Lockhart.

266. *Keys of the Kingdom*, Twentieth Century-Fox, (1944) starred Gregory Peck, Thomas Mitchell, Vincent Price, Edmund Gwenn, Roddy McDowall, Cedric Hardwicke, Peggy Ann Garner.

267. *The Eve of St. Mark*, Twentieth Century-Fox, (1944) starred Anne Baxter, William Eythe, Michael O'Shea, Vincent Price, Dickie Moore.

268. *The Raven*, American-International, (1963) starred Vincent Price, Boris Karloff, Peter Lorre, Hazel Court, Jack Nicholson.

269. *House of Usher*, American-International, (1960) starred Vincent Price, Mark Damon, Myrna Fahey.

270. *Tales of Terror*, American-International, (1962) starred Vincent Price, Peter Lorre, Basil Rathbone, Debra Paget.

271. *The Bat*, Allied Artists, (1959) starred Vincent Price, Agnes Moorehead, John Sutton.

272. *I Like What I Know—A Visual Autobiography* by Vincent Price. Doubleday & Company, Inc. Garden City, New York, copyright 1959.

273. *Diversions and Delights* by John Gay was directed by Joe Hardy and tells of the last year of Oscar Wilde's life when he was all but destitute. It takes place in a Paris theater where Wilde talks to the audience about his life, his writings, and even about his love for Lord Alfred Douglas that resulted in the scandal which brought him to ruin.

274. *Vincent,* Walt Disney Productions, (1982) narrated by Vincent Price.

275. *Edward Scissorhands,* Twentieth Century-Fox, (1990) starred Johnny Depp, Winona Ryder, Dianne Wiest, Anthony Michael Hall, Kathy Baker, Vincent Price, Alan Arkin.

276. *The Whales of August,* Nelson Entertainment, (1987) starred Bette Davis, Lillian Gish, Vincent Price, Ann Sothern, Harry Carey, Jr., Mary Steenburgen, Frank Grimes, Margaret Ladd, Tisha Sterling.

277. *Theatre of Blood,* Cineman Productions, United Artists, (1973) starred Vincent Price, Diana Rigg, Ian Hendry, Harry Andrews, Coral Browne, Robert Coote, Jack Hawkins, Robert Morley, Dennis Price, Diana Dors.

Gordon Scott

278. Sean Connery (1930) was just getting his career underway when he played the "second villain" in *Tarzan's Greatest Adventure* in 1959.

279. Anthony Quayle (September 13, 1913—October 20, 1989) was a highly regarded British actor and director. After a classical career on stage, he turned more to movies in the 1950s and was featured in such films as *The Guns of Navarone* (1961) and *Lawrence of Arabia* (1962). He was nominated for an Academy Award for Best Supporting Actor in 1969 for *Anne of the Thousand Days.* In *Tarzan's Greatest Adventure* (1959) he played the chief villain in the film.

280. *Tarzan's Hidden Jungle,* RKO, (1955) starred Gordon Scott, Vera Miles, Peter van Eyck, Jack Elam, Charles E. Fredericks, Richard Reeves.

281. Johnny Weismuller (June 2, 1904—January 20, 1984) was a 1920s Olympic swimmer who won five gold medals and one bronze medal and set sixty-seven world records. He was the sixth person to play Tarzan in films and is the actor most identified with the role.

282. Vera Miles (1929) was a film actress who is most known for work with directors John Ford (*The Searchers,* 1956, and *The Man Who Shot Liberty Valance,* 1962); and Alfred Hitchcock (*The Wrong Man,* 1957, and *Psycho,* 1959). She was under personal contract to Hitchcock and was to play the Kim Novak role in *Vertigo* for him but became pregnant and was unable to do the role, thus causing a falling out with Hitchcock who only used her in one more film. She retired from acting in 1995.

283. Jock Mahoney (February 7, 1919—December 14, 1989)), one of the great stuntmen of Hollywood, was the heavy "Coy Banton" in *Tarzan the Magnificent* (1960). The next year he took over the role of Tarzan from Gordon Scott. See my conversation with Jock Mahoney in this volume.

284. *Tarzan's Greatest Adventure,* Paramount, (1959) starred Gordon Scott, Anthony Quayle, Sarah Shane, Niall MacGinnis, Sean Connery, Al Mulock, Scilla Gabel. Many consider this the finest Tarzan film ever made.

285. *Greystoke: The Legend of Tarzan, Lord of the Apes,* Warner Bros., (1983) starred Christopher Lambert, Andie MacDowell, Ian Holm, Ralph Richardson, James Fox.

286. *Tarzan and the Trappers*, Sol Lesser Productions, (1958) starred Gordon Scott, Eve Brent, Rickie Sorensen, Cheeta, Lesley Bradley, Maurice Marsac, Scatman Crothers.

287. Steve Reeves (January 21, 1926—May 1, 2000) was a body builder who became an actor primarily in Italian "sword and sandal" epics such as director Pieto Francisci's *Hercules* (1958). He died of complications of lymphoma.

288. *Duel of the Titans*, Paramount, (1962) Starred Steve Reeves, Gordon Scott, Virna Lisi, Massimo Girotti, Ornella Vanoni, Jacques Sernas.

289. *The Tramplers*, Embassy Pictures, (1965) starred Gordon Scott, Joseph Cotton, Muriel Franklin, James Mitchum, Ilaria Occhini, Franco Nero.

290. *Danger!! Death Ray*, Asdrúbal, (1967) starred Gordon Scott, Maureen Delphy, Nello Pazzafini.

291. *Segretissimo*, Filmes Cinematografica, (1967) Emilio Arnaiz, Dali Bresciani, Aurora de Alba, Gordon Scott.

292. *Toronto Star*, 1987.

293. Adam Bernstein, *Washington Post*, Friday, May 4, 2007.

294. Frederick N. Rasmussen, *Baltimore Sun*, May 2, 2007.

295. *The New York Times*, June 4, 2007

296. Frederick N. Rasmussen, *Baltimore Sun*, May 2, 2007

George Takei

297. *Walk, Don't Run*, Columbia Pictures, (1966) starred Cary Grant, Samantha Eggar, Jim Hutton, John Standing, Miko Taka, Ted Hartley, Ben Astar, George Takei, Teru Shimada, Lois Kiuchi.

298. *The Green Berets*, Batjac/Warner Bros., (1968) starred John Wayne, David Janssen, Jim Hutton, Aldo Ray, Raymond St. Jacques, Bruce Cabot, Jack Soo, George Takei, Patrick Wayne, Luke Askew, Mike Henry.

299. Just for the record, the original *Star Trek* series that George was in ran on the NBC network from September 8, 1966, until September 2, 1969.

300. Gene Roddenberry (August 19, 1921—October 24, 1991) was a screenwriter and producer who created the world of *Star Trek*. He died of heart failure at the age of seventy. In 1992 his ashes flew in space aboard the space shuttle Columbia. In 1997 a small capsule (about the size of a lipstick) of his ashes was sent into space to orbit Earth for about six years.

301. Jeffrey Hunter (November 25, 1926—May 27, 1969) was a film and television actor, probably best known for his role of Martin Pawley in John Ford's *The Searchers* (1956) with John Wayne. He played Captain Christopher Pike in "The Cage," the first pilot for the *Star Trek* series. Hunter decided to concentrate on movies and so passed on the second pilot of the series. He died young of a cerebral hemorrhage.

302. Majel Barrett (February 23, 1932—December 18, 2008) is the one original cast member with whom the reader might not be familiar. She was in the initial pilot as the USS *Enterprise's* unnamed First Officer, "Number One." It was speculated that she acquired this major role as a result of being Gene Roddenberry's girl-friend, much to the dismay of NBC executives who insisted on a casting change. In following episodes she became Nurse Christine Chapel. When the original series ended in 1969, she became Mrs. Majel Barrett-Roddenberry and has been cast in some role in every incarnation of the *Star Trek* franchise. She died as a result of complications from Leukemia.

303. Leonard Nimoy (March 26, 1931), of course, was Spock, the half-human half-Vulcan in the original *Star Trek* series. He later played Spock in the *Star Trek* movies and directed *Star Trek III: The Search for Spock* (1984) *and Star Trek IV: The Voyage Home* (1986).

304. DeForest Kelly (January 20, 1920—June 11, 1999) played Dr. Leonard "Bones" McCoy in the original *Star Trek* series and movies. He died of stomach cancer.

305. *Fear in the Night*, Pine-Thomas Productions/Paramount Pictures, (1947) starred Paul Kelly, DeForest Kelly, Ann Doran, Kay Scott, Charles Victor, Robert Emmett Keane, Jeff York. This excellent *film noir*/mystery was DeForest Kelly's first film.

306. George may have known something that he was not able to tell me in 1977 when we talked. *Star Trek: Phase II* was in the works as a follow-up TV series to the original series and was tentatively scheduled to air in June of 1978 on what was to be a new television network, Paramount Pictures Television Network. Scripts were written with the original cast returning except for Leonard Nimoy as Spock because he was having legal disputes with Paramount at the time. The new network was ultimately deemed too risky at that time, and the success of the film *Star Wars* (1977) led Paramount to decide to go with a *Star Trek* movie instead.

307. *Baa, Baa Black Sheep* (September 21, 1976—September 1, 1978) was an NBC war drama TV series that starred Robert Conrad; James Whitmore, Jr.; and Dana Elcar.

308. This program was mentioned earlier in the Jock Mahoney chapter.

309. *Mirror Friend, Mirror Foe* by George Takei and Robert Asprin was published by Playboy Press Paperbacks, 1979.

310. *To the Stars* by George Takei was published by Pocket Books, a division of Simon & Schuster, Inc. in 1994.

Victor Sen Yung

311. Warner Oland, who had played Charlie Chan for some years, had just died, and the studio first thought of using Keye Luke in a "Son of" series.

312. Keye Luke didn't actually appear in the Dr. Kildare series; it had morphed into the Dr. Gillespie series by the time he joined the cast in 1942 in *Dr. Gillespie's New Assistant*.

313. *Charlie Chan in Honolulu*, Twentieth Century-Fox, (1938) starred Sidney Toler,

Phyllis Brooks, (Victor) Sen Yung, Eddie Collins, John King, George Zucco, Robert Barrat.

314. *Winged Victory* (1943) was playwright Moss Hart's warmhearted Broadway salute to the Air Forces of World War Two. The Broadway show was made into a Hollywood movie in 1944 with the screenplay also written by Hart.

315. When Fox decided to cancel the series, Sidney Toler bought the screen rights to the Chan films and made a deal with Monogram Pictures to continue the series, though as much lower-budgeted films. Eleven films were made at Monogram with Toler starring. When Toler died in 1948, Monogram continued the series with Roland Winters as Chan for six final films.

316. Mantan Moreland died of a cerebral hemorrhage on September 28, 1973.

317. Yes, Mantan was fast with a quip, but he was also famous for his "incomplete sentence" routines that he developed with his straight-man partner, Ben Carter. The act consisted of fast repartee between the two of them with neither man finishing a sentence but each obviously understanding completely what the other is saying. The hilarious routine, with many variations, can be seen in two Charlie Chan pictures, *The Scarlet Clue* (1945) and *Dark Alibi* (1946).

318. *The Left Hand of God*, Twentieth Century-Fox, (1955) starred Humphrey Bogart, Gene Tierney, Lee J. Cobb, Agnes Moorehead, E. G. Marshall, Benson Fong.

319. *Blood Alley*, Twentieth Century-Fox, (1955) starred John Wayne, Lauren Bacall, Paul Fix, Mike Mazurki, Anita Ekberg.

320. *The Hunters*, Twentieth Century-Fox, (1958) starred Dick Powell, Robert Mitchum, Robert Wagner, Mai Britt, Richard Egan, Lee Phillips.

321. *Bonanza*, a hugely popular western television series, ran on the NBC network from September 12, 1959, until January 16, 1973, lasting fourteen seasons. Only *Gunsmoke* was a longer running western TV series.

322. RCA owned NBC and the *Bonanza* series and wanted to use the series to push the popularity of color television sets, especially the RCA sets.

323. And sell color TV sets it did, as it became one of the top shows on the TV schedule. By the mid-sixties it had reached number one in the ratings, and by 1970 it had become the first series ever to be in the Top Five for nine consecutive seasons. It was the biggest hit series of the 1960s.

324. Lorne Greene was born in Canada on February 12, 1915, and died at age seventy-two on September 11, 1987, of complications from prostate cancer. He had a long television career after *Bonanza*. Highlights include the miniseries *Roots* in 1977 and another patriarchal role as Commander Adama in the science fiction TV series *Battlestar: Galactica* from 1978-1980. Shortly before his death he had signed a contract to appear in a revival of *Bonanza*.

325. Dan Blocker was born in DeKalb, Texas, on December 10, 1928, and died of a pulmonary embolism following routine gall bladder surgery on May 13, 1972. Probably the most beloved of the Cartwright sons, his death resulted in a decline in ratings for *Bonanza* and the series was cancelled after one more season.

326. Michael Landon was born on October 31, 1936, and died at age fifty-four on July 1, 1991, of pancreatic cancer. Landon's career continued unabated after *Bonanza* with *Little House on the Prairie* (1974-1983), and *Highway to Heaven* (1984-1989).

327. Pernell Roberts was born in Waycross, Georgia, on May 18, 1928, and is the only survivor of the Cartwright boys of *Bonanza*. Roberts left *Bonanza* at the end of the 1965 season and proceeded to guest star on many network series and specials. In 1979 Roberts began a seven-year run as Trapper John, M.D. in a CBS series of the same title. Pernell Roberts is now in his early eighties and pretty much retired.

328. *Kung Fu* was an ABC television series that ran from October 14, 1972, until June 28, 1975, and starred David Carradine, supported by regulars Keye Luke, Phillip Ahn, and Radames Pera. The Carradine character, Kwai Chang Caine, was a Chinese/American/Buddhist monk/martial arts expert who trod the American west in the mid-1880s. The series was sometimes referred to as a philosophical western and became quite a cult favorite during its run.

■

They say there's nothing like a good book...

We think that says quite a lot!

BearManorMedia

CPSIA information can be obtained at www.ICGtesting.com
Printed in the USA
LVOW100412210113

316503LV00001B/8/P